Department of History
U.S. Military Academy
West Point, NY 10996
April 1, 1988

Frank Simons is an extraordinary individual -- a real soldier -- and he naturally is infuriated by the willingness of officers of the US government, bureaucrats, and generally the American public to ignore the MIA problem. The statistic are ominous: very few of the men captured in Laos returned. The course of the Vietnamese government after 1975 was predictable: hold American hostages until the United States fulfilled its promise, given by President Nixon, to support the economic reconstruction of Vietnam. There have been many sightings of Caucasians, testified to over the years by the boat people. Although Vietnam now has been opened to tourism in an unofficial way -- Americans must obtain visas from other governments that maintain diplomatic relations -- and although Vietnamese officials deny they are holding Americans, it is presently impossible to check out either Vietnamese or Laotian protestations. It is a very uneasy situation. Colonel Simons even went to the length of scouting the Laotian border, walking for miles along the river, disguised as a local inhabitant. Here, in his account, written with real verve, are his experiences.

Sincerely,

Robert H. Ferrell

Congressional Records

Task Force Omega

Declassified CIA Reports

Wall Street Journal Articles

Sam Dunlap

William T. Fleshman

George W. Gill

Thomas V. Ashworth

Bob McEwen

Bill Paul

Robert R. Garwood

The work of the above organizations or writers is acknowledged and compiled from page 24 to page 69 and not under the copyright © 1988 Simons. The compilation is composed of data reports, letters, writings, and articles, some published, some not published. The compilation has great value as evidence to establish facts which point to the existance of live POWs in Southeast Asia being held there against their will.

***Published by The Civil Fact Finding Commission for POW/MIA in Southeast Asia a not for profit organization.**

# YOU DON'T CRY FOR HEROES

## (THE POW DILEMMA)

BY

FRANK D. SIMONS

LTC. U.S. ARMY RETIRED

## DEDICATION

The Vietnam war for me has not ended. It continues. It will not be over unti all the POWs have been brought home. The only disgrace and tragedy of the Vietnam War is that we left several hundred of our comrades in the hands of the enemy and I'm not sure they will be recovered before this book comes to press. Therefore, I dedicate this book to the on going crusade by those few who will not rest until the Vietnam War is really over--when our prisoners are releas-ed and the missing accounted.

## ACKNOWLEDGEMENTS

To Dr. Robert H. Ferrell. Dr. Ferrell, guest Professor of History at West Point during 1988 and Veteran History Professor at Indiana University, gave me the push and encouragement to write *"YOU DON'T CRY FOR HEROES."* His honest belief that we have left POWs behind in Southeast Asia and his desire to see this dilemma ended reflects his great humanitarism and a real feeling for the "Lost Battalion" of US servicemen still held in Southeast Asia. Dr. Ferrell proposes this interesting question. "What do we tell our young servicemen in future years, when they ask: 'if captured, will we also be left behind forever like the POWs in Vietnam and Laos?'"

In reviewing this book, Dr. Ferrell guided my efforts to produce a quality piece of work. The mistakes that remain are mine alone.

Thank you Dr. Ferrell. FDS

Without the help of Nita Coplen, who worked on the computer and waded through my poor hand writing, this journal would never have been written. Her pay days were seldom or non-existent as she became involved in the POW issue.

Particular mention is given to Dick Robison of Rochester, Indiana, a Vietnam Veteran, who furnished electronic data and updates concerning the POW issue. His actions as a combat infantry man of the 1st Infantry Division exemplified service rendered by the young men of this country who answered the draft call and served with distinction. He returned from Vietnam to build a business, become a property owner, own his own home and become a respected citizen of the community. His interest in the POW issue will without a doubt continue until the POWs are brought home.

The officers of the State of Indiana; the Commander of the 2nd District of the Indiana VFW, Phil Deck and Don Ochesky, Commander of Post 1343 of Rochester and the Knox, IN Post supported my POW/MIA investigation and contributed significantly to the POW issue.

Judy Burton of Rochester, Indiana contributed financially and with political support during the investigation and fact finding mission. Her advice and influence was of great help.

John Draga of Indianapolis, Indiana helped by keeping the computer on line and training operators.

## CREDITS

I have presented a compilation of information from various writers. I have used their work in good faith that we are all trying to bring home the POWs and account for our missing in Southeast Asia. I credit each writer (some unknown) for their efforts.

FDS

To my present wife Monika who has endured my restless nights as I recalled the Vietnam experience.

To my first wife Jeanne who lived through the Vietnam years with me and worried most I might not return.

FDS

## YOU DON'T CRY FOR HEROES

## TABLE OF CONTENTS



Our POW in Southeast Asia are real, alive and must be recovered.

**Special credits are given to the following:**

General William C. Westmoreland: For his ongoing effort to move our government to action to resolve the POW issue.

Ann Mills Griffiths: Without her efforts the POW - issue may have fallen through the cracks of our bureaucratic floor years ago.

Mark M. Simons: For his diligent reseach and compilation of statistics and data. He has made a significant contribution.

Ronald Reagan: Kept the POW issue at least on the back burner throughout his tenure as President. Although History may see the POW dilemma as his greatest personal failure, it was not completely swept under the rug.

H. Ross Perot: Discussed the issue with me. His ongoing efforts concerning the POW problem may well be its only salvation.

Bill Paul: Writer and investigator for the Wall Street Journal has had the guts to bring the POW issue before the public and the Wall Street Journal has brought some statesmanship to the World of Journalism by printing his findings.

The Homecoming II Project: Furnished information, real action and research that is without equal.

Bob and Joan Stewart: Of Bloomington, IN. Their exact support was important and is confidential.

Carla Zartman and Patsy Clark: Proofreaders.

Ladies Auxiliary VFW Post 1343: Continued support.

Col. Hopper: Gave me his son's story.

Senator Lugar, (Indiana): Helped as he could on my investigation.

Tom Burch of the Vietnam Veterans Coalition: He stands as a principal force keeping the POW issue alive with current information distributed monthly to veterans and veterans organizations.

Bill Bennett: Also of the Vietnam Veterans Coalition, his legal, modest approach lends a touch of class to the political and bureaucratic battleground in Washington, D.C.

American Defense Foundation: For the formation of a reward fund of over two million dollars for the delivery of two live POWs out of Southeast Asia by indigenous people.

## INTRODUCTION

My return to Southeast Asia to investigate the POW issue and suggest "*YOU DON'T CRY FOR HEROES*" should give the reader insight into the Vietnam War and the POW dilemma.

Over the years friends have asked me to write about the Vietnam War. Now after 15 years I decided to try. Unfortunately there seem to be only three basic stories of popular interest - the drug-oriented troops, crazy officers as seen in "Apocalyspe Now", and mythical POW rescue missions. The fact that a large measure of the war's objectives were realized is seldom discussed. The press convinced the world and the American public the war was lost. But, let's look at Vietnam today; a poor non-productive, lost nation...not a winner.

Somewhere behind the scenes of protestors and politics of the Vietnam era there was a very real war going on, conducted by the U.S. Military Services and some very dedicated civilians.

Today many people feel that we lost the war. Others feel the services should have been more strongly supported. Some feel that the federal government gave the war away. Was it a politicians' war only of economic value? Some say it was not even a war.

Every officer in the Military knows it takes 20 years to build an army. The war was turned over to the Vietnamese too soon. It took us 30 years in Korea. Now the Korean Army is the best trained in the Far East.

It should be considered that, by-in-large, the Vietnam War was a victory and still stands as a great deterrent in the Far East to Communist expansionism. The communist effort in the Far East may proceed, but it will proceed very slowly. The communist Vietnam Government really never wants to face the U.S. again in war.

The areas of Cambodia, Laos, and Vietnam were the countries from which we withdrew. We did not withdraw from Thailand, the Philippines and the other areas of the Far East where the U.S. has had a traditional and on going interest. The Vietnam Government, currently in power, understands very clearly that any aggressive action toward these areas will receive the wrathful attention of the American people. They fear the American Government will take action once again.

Most will agree there is a time when it is necessary to stand up to defend your allies or your friends. If they go under, you will stand alone to defend yourself with the enemy using the resources of those deserted friends and allies.

The idea that the Vietnam War was lost is absolutely preposterous. The war progressed; the security became better in South Vietnam; and about 1969 or 1970 the U.S. had, by any previous standards won the war. The idea that TET of '68 signaled the wars loss is false. The 68 TET Offensive was the last real effort of the V.C. **It failed.**

The II Corp area in which I operated in the early 70's was 100 times more secure than it was ten years before. "Well, did we really lose that war?" The timing of the withdrawal was a great mistake. Especially poor was the manner in which it was conducted. We had the air power to pressure North Vietnam to back off from Saigon. **It was not used.** The fact is that mistakes are made in every war. The U.S. Army was the best armed, and the best supported military that we've ever presented to fight. So as you turn the pages of *"YOU DON'T CRY FOR HEROES"* think about the title. It's time we quit feeling sorry for the Vietnam War. We must support efforts to account for our 2400 missing in action and conclude this war in a manner that history will be very kind to us. It is a fact that we didn't press the war home to North Vietnam and the ultimate extermination of the North Vietnamese people. Was enough pressure used to halt the communist expansion?

One thing that must be understood is that Laos, Vietnam and Cambodia represents a vast area of jungle and mountains where many of the villages are so remote that the villagers have never seen a white or black man to this date.

There are many facts and figures to substantiate the fact that the Vietnam War was not a lost cause. But, because of the poor withdrawal it's rather hard to look at it that way. The politician, the historian, the political scientist will give you the explicit and possibly boring details. I will relate to you a soldier's story from the point of view of a U.S. Army Adviser in the Laos and Vietnam War. I hope the reader will forgive this soldier's memory. I tend to only remember those days that were adventurous, stimulating, bizarre or at least do not cause me a great deal of pain to recount. Therefore, much of the daily routine and drudgery of the military service has been passed over. Also, I have not recounted the details involving the loss of close friends. Of course, as in all "war stories" some were not to return.

Sometimes its hard to describe a soldier's life without making him out a philanderer. The friendly flirtation with the ladies who enter a soldier's life may be mentioned in passing, but are not to be construed as anything except one soldier's casual encounter with fate.

My "return" was one soldier's effort to end the Vietnam era. It will not end until our POWs have come home.

*Throughout this Journal the term POW "Prisoners of War" may appear as POWs because of the current use by the press and writers.

*The different spelling of advisors and advisers appear throughout this journal. Webster accepts both.

*Southeast Asia may appear from time to time as South East Asia.

## THE RETURN

As I tried to relax on the pipe and web seats, the engines of the US Air Force KC-135 seemed about five times louder than a civilian jet. I was on my way to Southeast Asia seventeen years after three and a half combat tours.

But, this time everything was different. I was flying space available as a retired lieutenant colonel of the US Army. I was traveling alone without official sanction on my way to investigate the most intriging and challenging questions of this decade. "What happened to the US POWs left in Southeast Asia after the Vietnam War and can they be recovered or rescued?"

Years after the official end of the Vietnam conflict over 2,400 of our men were still listed as missing and over 200 of the 2,400 suspected held POW. The government seemed to be ineffective in all attempts to negotiate their recovery.

I had been picked up at Grissom AFB in Indiana for a hop to California where I would make my way to Hawaii, the Philippines, Bangkok and eventually the Lao border.

It was time to start my log. That is a military term for diary (it sounds more official). I had about eight hours to reflect on how I came to this point in my life. I was defying my government, to some extent, by carrying my POW investigation personally to Southeast Asia. Such intentions were considered nonproductive in nature. But since the Vietnam War, all administrations had failed to bring home even one POW. I felt I should try to at least find out why.

This was going to be a long and possibly dangerous trip. I had become involved but I was full of doubts about the POW issue. Now I had some time to reflect on my motives. Certainly this trip was not for my health. It also was not a one man crusade. Many Vietnam veterans and MIA families felt the government had deserted the POWs. Some felt there was a government coverup. I was fortunate enough to have the time, some finances of my own, personal friends to back me and the total support of VFW Post 1343 of Rochester, Indiana.

What would I be able to do? Could I make a difference? I had no idea. I only knew something needed to be done. I hoped to help in some way to bring our POWs home.

I used the sound of the jet engines to let my memory reconstruct the last few years. Possibly I could then better understand the irresistable force compelling me to take independent action on the POW issue.

I was not so foolish to think I might succeed where others have failed, but I knew I must make a maximum effort to help solve the dilemma. It would be tough. I had no illusions of grandeur. I was alone without government support.

Little did I realize that this venture would cause my mind to dredge up long forgotten memories of Vietnam and I would be forced to relive events of the war I entered as a youthful professional soldier.

I was re-entering the Asian environment that I had called home for several years. I hoped the personal involvement I developed during the war would be more clear to me as I became once again engulfed in what surely must be the last chapter of the Vietnam era.

As the jets whined my mind drifted and suddenly I was again an army captain in Korea; the year was 1960. Soon the war in Southeast Asia would become a reality for me. As I drifted in half sleep, the roar of the jets became the rumble of an army duce and a half cargo truck.

## Chapter 1

## ESCAPE FROM KOREA

I looked out through the small hole in the large box marked refrigerator, I could see the Korean hijackers working quickly to replace the cigarette shipping boxes with others of similar size and weight. The refrigerator box concealed my position in the military freight truck routed from Seoul/Kumpo area to Pabwani. It was a neat operation and if I lived the next hour or two my investigation would terminate the largest U.S. Post Exchange black market endeavor since the Korean War had ended in the early fifties.

The refrigerator box I had stowed away in was scheduled for the 1st Cavalry Division. Within fifteen minutes 20,000 cartons of cigarettes were on their way for sale in the many small towns of Korea where they would bring a premium price.

To my great relief the refrigerator box was untouched. This slick operation utilized an underwater bridge of some sort across the Han Gang/Imjim River and its use cut twenty minutes off the normal trip time. I found later the depth of the water was critical and this changed with the tide each day. Timing for the hijackers had to be perfect.

The trip to Pabwani was completed on time and luckily the refrigerator box received little attention as it was moved to a warehouse cover. An hour later I made my way out of the PX (Post Exchange) compound. After a quick report to the general, I changed clothes, turned in the .45 pistol and climbed the 567 steps up the mountain to the officers club. I needed to reflect on this assignment and a double scotch and soda would help. I had been stationed in Korea for almost a year.

This day's work was the result of several weeks of intensive snooping, on my part, to determine what was happening to all the cigarettes which were supposed to be arriving in our division area.

The Division Commander had appointed me to look into the problem after our Criminal Investigation Division (CID) had not come up with a solution to the dilemma. All ration stamps and monies were accounted, but cigarettes were never available. This problem was not just some administrative ''snafu'' and the excuse ''that it has just happened'' seemed a little inadequate.

Stowing away on the truck was a decision I might not have made if I had been a little older or a more experienced investigator. But, at the time it seemed like the most direct way to find out what the hell was happening to our cigarettes.

In Seoul, a week later, a Korean dump truck tried to run over my jeep. It became obvious I had made enemies in high places. PX employees at all levels were being replaced and some high government officials fired. Besides, I had dealt a blow to Korean organized crime and my continued good health in Korea was at best unsure.

Two days after the attempt on my life I was the night operations officer for the division TOC (Tactical Operation Center), when I saw a message requesting a captain, qualified in operations, for a classified mission. With a word to my boss the G-3 and the general, I put in my name and within three days I was on my way to Seoul to await a flight to Japan, Taiwan, The Philippines, Saigon and

Bangkok. My destination was Laos.

And so I began a new life. I was going to a real war. It was a "secret war" at the time, but nonetheless a war. I liked traveling for the Army in civilian clothes. My travel orders directed that I furnish my own weapon, so I had bought a fine K-.38 pistol from the captain of our Division pistol team. "Yes, I thought this will be an interesting assignment". In my briefcase I had 100 rounds and with the .38 in my raincoat pocket I left Korea. I am not sure what I expected in Laos but knew I was going to a Special Forces group known as the White Star Mobile Training Team. The trip to Laos would take several days and I had time to reflect a little on my army career to date.

I had enjoyed diverse assignments in my eight years of service and I had every intention of becoming a general officer. I had served with the 11th Airborne Division, the 9th Infantry Division in Europe, the 513 Military Intelligence group at Oberursele, Germany, instructed with the weapons department at Ft. Benning, GA, attended the infantry advance officer course and served as a ROTC (Reserved Officers Training Corp) instructor at Indiana University. In Korea I had been on the general staff.

Except in Japan where I got into a taxi and asked the driver to hurry (which is a great mistake) the trip itself was routine.

But in one respect it was not. I had a pleasant evening in Taiwan with more entertainment than I needed. The next day on the plane I was fast asleep when a young stewardess lost her balance and sprawled over me, spilling coffee and becoming embarrassed. Luckily, most of the coffee went on the empty seat beside me. Within the next ten minutes, as she cleaned up the mess, I realized that my stay at Clark AFB would be a most interesting one. I was hoping this good luck was not going to run out during the mission in Laos. But for now, I was not going to complain. The young Eurasian stewardess was a beautiful woman and I might add she was an accomplished athlete: as we lounged at the officers club pool the next morning I found she could also swim. Everyone seemed to know her, but it was not until later that I discovered she had been Miss Philippine Islands. Well, the soldier's life is not all bad or there just wouldn't be any professional soldiers. Later that morning I also soon found out she was the very close friend of a local General. It was well I had a flight out that afternoon.

Upon arrival in Bangkok, I was met by a White Star liaison NCO (Non Commissioned Officer) who whisked me off to a motel called, by locals, the Riding Stable. The name was somewhat significant. After a quick dinner and stop at a bar or two, I turned in. The next thing I knew there was a quiet knock on the door and I had company for the rest of the night. At dawn I departed for the airfield. I remembered thinking that "I'd try to revisit the Riding Stable."

At the airfield we found the Air America C-47 with props turning and as soon as I threw my bag on board the door closed. The old war horse was off the ground in less than two minutes. I settled back in the bucket seats alongside of the fuselage of the old bird. The jungle below was lush and emerald green. The color seemed brilliant since I had just left a rather bleak Korea. In an hour or so we crossed the Mekong River to Laos. WaTai air field was in the distance. As we made our approach, I noticed an aircraft taking off. It was a little longer than a C-46 with a nose wheel. At first I did not recognize it, then realized it was a Russian cargo plane. What the hell was it doing here? The Russian aircraft took off as we were on final landing approach.

Ten minutes after that I was in the back of a jeep passing the French-style villas on the outskirts of Vientiane. Between the villas were small wooden houses, and a local girl caught my eye, bathing nude beside her house, pouring buckets of water over her jet black hair. She did not wave as we came by, but neither did she cover herself. She only smiled and continued to bathe. As we approached the compound, the gate guard motioned us on and a few yards down the dirt road I was dropped off along with my bag in front of a rough wooden building.

I reported to the S-1 who introduced me to Major Brovo, the executive officer of the special forces team. As a greeting, he said, "Oh, you're the leg from Korea". (A leg is a non-airborne soldier as seen through the eyes of those who always wear jump boots.) I knew I would have trouble with him later, I just did not know how much. I had been airborne qualified probably as long as he had, but my last job in Korea had not been in an airborne capacity and therefore, I was not transferred on jump status. He made it very clear I would not be put on jump pay.

After I was told I was there on trial, I was taken to the CO's office. "What the hell kind of an outfit was this?" I was thinking as I saluted the team commander.

Lt. Col. Arthur (Bull) Simons was seated behind an old desk, a smirk on his face. Acknowledging my salute he said, "So your name is Simons. Well, let me tell you one god-damn thing. There is only one Simons in this outfit and don't forget it. If you send a message, don't sign it Simons."

"Now your job" he continued, "is to run the airfield and get those civilian pilots straightened out. They all work for Air America, which is a CIA operation, and we have a young inexperienced captain out there who has the job fucked up. He needs an A team upcountry and not an airfield, which requires some tact to deal with pilots and the civilians of the embassy. Also, there is a logistics problem to coordinate and some operations to keep up with. Now, god-damn it, get out to the airfield and relieve that captain and if you fuck up this job I'll have you killed--get out!"

That was the "Bull". Later he was destined to gain fame as the leader of the ill-fated special forces mission to rescue the U.S. prisoners at San Tay, twenty-three miles from Hanoi. After that he retired and once worked for billionaire Ross Perot, of Electronic Data Systems of Dallas, on a mission to break out two of Perot's executives from an Iranian jail. The Bull was the subject of Ken Follett's *On Wings Of Eagles,* published in 1983.

In about two minutes I had received explicit orders. The colonel left me in no doubt about his sincerity and I remembered thinking that he did look like a bull. At the time, I did not realize that he was as dangerous as he looked.

I left for the airfield. It was not yet noon, and I had a half-day's work ahead of me. It took longer to find a jeep than to get back to the airfield I left my bag to be picked up later.

The captain seemed delighted to be rid of his job and looked forward to being sent upcountry. In the office three Lao soldiers and one U.S. special forces soldier were waiting for a plane. Ten minutes later they took off for Pakse. They were never seen again; the plane disappeared without a trace. No wonder pilots were hard to get along with. In recent months there had been seven planes lost, most shot down by ground fire. That afternoon I surveyed the airfield, got an idea of what was expected, and took over. I remember thinking, "I have made good my escape from Korea, but what the hell have I gotten myself into."

Next morning I got to the office early, after first light. The office was bleak. There was one telephone, a desk of sorts, an antique two-way radio, one lamp, and three cobras. Where did they come from? I got rid of them fast, but was hunting others the rest of the day, and for some weeks I inspected the office each morning before I sat down to work. The cobras must have come in with a load of rice. The office was at the end of the storage building on the part of the runway nearest the road to town. The Russians were using the other end of the runway for their operations. This was a strange war. At first I didn't have the slightest idea what I was doing. But I knew I was having a hell of a time getting back and forth to work. I opened the air operations office before 0600, after checking the operation and intelligence map at HQ each morning. There was never any transportation. At the end of the first week I went to town during lunch and bought a small motorcycle. I had never ridden before.

One sure gets wet when it rains, and it rains half the year in Vientiane. Problems began to smooth out. The pilots were not hard to win over. I could understand them. They were making $3,000 a month and wanted to live to spend it. That was a lot of money early in the 1960s. The intelligence briefing I gave before each mission was keeping them alive. For a change they were getting enemy troop locations and proper updates. The Bull never said a word. The S-3 and XO were on my back about not having a "need to know" about special force team locations. But that intelligence was keeping my pilots alive. Of course, teams in the field also needed security. Their locations were all classified. It would take weeks for me to gain their confidence. It must be understood that special forces troops are special men in more than one way. As augmentation to Special Forces, I was not a real member of the group. Even though I had been airborne qualified for eight years I was never put on jump status with the White Star unit in Laos. Also, since I was not authorized to wear the green beret, it took me more effort to win personal friendship of the special forces team. I am not sure in those early years of the war that I ever really understood them. They were a proud group and almost as good as they thought they were, but over the months I did develop friendships. You had to prove you could do any job. Then once accepted you could do no wrong. At least I could drink with the best, including the Bull, and that was a start.

Colonel Simons had the reputation of a field commander. Tact was unknown to him. However, he could be charming when required. We would drink medical alcohol and rose lime, when the Beefeaters ran low. I got to know him, but he was not one to get close to. Besides I was a captain and a wide gap in age and experience existed.

He carried a Colt Phytham on a Texas-style belt. With his bulk it never showed under his jacket or shirt. On the belt, which had at least 25 loops for 357 cartridges, he also carried a Finnish fillet knife. I have seen him carry a Swedish K-9mm submachine gun when he headed for jungle "A team" operations. Once you met him, you better understood the Special Forces Soldier. Tough, well trained, but maybe a little too brave.

After a week or two at the air field and learning to ride a motorcycle in French-style traffic, I got into the routine of Air America support for special forces. A special forces captain befriended me. He was leaving within a few days so one evening I got his personal tour of Vientiane. He introduced me to his five girlfriends and made it clear he was leaving and that if they needed anything they should see me. It was the most beautiful clean break repeated five times I have ever seen. The embassy girl was a little strange but not bad. The French nurse was very very French. The other three were within acceptable standards.

Lunch was a little bizarre every day at a French restaurant halfway down the airfield on the west side. It was near the Russian support aircraft. Almost every day Russian pilots would jokingly ask me to defect to Xeing Khouang, communist headquarters to the north. It became worse after they found out I could get along in Russian (a little basic Russian picked up working in army intelligence in Europe). It broke up the day and gave us a laugh at dinner. I am not sure the special forces team believed any of my stories.

The first time I got away from the air field for a short flight was in an old L20, the Havilland "Beaver". This single-engine workhorse would carry a load of 1,800 pounds of people or cargo, a really great aircraft, very forgiving. Even I could fly it. My pilot was forty-two or forty-three, a bush pilot from Alaska and, before that, Africa. We were going north 150 miles to pick up a wounded special forces advisor. I had a sergeant who would cover me at the office when I was on a mission. From time to time I had to go along to assure the pilot I was not sending him into an area I would not go.

I cannot remember why I was on this mission, but I had a chance to get a few hours in with my instructor pilot. That afternoon I was to see some flying that in the old days was described as "seat of the pants". We were approaching two mountaintops and I had assumed we would go over the cloud cover. The peaks were a half a mile apart I could not believe it when he did not pull up. Before I could object we were in the soup. He reached over past me and opened my window. When I asked what he was doing he said, "Shush, shush, not now." The plane rolled a little right. In a moment he closed my window and opened his. The plane banked left and in thirty seconds, which seemed longer, we broke out of the clouds into the sun, the mountaintops behind. I got out one "goddamn", then another--"What the hell were you doing?" He answered casually, "I was listening for the echo of the motor off the mountainside, no big deal." We went back another way. The special forces advisor was not hurt seriously. As an instructor Mike was off my list for a while. Possibly my escape from Korea was like going from the frying pan to the fire.

## Chapter 2

## THE DRAGON LADY and AIR OPS

The following week was uneventful. Then it happened. When I reflect on that day; I now realize it affected my entire life.

I was at the desk trying to write a report when the telephone rang. It was about 10:00 a.m. The office was hot and any diversion was welcome. I would be there until about 7:00 p.m. until I got the last helicopter off the Udorn in Thailand, where they were overnighted and maintained. The voice on the phone was known. I had been at an embassy affair the night before and talked with the owner for half an hour. The voice told me a message was on the way from the embassy and it was the ambassador's order that I was to comply immediately, I asked him to notify my headquarters. I had a helicopter on the pad as standby and told the pilot to warm up.

About 15 minutes later a car delivered the message and we were on the way. The order was clear. I was to pick up a U.S. agent near Ban Houei Sai and return to Vientiane.

Why was I needed? The villa marked on the map was near doctor Tom Dooley's area. Tom did a lot of work in northern Laos and had become well known around the world. The trip was going to take an hour over the jungle. When flying I usually carried a doublebarrel twelve gauge with 50 rounds of buckshot and my new "old" .44 mag ruger pistol. One of my pilots had fallen in love with my .38 special and talked me out of it with two $100 bills and a good .44 mag. He called it a trade, and I must admit it was one of my better deals. I slept in the helicopter seat for the hour and awoke as we were ready to land. I had been to Ban Houei Sai before on an orientation flight and the area was familiar. The villa was surrounded by a ten-foot wall.

As we touched down about two hundred yards from the wall, a door opened and out came the best-looking woman I had ever seen. She stood 5′10″ in black breeches, high boots, tight green blouse, and bush hat. She looked as if she had stepped out of a Phantom comic book with a centerfold Playboy style. I was thinking, "How did this happen to me?" I walked toward her and we met halfway (about a hundred yards) from the villa door. She handed me the small round bag she was carrying. She wore dark glasses. I tried to see behind them but only got my reflection. There was a nod, a faint smile. I dropped back a step to admire the view but it was a short dream. A bullet zipped by my ear, then another tore into the bag. I had thought the enemy was forty miles away on the road north from Nom Ta, but we were being shot at here and now. I turned, and in the same motion threw the bag to the dragon lady and yelled, "Make the helicopter!". There were two more shots as I knelt down and drew the .44 mag. I did not know where the shots were coming from. It was small caliber, probably .22. Damn! I was hit high in the leg. Then I saw him, standing in the villa door with a rifle, still shooting. I had my knee on the ground, both hands holding the 7½ inch .44 mag. A bullet tugged at my shirt. I squeezed off three fast, really fast, shots. On the third shot I saw only boots about two feet off the ground as the man fell backward through the door. I had hit him somewhere high in the chest. I fired two more rounds at the black area at the bottom of the door and headed toward the helicopter.

The pilot was taking off and I barely made the door. I could not blame him. No one expected to get shot at on this mission. What had gone wrong? I was hurt and bleeding. The small bullet had gone through like a hot wire. I cut open my trousers leg to inspect the damage. Shaking my head I looked up to see the coldest expression I had ever seen on a woman's face. "What was that about?" I asked. Without emotion she said, "Well, that was Jaques. We have been living together for about a year now and he just doesn't understand all this." My mind was numb. She had seen me shoot down her French lover and her voice was cold as the midnight sun. She added, "Can I help you? I am a nurse." I said nothing, shook my head and leaned back. I had learned a little more about women. God, how many were there like that around? How was I going to explain getting shot by a jealous lover? It couldn't get worse, but then I'm often optimistic to a fault.

We landed. In front of my office an embassy car was waiting. She got in the car, never looked back and disappeared in the rain that had just started.

My troubles were over, or so I thought. As I entered my office the radio was blasting, the phone ringing. I answered the radio, asked them to wait, and picked up the phone. I didn't get a chance to say a word; it was the S-3, my boss, madder than hell. Where had I been? On whose authority? He wanted to see me after I left the field at 7:00 p.m. My friend at the embassy had not called my boss. I'd get it straight tomorrow. Who was it on the radio? I had forgotten the call sign. Some days are better than others.

But the next day was not going to be one of them. I'd put my boss off telling him the embassy would straighten out the problem. I called my embassy contact to discuss yesterday's mission. My boss wanted something in writing. You can possibly guess the next event if you know anything about our State Department. My contact, who will remain nameless, told me in short cryptic voice that there had been no embassy mission authorized yesterday. The ambassador had been in Bangkok and was not expected to return for a few days. I told him what an ass he was and that if there was no mission yesterday then no Frenchman could have been shot. The phone was quietly hung up and I never heard anything more until much later, when I got an efficiency report for that day's work. Ultimately it would cost me a year date of rank. Maybe the Bull got wind of the real story but the pressure dropped off me sharply. I often wondered who was the Dragon Lady. What was her mission and would I ever meet her again?

Things were quiet the next few days and then another strange thing happened. A P-51 buzzed the airfield. I had only seen photographs of this fighter from World War II. The next pass over was a barrel roll the length of the field at about three hundred miles an hour, only thirty feet off the ground. A few minutes later it skidded to a stop in front of my office. A not so young man stepped off the wing. "The guns are loaded, I'm ready for a mission. I get $5,000 a month, maintenance, and fuel for myself and my plane." He had a World War II leather helmet, goggles, white scarf, and was carrying an Army .45.

It sounded like a good deal to me but I explained that I did not do the hiring. I knew the Bull would want him out of the area. I told him to go to Taiwan, headquarters for Air America. Perhaps Air America would hire him. I fueled him, and within minutes he was out of sight. Now, who was that? When I told the Bull that night he did not say a word just walked away. Maybe I did the right thing that time.

My good fortune was shortlived; a week later I got word that one of our teams was in trouble with the locals and needed an L-20 immediately. It was in an area where none of my pilots had landed. The other Air America support had been making supply runs. I went with the mission. When we arrived, I found they had a small girl and her father to transport to the French hospital in Vientiane. She had swallowed a carbine bullet that the father insisted came from the advisors' house. He had aroused the village people and the team commander had called for an evacuation. The landing was interesting, the take-off something else. The runway was nine hundred feet long but not quite wide enough. It had been cut out of the jungle. It seemed we would never get off the ground. But the pilot was a former test pilot so I never doubted we would make it. I saw the end of the runway approaching, about the time I knew we were dead, Jake pumped in a little more flap and we sort of popped up over the jungle.

As we rolled to a stop in Vientiane, I got out to help the old man and child. I reached behind the seat to pull out his small bag. I almost broke an arm; it weighed ninety pounds. What was this, I opened it and still did not know. I tried Lao on the old man but got no answer. Then the pilot came around, took one look, and said, "That's raw opium". I had just transported opium into Vientiane. It was the village's entire output for a year. The ambulance arrived for the little girl; the suitcase went to my office. "Wait till the boss sees what I got this time", was my thought. I did not have to wait long. I got a call in an hour that started out "goddammit" and ended more explicitly. I was ordered to give the man his suitcase. There was no law in Laos concerning opium. The little girl did have a bullet in her stomach, probably put there by her father to get a free ride over bandit country with the entire product of the village. It sold that night for $5,000. In Bangkok it would bring $25,000 to $50,000, and who knows what on the streets of New York. The little girl was all right in a few days. I got them back to their village. Again the Bull said nothing. We were not losing planes or pilots. Air America was not any longer complaining and in general the job was going well.

A week later on an air resupply run over southern Laos I had another interesting experience. It was a low-level drop and the C-47 was having a rough time as wind currents and drafts were bad. The civilian Air America crewman fell over a tie-down, hit his head, and broke a leg. I had never pushed a load before but, it looked like today was the day. All the drums of fuel were on rollers and moved easily once the tie-downs were loosened. The ground team needed supplies. I gave the injured man a morphine shot, and we made the next pass. Everything was fine until the drums of fuel pushed a little too easily and I found myself in the air with them, at three hundred feet. The only safety line had failed. I grabbed for the handle of the reserve parachute. A helicopter was sent for me the next day. That wouldn't happen again. I'd been lucky. I tried to explain what happened to the Bull but with his jaw set, he said, "You still are not on jump pay, get out."

A few weeks later I had a chance to fly into Site 21, an airfield on the "Plaine de Jares" of North Laos, locality of the Meo tribe. Actually the Meo, who prefer the name Hmung, are a series of tribes and villages that stretch through northern Laos, Thailand and Burma, and seemed to me similar to the mountain tribes I dealt with later in Vietnam. They are a small people with a darker skin than the Chinese or Thai. They look like American or Latin American Indians. American special forces, in conjunction with the CIA, had been training the tribes to resist incursions from Vietnam and the Hmung had received the training well. Some young men had been given jump training.

There was to be a celebration at the end of basic training and I was invited. As we flew over the village, I noted hills all about and the name "plain" seemed a misnomer. The airfield was in what appeared to be the basin of an old volcano, and the pilot had to circle and bank severely on approach. The runway was in three levels and I remember thinking that if I got on the ground I would buy the pilot a drink or maybe two. It was a rough landing even for a C-123 and I could see no way it would ever get off the ground from such an airfield.

There was shooting as we arrived, and I was pleased to find that it was a shooting match between the tribesmen. The match used old flintlock weapons, combinations of rifles and pistols. Barrels were four feet, fitted with pistol grips. Rifles were fired at arms' length. Barrels were held to the wood by bands of pounded coin silver and the smoke that belched from the smoothbores covered the field.

These weapons were being replaced by U.S. rifles, and the match was more symbolic than competition. I found it hard to believe the Meo had killed tigers with these guns. The tigers must have won the confrontations often.

After the shooting, the feast began and lasted several hours. The meat tasted strange and it was not until later that I noticed the village did not have many dogs.

We had brought in some ice so that night the special forces team had cold beer. One of the members had too much. He was unceremoniously thrown on his bed. The next morning it was discovered he had landed on a very large snake, which the weight of his body had killed.

The flight back to Vientiane was good, after a take-off as bad as the landing. We only had one pilot who would fly a C-123 into Site 21. He would never have a chance to do it with me again. It took me a week to recover from the dog meat. Site 21 could get along without my personal attention. Besides the team was well supported by other CIA aircraft.

One of the interesting places on the outskirts of Vientiane was a night club quite popular for special forces troops when they came out of the jungle. It did have entertainment; there was plenty of music and young ladies. It was the sort of club where you did not take a date, girlfriend or wife. One visited it with several men and during the evening young ladies were available. They were expected to get tips and the drinks increased the profit for the house. The news people would hang out there and prey on the special forces troops. But, I am not sure who preyed on whom. A reporter would spot a soldier out of the hills and start asking what area he was from and what action was going on. The reporter got his dispatch without leaving town. Now this was all right but it got to be pretty apparent where the Lao War was being fought and very few special forces troops would break security. When a young man would come into town, he knew that if he went to the club and told a good story he would get free drinks and dinner. If he told an outstanding story about battles, he would get drinks, dinner and maybe a girl for the evening. A lot of stories were told and to this day no one knows if they were true. I've often wondered how many of them actually got printed back in the States relating the Laos War "as it really is out there in the hills".

Another place was the Continental Hotel. The reporters lounged there, sipping drinks at the outside restaurant. We all had entered the country in civilian clothes, then changed into fatigue uniforms. We used no unit patches and very shortly after we got there we took off our name tags. If a reporter saw a tag, he would quote you in the New York paper.

Reporters created problems. I remember a young woman reporter at the Continental. She represented several prominent papers but called herself a free lance. She was extremely effective. Several times I had trouble with her getting into inappropriate areas of the country. There were areas where she really had no business. She was going to get herself killed and I made up my mind it was time to talk to her. I told her certain places were off limits and she could not travel to them and that I had the authority of the Laos Government behind me. In fact, there was a Lao colonel present at the time I related this order. The young lady did not take "no" for an answer. A few weeks later I found she was getting into anyplace she wanted to. She would meet one of my pilots in a bar, spend the night with him, and as he took off on a flight the next day, she would meet him at the end of the runway when he turned the plane around, get in on the side where we could not see her, and be off on a flight. After observing the operation a few times. I gave the pilot a warning letter, called her into the office, gave her a pass to parts of the country where she could go, and told her if I found her in any other area I would have her jettisoned out of the plane. I'm not sure she really believed me but I never found her again going in the wrong direction on one of my aircrafts.

Another night spot was the White Rose Saloon, it was located in the middle of a commercial district, and was a very nice little bar. I think it was the first of the modern massage parlors. The girls there were all Thai and well selected. The group was probably the most acceptable that could have been gathered together. At that time the special forces medical captain insured our young men against coming back to the United States with problems that they would have for many years. He inspected the White Rose girls and had a Lao doctor keep them cleaned up with antibiotics. Surprisingly not one of our men came down with disease. The beer was reasonable and the girls exceptional. The price was $5.00. They would check out a massage machine and take their customer to a room upstairs. They were either extremely good actresses or these young ladies enjoyed their work. Of course, I was only told about all of this.

Things went along well for a few weeks until we had a confrontation with the Russians. For some reason from time to time the Russians caused a problem. I have a feeling it comes as an order from above to find what will be the Americans' reaction. It was against rules to arm the helicopter. I could not put machine guns in the door. We did not have rocket pods or armament and to the best of my knowledge neither did the Russians. But, one morning as our aircraft took off, there was a Russian helicopter also taking off. It had been just a little ahead of ours. Suddenly the Russian helicopter turned, came up beside ours, opened the doors and everyone in the Russian helicopter pointed rifles at our helicopter. Naturally the people in our helicopter responded in the same way--rifles readied. The helicopters proceeded for four or five minutes, both crews and passengers at the ready. Then for some reason the Russian pilot waved at ours and veered to the right and ours turned to the left and each went about its own mission.

These small confrontations were interesting because they kept us aware who was supporting the other side. Why was this done? I have no idea why these confrontations took place. They were never serious. There was never any shooting. But about the time a friendly situation was developing, something would happen and we relearned about the Russians. This way we got a little insight into the Russian character--their ability to keep things on the brink of disaster.

Confidential American Source (C.A.S.) was the agency behind most covert action in Laos in the early 1960s. It was common knowledge in Vientiane that American special forces worked in conjunction with C.A.S. The White Star mobile training team was a covert special forces unit. At least there were attempts to cover the fact that U.S. forces were in Laos. But in Laos it was no secret; with reporters everywhere no secret could be kept. The actions of C.A.S. were covered with a veil of whispers. Their involvement in furnishing supplies to the tribes and special forces was not discussed openly. Air America was a company using C.A.S. funds and it was my duty to help coordinate operations. All the pilots were civilians, supported through a headquarters in Taiwan. Funds were no problem if some justification could be given. Pilots and maintenance crews were paid well. Air America would be active all the way through the Vietnam War and there should be no surprise if it appeared in Latin America today.

Each month I had to transport $2 million from Thailand to Vientiane. The money was used at the ambassador's discretion and in accord with U.S. policy. I have no idea how much went to the U.S. effort and how much to support the Lao Government, but it made for an interesting trip. One day a month I was rich.

The fact that I was not on jump status in this all jump qualified unit was always good for an argument. This was especially true after a few drinks.

One night I challenged the unit doctor to a PT (physical training) test. I lost, but from it came a challenge on the range the following day from Major "Brovo" He and I were never on good terms but after awhile we had a mutual respect. Sunday we were off to the range to decide if his old Colt .45 or the modern .38 was more accurate at a hundred yards. These diversions were some of the good times that all soldiers need when far from home. The winner of the match is not important but the .38 proved far superior to the old Colt. The match was not quickly forgotten and any animosity he felt was only redoubled. But it ended shooting challenges to me for the tour in Laos. I never mentioned I had been a national match shooter and fired for a U.S. team in the Olympics, but it was time I got one up on special forces.

For the American in Vientiane there were only a few rules--always be armed, keep it concealed, and do not cause problems.

We never had anyone mugged and few incidents were ever brought to light. I can only remember one time a soldier got in trouble and it was all over in a few hours. One of our men had been cheated in one of the bars, or at least he thought he had been. He was thrown out. He returned to the team house, got a submachine gun and returned to the bar. When he finished, he had destroyed the bar. He had fired over a hundred rounds. This indiscretion cost him a stripe and he was out of the country the following day.

## TET

One of the most pleasant times of the year is the new year's celebration. Young girls stand along the road and throw buckets of water on passers-by. The military jeep is open and a made-to-order target. It is all in fun, and a sign of good luck if you get wet. If not, it is still in good humor. However, when you're on the way to dress-up affairs this surprise baptism is not always welcome. After 6:00 p.m. the water is supposed to stop. Sometimes it does, sometimes not.

The rain came every day in Vientiane and the motorcycle I used to get to the airfield was my only transportation. I remember one day as I passed the center of town I ran the stop light. There was not much traffic, but there was a cop and he blew his whistle until I stopped. The lecture I received was a classic. "Sir, we of this country do appreciate what you are doing here, but we must insist you pay attention to our traffic lights. Now this is a big modern city. These lights have a purpose. When the light is green you may pass; when the light is red you must stop. Do you have any questions?" I tried not to laugh. I received no ticket, but for weeks I kept an eye out for that cop. I guess he thought I had never seen a stop light before.

In Vientiane the worst traffic problem was the dogs. There were so many that you hit one every day or so. I felt the dogs had a better chance of survival than the motorcycle rider, so I started to look for a jeep or a truck or anything with four wheels.

I used the motorcycle for two months. I never did learn to ride it well, but at least I did not kill anyone.

I was at work one morning across the runway from my office overseeing the loading of one of my aircraft. When I returned I found an old jeep outside my office. It was painted an off black, and the key was in the lock that secured the gas cap and the steering wheel. I thought, "Surely someone had left it in haste and would return". It was still there at 7:00 p.m. I drove it to the team house. I knew if it was left on the airfield overnight it would not be there the next morning. Whose jeep was it? I never knew. I drove it for the rest of my time in Laos and left it for my replacement, key in lock as I found it.

I guess no modern war story is complete without a description of rest and relaxation (R&R). It was a break, a pass to life away from war. In any combat area movements are restricted, social life is nothing, a married soldiers' family is 10,000 miles away; the bachelor separated from girlfriends. Not many businessmen throughout the world spend very much time away from home. If they are gone more than one weekend the wife raises so much hell that business trips are rescheduled. Uniquely the armed forces have been obliged to station people in places around the world where they are without families for a full year. This is one reason why service retirement pay is "earned pay" upon completion of twenty years. In winter you freeze because you are always in the field, and in the summer the army sends you off to the jungle where it's hotter than it would normally be past the gates of hell.

In most cases leave is not charged for R&R. During the Lao War two R&R areas were popular with troops. One was Bangkok. The capital of old Siam was only a couple of hours away by air. The other was Hong Kong. Later in the Vietnam War one could go to Taiwan, Manila, and Australia. However during the first few years of the war men would take R&R either in Bangkok or Hong Kong. Both boasted of many jewelry stores. Everyone wanted items for families, wives, girlfriends, and sisters. Particularly interesting were star sapphires, both black and blue. There was a store in Bangkok run by a fellow who called himself Johnny Gem, who would be notified that several men would be arriving on a particular date. They were ready for a good time and would have plenty of cash. Johnny was a real businessman. He met them at the airport with a sedan and transported them to his motel. As they settled into a spacious room, things began to happen. The refrigerator would be full of beer and within a few minutes the waiter arrived with glasses, a bottle of scotch, and sodas. This was "on the house".

Shortly afterward Johnny Gem arrived and asked what you wanted to purchase in Bangkok. What did you want to see? In what price range? He would arrange a trip to his shops or other shops if he could not provide what you wanted. This was done discreetly, businesslike, and Johnny Gem was known to make the guarantee that if you could not get twice the price for the article back in the U.S. he would refund the full price. He knew he would be dealing with the same people the next few years so this was not an idle guarantee. As far as I know, no one ever brought anything back.

After he found what you wanted, his car would take you to a fine restaurant. Johnny Gem always furnished meals and if you wanted anything to drink while away from his motel it was up to you. This was acceptable, so we would take advantage of his courtesy. After a quick drink at the motel you'd be off to the Star Lite, sort of a dance hall. It was a nice place. As I remember it was a large room with a beautiful floor and some of the most beautiful dancing girls in the world.

This place lived up to the reputation of the old days of Siam. There was a culture trip the next day, which included the Wats, the religious shrines, a tour to the Buddhas. If you wanted, you could take a tour of the river market places and see how the river people lived.

That night you went back to your motel. If you were unaccompanied you did not stay unaccompanied long.

When R&R in Bangkok would end, you would have bought everything you wanted and probably had money left over because of the fine deals.

Everyone was satisfied and I am sure Johnny Gem made millions from special forces troops and other Americans who came to know his establishment.

It is difficult when you are trying to describe the soldier's life and still not make him look like a philanderer. But when you take someone away from their home for a year it is a difficult, emotional time. Usually wives and families at home are with friends or relatives. They are with people who support them. Young soldiers were in a foreign environment. R&R helped get them back to their families.

Colonel Simons finished his tour as commander of the WSMTT and dropped out of sight. He did not leave the country, but went to the Plateau de Bulivans to attempt to organize the Cau tribes. He had some of his best troops on the plateau and stayed for at least four months.

Most of us rarely knew where he was, but reports were received every day by coded radio messages describing the combat actions the Bull was conducting. The extent of his success may never be known.

Certainly the Cau fought well near their villages. They did not do that well when units moved away from home to fight. Possibly no government will ever again control either the Cau or Hmong. They were armed, independent, and would fight any control. Their areas are so remote no information is available, but the Bull will be talked about around village campfires and tribal meetings for years to come.

At the end of my Lao tour the military advisor group's commanding general gave me a goodbye dinner. I was preparing to return to Korea where I had four or five months to complete a hardship tour. President Kennedy had given us all a Christmas present by extending the twelve-month tour to eighteen. This was to save federal money. It cost soldiers an extra six months away from their families. Who knows how many marriages bit the dust during that last six months.

I was looking forward to a slow trip back to Korea with a stop at Clark Air Force Base and a day or two layover in Japan. I did not have a replacement so I was still at the airfield two days before my departure. I was trying to write instructions for whomever was to take over. There was no use letting the next officer make the same mistakes I'd made.

But, the report would have to wait, a Thai colonel came storming into the office. His English was not bad, but it took awhile to understand what he was trying to tell me.

The colonel told me he had a Thai special forces team in trouble about a hundred miles from Vientiane. His unit was surrounded by a Vietmen unit and would be overrun or captured if he did not get them out.

I sent for the pilot of a standby H-34 that we had just refueled. He was at the French restaurant and returned in ten minutes or less. The colonel had maps and radio frequencies. In a few minutes I explained to the pilot that he likely would be going into an area under fire.

He was the best we had and had flown in Laos for three years. He looked at me and asked, "Are you going? I'll need someone in the door with an automatic rifle or .30 cal. machine gun." I nodded and picked up an old BAR (Browning automatic rifle) I had scrounged along with thirty magazines I kept in a small duffel bag. In five minutes more we were clearing the south tower. I had failed to call my headquarters this time, on purpose. There would be questions and a delay that might cost the team members their lives. Also, I might have been told I could not go. But what the hell; I was leaving. What was anyone going to do? Send me to Korea? I'd explain later and if we made it, then my decision would be justified. I'd learned a little about how special forces people think.

In forty minutes, with the air speed indicator red-lined, we were circling the area. The colonel was now standing in the door and I was lying at his feet on the helicopter floor deck with the Browning ready.

As we circled the hill, to which the special forces team had withdrawn, we began to pick up ground fire. I selected areas where the fire came from and fired as fast as I could. I had been a BAR instructor at Fort Benning, and I liked the old weapon. Some of the ground fire stopped. The colonel had spotted his team and they had recognized him standing in the door. He motioned them to the far side of the hill and the pilot picked a landing zone.

There was a lot of luck involved. The enemy had failed to cover that side. Maybe they would have done so shortly, but we were clear for a few minutes, and the team, with two of their wounded, was able to get on board.

I could not see any enemy, but I had gotten out of the helicopter and continued to fire in all directions all thirty of the twenty round magazines. I figured I would not need them anymore so left them on the ground as we took off low over the green jungle. The pilot took his time on the flight back and I wondered how much hell I would catch about this mission. The Thai colonel called by radio to have medical help at the airfield. We landed; the mission was a success.

I checked in by radio to headquarters as soon as we were on the ground. To my surprise no one had missed me for the three hours and I was not going to bring this mission up at dinner. I had learned a little in that regard. That night I was invited to the pilot's house for a little celebration.

The next day, my last of duty, the Thai colonel came into my office with two of his staff officers. He asked for the pilot of yesterday's mission. Again I sent for him and within a few minutes he arrived. The look on his face when he saw the colonel was a classic. He said, "Oh, no, not again." But the colonel quickly raised his hand and assured him he could relax; there was no mission. The colonel then asked us to stand side by side and his two staff officers stepped forward with two small boxes. Was this to be an award ceremony?

The colonel stepped forward and placed a large three-ounce gold chain over my head. On the chain hung a gold Buddha. The pilot got one also and the colonel explained that I had received a very old "soldier's buddha" which would keep me safe in any war. He told us these were presents from the families of the team we had rescued. I doubted this; I thought he had bought the gold, but it seemed right not to argue the point. I thanked him and decided to learn a little more about the "soldier's buddha". As usual, I got busy packing, saying good-bye, arranging my flight, and forgot to ask more questions.

In future years I would reflect many times on the colonel's words. I decided I would take no chances on the authenticity or value of this soldier's buddha.

I wore it for three more years in Vietnam and still wear it every day that there is the slightest chance I might get shot at.

My return to Korea and the following months were routine, but rather dull after Laos.

## THE RETURN (Cont.)

The Air Force Senior Master Sergeant was speaking to me, his hand on my shoulder, "Sir, would you like to observe the refueling of four, A-10 fighters? Come with me." He took me to a reclining control deck in the KC-135 tail section. We each took a position on opposite bunks facing aft to watch the A-10's approach.

During the next fifteen minutes he methodically refueled the fighters. The sergeant talks directly to the pilots and flys the fuel nozzle into the fuel intake orifice. Speed must be coordinated perfectly and frankly in twenty-one years of service I had never witnessed such team work. For the Air Force it is daily routine-for me a great experience to witness first hand at close range.

For the rest of the flight to California I was wide awake and had some time to think about the POW dilemma which had increased during 1983-85. I became more involved as I collected information and tried to unravel the last remaining issue of the Vietnam War. By understanding my personal confusion about this national issue and the maze of information not readily available to the American public, the reader will quickly realize it was necessary for me to return to Southeast Asia in 1986 to explore in depth the POW problem. How could I otherwise state facts unless I could say I know this to be true, **because I was there.**

Facts about the POW problem were hard to come by. They were elusive, almost as if they were being kept from the public. Only the Vietnam Veteran Coalition seemed active in trying to inform veterans and the public. The League of Families and our government backed off concerning the POW issue, for fear Vietnam might quit talking about the MIAs.

I wrote plans and attended VFW National Conventions. Except for the VFW, the Vietnam Veterans Coalition, the League of Families, and H. Ross Perot no one seemed to be doing anything. Our Defense Intelligence Agency seemed intent on discrediting live sighting reports. What was going on? There were rumors of a coverup.

In December 1985, after long discussions with my wife, I made the decision to return to Southeast Asia to explore the POW/MIA issue. The League of Families had done what it could. Headed by Ann Mills Griffiths it was dedicated to accounting for the 2500 MIA/POW. There had been eighteen Defense Intelligence Agency personnel working full-time on the problem of several hundred live-sighting reports. By December, 1985, this figure had been worked down to 100. Almost reluctantly, it seemed, the federal government had to start supporting the League of Families and use them to get the Vietnam Government to cooperate in an accounting. No President until Reagan had paid attention to the League of Families. Pentagon and State Department personnel were assigned to deal with the League of Families. Was the League used for political purposes? Ann Griffiths was finally getting attention. She would be able to represent the U.S., but the effort to recover POWs seemed downgraded and an effort was mounted to account for aircraft crashes. Of course in meetings there were always references to the POW issue but the Vietnamese Government denied POWs existence and the League of Families and the U.S.Government representatives would back off and be grateful that the Vietnamese would meet for such discussions. I met Ann Griffiths to discuss the possibility of working in this effort. She informed me she had the ear of the President and had "real experts" in Southeast Asia. Of course, the term is relative. The fact that a man is married to a North Vietnamese does not give him expertise to conduct the effort required to gain cooperation, set up an intelligence collection, and select personnel the Vietnamese would work with. Although the above thoughts weighted heavily on me, I was willing to step back for awhile. But after two years of small concessions from the Vietnamese Government the results were unsatisfactory. The U.S. received bodies that would not check out forensically.

We sent delegations to plead with a government that cannot feed its own people. We were acting like a nation that lost a war. The U.S. was told in late 1986 that "possibly" POWs exist in Vietnam. Maybe all the POWs have been moved into Laos or traded to Russia. U.S. Delegations did not press the issue for fear Vietnamese might take offense and stop sending a few bodies each year. The statement "all is being done that can be done" was unworthy of any U.S. effort, a defensive move. The only satisfactory government action would have been to recover a few POWs from the suspected two to four hundred.

In the years, from 1980-85, there had been over 800 live sighting reports that the National Intelligence Agency has investigated. (By 1986 there was almost 1000) There remained in December 1985 at least 95 live sightings that could not be disproved. Of these, 43 are "most likely" real. Reporters of live sightings had been given lie detector tests, or the same sightings were reported by more than one reliable source. Yet still no pressure was being exerted on the Vietnam Government. Our government was satisfied with the League of Families' effort and hoped it would quiet the voices of veterans. To some extent these minimum efforts did what political Washington wanted done and some veteran organizations accepted that "all is being done that can be done".

Then Major Mark A. Smith and S. Sergeant McIntire, former soldiers, brought suit and named President Reagan as defendant for lack of U.S. action.

Although I had been keeping people near me aware of the POW/MIA issue, I was not satisfied with the information from our government. The questions were becoming more urgent. Are there POW in Southeast Asia? That was the question.

On December 1, 1985, I decided that nothing short of a trip to Southeast Asia would give the answers I needed. I was not sure a trip was the solution. The message from Washington was clear. Ann Griffiths and her associates wanted no civilian interference. Of course I disagreed. It is of concern to veterans how the government will support POWs. I thought that our government probably "will not kill me for taking my own action in accord with my conscience." Certainly the woman most veterans refer to as "that traitorous bitch", who went to North Vietnam during the war, was not put up to much official criticism. I was not proposing across border intrusions "Rambo" style, only a fact finding mission. Of course I did not rule out that I might be able to do something to recover a few POWs.

During January, 1986, I collected what cash I might put in the project, borrowed from friends, got other backing, leaned on my VFW post, got support of Vietnam veterans in northern Indiana, wrote for a Thailand visa, and wrote the chief of the Bangkok police for a pistol permit. I established myself as an import/export buyer, a real position with a southern Indiana company. I obtained recommendations from the local sheriff and made sure my passport was valid. It seemed the details would never end. I brought my will up-to-date and talked to the Air Force about flights west. I could fly space available as a retiree. The preparation period I set was sixty days. I was to leave for Thailand about March

1, 1986. Funds were slow to arrive. I did not have a pledge for enough money by February 28. I would need cash if I could make arrangements to have some POWs freed.

I do not know why I felt I must do this--the return to Southeast Asia could only mean financial burden, and a chance of alienating the only President I had respected since Truman. If I found that our POWs are not being recovered when an opportunity existed, the scandal would make Watergate look like a Sunday School picnic. There was danger that some duty-conscious protector of the President's reputation would order me killed while on this mission. There would be a million easy ways to dispose of me. My intention was, of course, only to collect such information that might convince the administration to take whatever action was required to recover our POWs.

Some may feel I'm presumptuous to assume I might be successful at this, but one thing is for sure-if I can arrange for a POW to be released for a price, then it could have and should have been done years ago with all the "high powered" American help and intelligence available. To leave our men in captivity would be the crime of this century. But why would they be forgotten by our government?

The possible reasons stagger the imagination. Somewhere behind a "POW coverup" there would have to be a mammoth reason. I can only guess at possibilities because understanding big money, which by and large dictates all world political action, is not my expertise. Is there off-shore oil to be developed off Vietnam? Or is it just simply the Vietnamese want the $3.25 billion promised in Paris for war restoration. Whatever the reason (if there is a coverup) it must be good. Or has the problem lasted so long and now it's a personal embarrassment to our intelligence agencies and directors, a subject no politician wants to touch for fear of failure.

I had begun to think that this might be one of the most dangerous missions of my life. It's bad enough to have to worry about one enemy, but on this mission many entities could be against me-U.S. Intelligence agents, the political structure, the embassy, CIA, and big business enterprises. This danger is most likely just a fancy of my imagination I keep telling myself.

All plans were made for the Southeast Asia trip. A SAC aircraft would pick me up 7 March for the flight to Mather AFB in California, then to Travis AFB for a flight to Clark AFB in the Philippines. In the Philippines I would get a flight into Bangkok.

The month had been filled with details-getting the money together, registering the guns, packing, and getting my wife, Monika, ready to take care of our business for three months. She had a lot of bills to pay, spring taxes, etc. I had revised my will and fixed things around the house, repacked one week prior to departure and contacted the Air Force base to check on air transport.

As of 1 March all final plans were made, the will signed.

The week prior to leaving was filled by completing short range projects. Then the brakes on both vehicles went out and I had a final dilemma of last minute mechanics. I did some of the work and had some done.

I departed Grissom AFB 1020 hours 7 March, 1986. Preparation had continued up to the last minute of departure day. It might be said my departure only interrupted preparations. With car maintenance finished, the morning of departure

Monika drove me to the SAC base where five weeks before I had made arrangements for transportation to Mather AFB, California. The Strategic Air Command is probably the only entity of the U.S. Government or any civilian company that could make an exact five week aircraft arrival predication, make it, and then rendezvous five hundred miles from that point with four A-10 fighter bombers for refueling.

As I entered the California SAC base I had no idea how I was going to get to Travis where the Military Air Command would lift me to Hawaii. The adventure had begun and possibly a last chapter for my book. All ahead was unknown. I hadn't been to Southeast Asia for 15 years, and times, people, and places change. I had no idea if the embassy in Bangkok would support me in any way.

At Mather I looked around base operations and asked about a bus to Travis or if there might be some base transportation going that way; the hour was now about 1445, California time. The sergeants were helpful, but nothing was going my way. Then luck caught up with me again and I got my first good sign. I met an Air Force Lieutenant Colonel, Jon Perney, and after a few minutes of conversation he offered me a lift to Travis 50-60 miles southwest toward San Francisco. He had served 23 years, from NAV to base operations commander. He had been professor of aero space science at a prominent university and was considering retirement. We talked politics during the next hour and he went out of his way to deliver me to the MAC terminal, where I requested a flight to Hawaii the next day. I hoped I might get out. Then the first snag I ran into was I'd need a Philippine visa, even to stay at Clark AFB in transit to Thailand. This meant a few days in Hawaii, which would increase the cost of my trip. So far in getting to Hawaii I had spent $30 of the $2,000 I was carrying. Well, we would see how that would go: there might even be a delay in receiving the visa. I'd also need visas for Japan and Korea. I might have to go through Singapore and take a train north to Bangkok. Things were beginning to happen, and I only had partial control. When traveling Air Force space available, you have to be ready to take any route to your destination.

That night I went to the officers' club at Travis for dinner, and when I arrived at the visitors quarters, I had to wait until after midnight to get a room.

My flight to Hawaii (Hickam Field) would be set up at 0600 Saturday 8 March and that meant a 0500 get up call. It had been a long day, I was beat and yet didn't sleep well. Flying space available is always a trying experience, to say the least. The retired military officer is given no priority and loads only after the goats, sheep, and chickens. But the price is just about right.

Next morning I was up at five, but not awake enough to get it altogether. I forgot to shave. When I got my bags downstairs I lucked into a ride to the terminal. There would be 73 seats, enough for all to go who were standby. We were delayed an hour because of some problem of loading cargo.

Again I would be in Hawaii on a Saturday night, probably no quarters available and no transportation anywhere, even if I knew where to go. Scheduled to leave at 0900, we boarded at 1130, only to be brought back into the terminal at 1400. Then we did it again; this time it was 1600, when we were told that possibly because another C5 had trouble and returned we might be able to go on that one if it was repaired. What the hell did they mean "repaired". That's the second aircraft today that didn't make it and it might fly in two hours or did they say loaded in two hours. The waiting goes on and on. I found a place in the terminal to buy a beer, then one more. Everyone was patient and it was only after ten and a halt hours that some appeared to wear a little thin. I bought $25,000 worth of flight insurance for $2. At this point it seemed a good investment. It would cover the next thirty days and the trip from Travis to Bangkok. At 1730 we were still in the holding area. The plane was not repaired. It seemed a landing gear would not go up.

By 2115 that night I had been out of the terminal three times to board. At that time the flight was scratched and all passengers had to find a place to stay until the next morning. I elected to stay in the terminal and catch what sleep I could. The seats were intentionally made not to sleep in and it took me a while to arrange my accommodation. I bought two beers, went for a long walk in the rain and turned in.

I awoke at 0200 and again at 0430: it was no use, the night was over. At 0600 one flight was set up and I passed on a C130 ride, hoping to get the same flight I was scheduled on all the way to Guam. But the flight to Guam did not work out. I would have to get the Philippine visa in Hawaii. We departed for Hawaii at 1230, March 9, 1986, on a C-5, the world's largest military aircraft. I was trying to think ahead. Between catnaps I was considering:

To gain information of value on the POW issue, or arrange to recover POWs if possible.

That there are POWs in Southeast Asia.

To do this without violation of the Neutrality Act.

To do this without expenditure of large amounts of money.

To obtain money for payment "COD" of one or more POWs.

Should I: 1. be up front with officials at the embassy; 2. use covert operations with only paid agents; 3. a combination of the above; 4. try to become employed by CIA; 5. use covert intelligence methods only; 6. use embassy secretaries as contacts; 7. use embassy as contact for import/export business and thus have a good cover; 8. try contacting other U.S. civil efforts.

Discussion of each of the above methods: 1. In the past all problems seem to rotate around the embassy: if there is a cover up that's where it starts: possibly new personnel may now have other orders; 2. This seems to have been the most effective intelligence production; 3. Possible but dangerous; 4. As I have learned, CIA agents cannot be trusted; 5. This means a border crossing at some date, dealing with the underworld; 6. This will be hard to do and keep my mission secure; 7. A civilian contact is necessary.

My thoughts were running in circles. I'd had some discussions with the CIA. A congressional task force was getting nowhere. Open or closed hearings and more than sufficient information was available indicating live POWs in Southeast Asia. Yet our government was still at top dead center in this effort to recover POWs.

What is going on? There is so much smoke we can't see the fire. But there is fire. There has to be with so many men so sure we have POWs left behind. The men in some cases are heroes. Smith and McIntire are highly decorated soldiers. Are officials so blind they can't see the truth? These retired Army officiers are not committ·ng perjury.

I thought about some of the code phrases I'd set up with Monika. "How are the dogs getting along?" means I have made contacts, things look good. "I have not heard from George at all" means things are bad, no cooperation. "Have trouble getting mail" means I've made a contact. Contact news media for money to pay for delivery to get a POW out of Laos, and so on.

But now I'd leave my future to luck. I was tired, the beautiful sergeant from Panama seated beside me was on her way to Korea to marry her "true love". She was reading and not interested in conversation. It would be a long flight to Hawaii. Strangely I found she was part of M.I. 470 (military intelligence unit). But she was not tracking me or she at least would have acted more interested.

Two days later in Hawaii I was still at Hickam. My usual luck seems to have taken a vacation. I had learned a lot about space available travel and how to get by on an air base without quarters. You must remain near the terminal. Flights, unscheduled, are posted at all hours. You must be ready. I otherwise would have been on Waikiki trying to enjoy my wait. There were no quarters and everyone was solving his own problems. I slept under a pool table for three nights in the USO, really not bad, but not exactly what I'd have selected. I concluded after four days and nights that there is no skill in space available travel, just luck.

One night trying to sleep under the pool table next to a very nice lady staff sergeant I reflected on the things I had learned concerning the POW issue.

I needed to talk so I got my friend up and we met Steve, the air force master sergeant, who we found lounging in the coffee shop.

We were all tired but not able to sleep. I broke open my old leather brief case and started to present to them the POW data I had been able to collect. I thought they would soon tire of these facts and want to return to our second class accommodations, but as I brought out more and more material and passed it around there developed a silence so intense you could hear it. The night passed quickly. Some of the material following is mine but mostly it is data and information others have dug up and furnished to me. Here is what Lisa and Steve became absorbed in.

## CHAPTER 3

### (The Longest Chapter of our History)

### THE POW/MIA STORY

### Myth or National Disgrace

In recent years, for over 2,400 American families, the POW/MIA dilemma has kept the Vietnam War from ending. Most of the public has little knowledge of facts concerning our missing men.

At the end of the war 591 POWs returned from North Vietnam, but 2,430 Americans are still missing. The latter figure includes U.S. Government or United Nations civilians.

When the POWs returned from Hanoi in 1973, most of us in our celebration did not realize that of all these men, not one was an amputee, badly burned, blind, or emotionally debilitated. Many missing men made emergency ejections from burning aircraft or were captured in firefights and other actions. Where were the seriously injured? From those who returned we know that many were tortured. Where are those hurt by torture?

Nearly 600 men disappeared into Laos, but only a handful came home. Pathet Lao officials said they had many American prisoners, but Laos did not participate in the Paris peace talks and facts indicate the POWs held in Laos were never released.

After the talks ended and the United States pulled out of Southeast Asia, refugees began to flood the world, bringing stories of Americans held in captivity. As of January 1986 the United States government received and analyzed nearly 4,000 such reports, which included over 800 eyewitness sightings.

In April 1975 all but a few of the 2,400 men were legally declared dead in an attempt to put to rest the Vietnam War. But this action did not work. Families of these declared dead and others, who questioned the government's MIA accounting, continued to press for a full accounting.

The Paris Accords and release of some of the POWs, officially ended the war. Since the end of the Vietnam War in 1973, other civilians and military were taken prisoner in Southeast Asia, but the following figures reflect those American MIA/POW prior to 1973.

The statistics of the POW/MIA are difficult to analyze when the large picture of all of Southeast Asia is considered. Losses were reported over North Vietnam, over the ocean, over China and adjacent seas, Cambodia, South Vietnam, the South China Sea, and Laos.

Correlation of figures comes only when one compares aircraft crews lost over North Vietnam and crews lost over Laos.

## AIRCRAFT CREWS

| | | |
|---|---|---|
| NORTH VIETNAM- | | % |
| Total Losses | 1069 | |
| Air Crew POW released | 469 | |
| Bodies returned | 106 | |
| Total accounted for | 575 | 53.8 |
| Unaccounted for | 494 | 46.2 |

NOTE: In North Vietnam only 23 of the 106 bodies returned were of men who died in captivity; therefore, 492 or 46% of crew members were in North Vietnam captivity at some time. This would put the survival of POWs in NVN captivity at 95.3% (This seems high and may mean that more were in captivity and died or were killed.)

| | | |
|---|---|---|
| LAOS- | | % |
| Total Losses | 533 | |
| Air crew released | 12 | |
| Bodies returned | 19 | |
| Escapes | 2 | |
| Total accounted for | 33 | 6.2 |
| Unaccounted for | 500 | 93.8 |

NOTE: If North Vietnam was an example of aircrew survivability, then approximately 250 POWs should be in Laos and even with an expected mortality rate proportional to N. Vietnam well over 200 should have survived and are still being held if they were not executed or allowed to die of neglect.

*Figures may vary slightly from one Government paper to another, but these are as good as any to date.

Intelligence reports present a compelling case. Following are examples:

1976- In the first half of 1976, a South Vietnamese girl (name protected) stated that on several occasions North Vietnamese Army officers told her American prisoners were still in North Vietnam. They told her that because these prisoners were sick or badly injured, the Democratic Republic of Vietnam was afraid of a possibly unfavorable effect on public opinion should they be released. (CIA communique bearing notation "FIR 317/09155-76" released 4 June 1982).

1979- "I was a bus driver on the Saigon-Hanoi route. I arrived in the U.S. February 20, 1980. In December 1979, I took a Communist colonel who said he was in charge of a prison and returning to his prison camp to deliver merchandise. He took me on a tour of his prison camp. During the tour I saw that the prisoners were Americans. They were in a sorry state, very thin and pale. I asked why our government kept those people. The answer was, 'Our Party and our State are not stupid...we want to use them to bargain and set a price for their release with the U.S. Imperialists. Our children will enjoy the claims we make against these flying bandits that have killed many of our comrades.' I asked how many 'flying bandits' we were keeping in our country and he told me about 300 of them." (Condensed from a refugee letter to the National League of Families).

1982- "I respectfully sent to you information regarding a prisoner of war camp for Americans in the Northeast of Laos which we personally saw during a special trip into that area. We were then part of the Vietnamese resistance. We established contacts with the Royal Lao Resistance Forces to ask for supplies; it was during April 1982. The prison camp we saw detained about 50 Americans kept in two rows of very solid wooden houses. The camp was guarded by Lao border security guards." (written by a master sergeant in the South Vietnamese Army working with the resistance against the Hanoi regime until April 1983).

1985- "During my imprisonment (1976) at Yen Bai, the group from my barracks was sent to whitewash the tombstones of 17 Americans there. I can draw a map and a sketch and show where the 17 are." Regarding live American POWs: "Your Americans are kept roving, they take them to North Vietnam to the same area they have kept the French prisoners formerly." (from a former colonel in the South Vietnamese Army, who escaped in 1980).

Following are stories of a few of the men:

ROBERT ANDERSON, USAF - His aircraft went down over North Vietnam on October 6, 1972. He and his co-pilot both ejected safely and talked to rescue planes. Anderson said, "I have a good chute, am in good shape, and can see no enemy forces on the ground." His co-pilot was captured and returned in 1973. Anderson is still missing.

DAVID HRDLICKA, USAF - Hrdlicka was observed during ejection from his aircraft and on the ground. A flight member said he saw him being led away by natives. Communist newspapers later printed his picture. Reports believed to pertain to him have been monitored for years.

COLONEL CHARLES SHELTON, USAF - was seen captured by the Pathet Lao in 1965. Even though indigenous rescue teams confirmed he was a prisoner and reports about him came in for years, admission of his capture was never made by Lao authorities. A highly credible report from 1976 indicates he was rescued from a cave complex near Sam Neua Laos by a friendly indigenous team. During the long cross-country trek to Thailand, the Lao team was confronted by a Vietnamese patrol which demanded that the "prisoner" be given to them. Reports over the years suggest a real possibility that Shelton may be alive today.

COLONEL PATRICK FALLON, USAF - Fallon's A-1 Skyraider was shot down near Xiangkhoang, Laos on July 4, 1969. Ejecting and landing safely, he reported only a stiff neck. He was quickly surrounded by Pathet Lao troops, but U.S. aircraft drove them back. Again the enemy approached and Fallon radioed a request for a second strike. His last transmission, "Put it all around me, I'm hit."

COLONEL JOHN F. O'GRADY, USAF - On April 10, 1967, O'Grady became one of over fifty American airmen lost in a small window of the world known as the Mugia Pass, one of the most heavily traveled sections of the Ho Chi Minh Trail in Laos. Not one of these men has ever been accounted for. Recent reports from Southeast Asia suggest that many of the men of the Mugia Pass may have survived.

S/SGT JAMES M. RAY, USA - On March 18, 1968, Ray was captured by the Viet Cong in South Vietnam. In April 1969 a POW who escaped from the camp where Ray was held reported he was among the healthiest POWs both mentally and physically. Another POW said of Ray, "He wanted more than anything else to be free." Ray was awarded the Silver Star for gallantry as a result of two unsuccessful escape attempts, after each of which he was chained and severely beaten. His records are a tangle of inconsistencies. No POW witnessed his death or knew with certainty what happened to him.

These are just a few of the hundreds of Americans who may have survived, waiting for the day the Vietnam War will end for them.

## LT.COL. EARL P. HOPPER, JR.

Earl P. Hopper, Jr., was born in Santa Maria, California, graduated from high school in Glendale, Arizona in June, 1961, and immediately entered the US Air Force Academy graduating in June, 1965.

Following graduation from the Air Force Academy, Hopper entered flight training at Laredo, Texas. He was selected as the most outstanding officer in his class and awarded the Commander's Trophy. Following his graduation from Laredo, he took training in aircraft with final assignment made to the F-4, Phantom fighter-bomber.

Hopper was transferred to Udorn AFB, Thailand, with the 13th Tactical Fighter Squadron in October, 1967, and was assigned to fly as "backseater" with Colonel, then Captain, Keith Hall.

Hopper had flown over 35 combat missions when he was shot down on January 10, 1968, while on an "aircap" mission over Hanoi. During the mission, the North Vietnamese fired three surface-to-air (SAM) missiles at Hopper's flight, two of the SAMs missing their target but the third exploding a hundred feet below and to the right of Hopper's F-4. The explosion caused damage to the hydraulic and fuel system. The crippled aircraft was able to climb to 18,000 feet before it caught on fire, causing one engine to flame-out. With the front on fire the flight leader instructed Colonel Hall and Hopper to eject, neither man had been injured in the incident. Colonel Hall ordered Hopper to eject, but apparently he could not. Hall then ejected.

Hopper turned the aircraft southwest towards Laos and was able to fly for 8 to 10 minutes before he was seen ejecting as it was entering a 5,000-foot undercast. Four of the six pilots in the three aircraft escorting the crippled plane reported seeing two objects leave the plane just as it entered the heavy clouds. These would have been the aircraft's canopy and Hopper in his seat. No parachute was observed because of the clouds.

Within minutes, the other aircraft monitored two emergency beeper signals, one strong which was Colonel Hall and one very weak which would have been Colonel Hopper, thus attesting to the fact that both men were alive and on the ground. Within thirty minutes after landing, Hall was captured by the North Vietnamese, imprisoned for over five years, and released in March, 1973.

Before returning to Thailand the other aircraft picked up a muffled radio transmission and continued to receive faint beeper signals. A search and recovery aircraft also picked up the two beepers but was unable to establish voice radio contact with Hopper. Because of weather and the lateness of the day, the search was discontinued but renewed the following morning.

For three consecutive days emergency radio signals were detected in the vicinity of where Hopper's aircraft went down. It was rugged, mountainous country, and weather worsened so no rescue attempt could be made. On the third or fourth day a ground search team was inserted into the area which located and recovered Hopper's emergency radio, transmitting weakly, but no trace of Hopper was found. There has been no word of Hopper since his shoot down. But one incident remains a mystery. Two and one-half years later, Hall was interrogated for twenty-five to thirty minutes by a North Vietnamese interrogator, with questions centered on information concerning Hopper, i.e., marital status, family, schooling.

Hopper was carried by the Air Force as missing from January 10, 1968, until July 14, 1982, at which time his status was changed to killed.

The change in status and presumption of death was "due to the length of time missing with no new information to prove he is alive."

Hopper was among the last five MIA to be declared dead and was the last who went down in North Vietnam.

The Department of Justice, after reviewing Hopper's case disagreed with the status assigned by the Air Force. In a decision of September 13, 1982, two months following the change to a Killed in Action status, a three man commission found that Hopper had been captured: "the Commission requested the Air Force to provide any information which would shed light on Lt. Hopper's status after the airplane crash. Having examined all available evidence...which provided details of the crash, the surrounding countryside, and the voice contact established with Hopper's commander, the Commission finds that...Earl P. Hopper, Jr. survived the crash and was captured on or about 10 January, 1968."

Alexander Solzhenitsyn, speaking on American prisoners held by the communist governments of Indochina, said that, "If the government of North Vietnam had difficulty explaining to you what happened to your brothers, your American POWs who have not yet returned, I can explain this quite clearly on the basis of my own experience in the Gulag Archipelago. There is a law in the Archipelago that those who have been treated the most harshly and who have withstood the most bravely, who are the most honest, the most courageous, the most unbending, never again come out into the world. They are never again shown to the world because they will tell tales that the human mind can barely accept. Some of your best people. These are your foremost heroes who, in a solitary combat, have stood the test. And today, unfortunately, they cannot take courage from our applause. They can't hear it from their solitary cells where they may either die or remain for thirty years."

In July, 1986, seven members of the House of Representatives POW/MIA Task Force sent a letter to President Reagan informing him of their conviction that many of our men are alive.

The congressmen wrote, "Our analysis of the data is now complete. Based on the extensive classified briefings we have received and the volume and clarity of the information we have seen, we write to inform you that American POWs remain captive in communist prisons in Southeast Asia. We are firm in this belief and we have not been, nor will we be dissuaded by the arguments to the contrary made by bureaucrats who have handled this issue since the end of the Vietnam War. The congressmen signing the letter were: Robert Dornan (R-Cal), David Dreier (R-Cal), Bill Hendon (R-NC), Frank McCloskey (D-Ind), John Rowland

(R-Conn), Christopher Smith (R-NJ) and Robert Smith (R-NH).

The six Republicans and one Democrat asked the President either to establish an independent commission or support legislation for a commission, so as to recommend ways to win release of the captives. They asked that H. Ross Perot head the commission.

One of the signers of the letter, Rep. Bill Hendon, is the author of the proposed legislation, and has been to Indochina eight times to investigate POW reports. Interviewed, he declined to estimate the number of American prisoners. He did say, however, "It's a large number of men, there's no question. it's three figures and up. We feel two things can be said with certainty: our men remain prisoners against their will, and it is long past time to bring them home."

We too, think that Perot is the man for the job. Called a "superpatriot , he has demonstrated a combination of qualities that makes one believe that he would be by far the best choice.

At the request of Secretary of State Henry Kissinger in 1969, Perot financed a monumental effort to sway worldwide opinion against the North Vietnamese for their treatment of American POWs. He filled a cargo plane with medical supplies, food, blankets, and clothing, and flew it to Hanoi, attempting to deliver the material to the American POWs. He was not allowed to do so, but his effort so embarrassed the North Vietnamese that they immediately improved treatment of the POWs.

Ten years later, Kholmenhi imprisoned two of Perot's employees. Perot's giant computer software company, EDS, had held the contract for administration of the Iranian social security system under the Shah. When the Ayatollah gained power he judged Perot's top two men in Iran "capitalist criminals" and arrested them. After repeated attempts by the State Department to obtain their release, Perot made a decision he would get them out. He mounted a paramilitary operation sent a team into Tehran, started a riot, and broke open a prison, freeing 11,000 prisoners, including his two employees. The team moved overland through Iran to Turkey and freedom.

But the Perot Commission for Vietnam could not perform a rescue. It would have two responsibilities: to determine whether our men were there; and; to recommend to Congress appropriate action to obtain their freedom.

HRC 129 presently has over 160 co-sponsors--160 plus congressman who believe the best solution is to get this problem out of the bureaucracy and into the hands of Perot who has shown that when he starts something he finishes.

Action is being taken in other ways; officials are getting involved. The Senate Veterans Affairs Committee has held hearings intended to look at the allegations of suppression of information by individuals within the U.S. government.

Testimony has had a strong effect on Committee members. Senator Dennis De Concini says he is "disturbed" and "wading in" to find the truth and bring men home.

The two million members of the VFW have passed a resolution asking the President to form a commission in lieu of Congressional commission.

Perhaps the most disturbing testimony has come from three highly decorated veterans of the Vietnam War, members of Special Forces (Green Berets). Major Mark Smith, Sergeant Melvin McIntire, and America's most decorated soldier,

Lt. Col. Robert L. Howard, presently commander of VII Special Troops Battalion in Stuttgart. According to these American prisoners were still held, specifically in Laos. When they reported that information they found no interest, their operations were shut down by superiors, and they were transferred out of Southeast Asia.

Smith and McIntire, along with more than 25 POW/MIA family members, filed suit under the Hostage Act against the government. They are seeking "declaratory relief," a court finding that American prisoners remain in Indochina. If the court so rules, the court may find those men have constitutional rights. Howard has filed an affidavit in support of the lawsuit in which he declares that at least a hundred POWs are still in captivity and that the Defense Intelligence Agency is discrediting reports of their existence.

If what Smith, McIntire, and Howard say is true and it appears they would have had nothing to gain and much to lose by inventing it, nothing can be accomplished until changes within the system are made. There is reason to believe that may be happening. The recently appointed Director of DIA, Lt. Gen. Leonard Perroots, has moved to change information handling within DIA, and has said privately that in meetings with Smith and McIntire he has come to believe they are telling the truth.

General Perroots has removed one DIA senior analyst. Another has admitted in a meeting with six congressmen that "for 13 years we've been doing it wrong" (analyzing live POW intelligence reports).

One congressman long involved in the POW issue has said, that Perroots is "absolutely all we could ask for in a DIA Director...but his ability to guide the government POW effort is limited". Seeming confirmation has come from General Perroots: "Sometimes I wonder who's running my agency".

The difficulty, it seems, is misrepresentation of facts which have been made over the years, for whatever reason, to the American people. Now, those who have been less than truthful, even though ordered to do so, are afraid to admit the real truth. President Nixon and Secretary of State Kissinger told us in 1973 that no secret agreements had been made with the Vietnamese in Paris. We now know this is not true. In 1977 the Carter White House declassified a Presidential letter of February 1973 explaining Article 21 of the Peace Accords. In that letter, Nixon promised the Vietnamese $3.25 billion in reconstruction aid over five years, and between $1 billion and $1.5 billion in humanitarian assistance "as needed". The Vietnamese kept our men, specifically those in Laos to ensure payment of that money. On April 13, 1973, however, the U.S. government ceased demanding return of prisoners in Laos, and declared, "There is no reason to believe that any American prisoners remain alive in Indochina". But time is not on our side...each day that goes by threatens the life of an American prisoner. Many of them are nearing 60 years of age, in a part of the world where the average life expectancy is 37.

*Taken from The Wall Street Journal, Tuesday, August 19, 1986.*

## PAY FOR U.S. PRISONERS IN COMMUNIST HANDS

By Bill Paul

Call them the legion of lost souls-hundreds of American prisoners of war who today are scattered throughout the Communist world: Russia, North Korea, Vietnam and Laos.

The U.S. government knows they're there but it doesn't want the American people to know because they might demand their return, even if it meant paying for them. The U.S. can't afford to be blackmailed, the Reagan administration says.

I say pay. In hard currency, if absolutely necessary; otherwise, in economic assistance or medical aid. There's precedent. The French quietly paid to get back men taken in its Indochina conflict. We paid to get back Bay of Pigs invaders.

Vietnam is desperate to cut a deal. At least that's how Washington observers view Hanoi's decision to release an American civilian it previously denied knowing anything about. The American, Robert Schwab, disappeared after sailing into Vietnamese waters. He was let go, apparently for a ransom.

What's needed now is for President Reagan to seize this initiative and buy the men back. The American people can't allow their government to continue lying that there is no proof these prisoners exist. They do exist, and here's more evidence that Washington knows they do.

In March 1984, John Noble, and American author and lecturer who rotted in the Gulag between 1945 and 1955, introduced himself to Secretary of State George Shultz at a banquet at a Washington hotel.

Mr. Noble, who now lives in Muncy, Pa. is living proof that when a government really tries, it can save anyone. Mr. Noble was originally imprisoned by the Germans in 1939. (Michigan born and bred, he was working in one of his father's German factories.) In 1945, when the Soviets moved in, he was imprisoned by them at Dresden. In 1950, he was shipped to a Siberian prison camp.

For years the State Department sent notes to Moscow asking that Mr. Noble be released. Each time the Russians denied holding him. Then, in 1954, Mr. Noble smuggled out a postcard to relatives in Germany signed, "Your noble nephew." Michigan Rep. Alvin Bentley got the card to President Eisenhower, who then personally pressed Soviet Premier Malenkov for Mr. Noble's release. At first Malenkov again denied holding Mr. Noble, but as publicity surrounding the case grew, the Russians suddenly released him-and his two American cellmates.

Mr. Noble says that when he told Mr. Shultz that many Americans remain in Russian prison camps, the secretary replied, "I know that they're there."

Then Mr. Shultz indicated that the State Department knows the names of Americans imprisoned in the Soviet Union. He said that occasionally the State Department sends notes to the Kremlin demanding the return of these Americans but that the Soviets, in Mr. Shultz's words, "throw (the list) back in our face." When Mr. Noble then asked what else the U.S. does besides send notes, Mr. Noble says Mr. Shultz replied, "That's all we can do."

(Calls to the State Department yesterday yielded no official comment on the matter.)

Mr. Noble didn't ask Mr. Shultz how many Americans are in the Gulag, but the New York Times once reported, on Jan. 5, 1954, that the State Department knew of more than 5,000 American prisoners in the hands of the Soviets and their European satellites.

While publicly the Pentagon hasn't ever admitted leaving men behind after the Korean and Vietnam wars, a few weeks ago Col. Henry Land, the number two man in the Secretary of Defense's POW office, acknowledged to Robert Dumas, the brother of a Korean War soldier still unaccounted for, that American soldiers are still imprisoned in North Korea.

Col. Land discussed the continued presence of U.S. POWs in Korea during a telephone conversation that Mr. Dumas tape recorded without Col. Land's knowledge. On the tape, Col. Land is heard to say. "The bottom line is that until the North Koreans get to a position and they want to release the prisoners and the remains that are up there. (Pause). They will do it when they feel it is to their advantage."

A careful listening to the 10 minute tape leaves no doubt that Col. Land is knowingly differentiating between live prisoners and remains, and that he is telling Mr. Dumas that both are still in Korea.

Contacted yesterday, Col. Land said he has "no recollection" of what he told Mr. Dumas. He also said, contrary to what is on the tape, "We honestly don't know if American POWs remain in North Korea.

While Gen. Eugene Tighe, who retired in September 1981 as head of the Pentagon's Defense Intelligence Agency, has frequently stated that he believes American POWs are still alive in Southeast Asia, none of his staff has ever publicly backed him up. However, in a recent interview, one of Gen. Tighe's former top assistants, who because he is still on active duty asked not to be named, backed him up unequivocally.

Indeed, this officer told me that when he reviewed the U.S.'s POW intelligence in 1981, he found that, as of 1978, the Pentagon had "hard evidence" of Americans still imprisoned in Southeast Asia. He wouldn't tell me what this evidence was, just that, "I came to the conclusion that (POWs) were there.

He added that, in his opinion, the Pentagon hadn't acted on this hard evidence because it was afraid that military morale would suffer if the troops learned that fighting men had been left behind when the U.S. pulled out of Vietnam.

In 1981, just weeks after President Reagan took office, the new administration learned that Vietnam wanted to sell to the U.S. an unspecified number of live POWs still in Southeast Asia for the sum of $4 billion (less than the U.S. had promised Hanoi in post-war rebuilding aid).

It's unclear whether the offer was made to Mr. Reagan or that he inherited it from President Carter. The proposal was discussed by Mr. Reagan and his advisers at a general meeting on security matters, according to one person who says he was in the room, and whose story is supported by another attendee.

During the discussion, it was first decided that the offer was indeed genuine. Then a number of the president's advisers said they opposed paying for POWs on the ground that it would appear as if the U.S. could be blackmailed. Mr. Reagan concurred. At that point, the president's men were prepared to let the matter drop.

To his credit, however, Mr. Reagan told William Casey, director of the Central Intelligence Agency, Richard Allen, then the national security adviser, to try to find another way to get the men home.

Mr. Allen subsequently proposed a reconnaissance mission into Laos which, if successful, would lead to a military rescue of prisoners presumed held at a jungle prison camp. The secret mission failed and word of the failure leaked to the press.

After that, the administration went to work to make sure there would be no more publicized violations of another country's sovereignty. A new POW policy was concocted by the State Department and the Pentagon. It maintained that the U.S. can neither confirm nor deny that POWs remain in Southeast Asia, but operates on the assumption that they are there.

Through this turn of phrase, the U.S. government is now able to appear steadfastly committed to getting the men home-without having to take any decisive action.

## THE GARWOOD LETTER

MESSAGE TO: The Congress of the United States of America

ATTENTION: Congressman Stephen Solarz, Chairman House Subcommittee of East Asian & Pacific Affairs

FROM: Pfc. Robert R. Garwood, USMC

I want to briefly outline what I know about American prisoners who are alive and being held against their will in Vietnam. Allow me to call to your attention the attached 'Washington Times' article dated May 21, 1985, as an accurate summary of what I saw and heard of other Americans while I was in Vietnam. I am concerned that you as congressmen have not taken steps to bring my brothers, fellow American prisoners, home. It's time for you to outline what actions you have taken, besides holding hearings and writing letters, to rescue these live POWs. I fought communists in a war in Southeast Asia in which Congress walked away in 1973 and left me, as well as many other Americans, behind.

I have been told repeatedly by officials of the U.S. Government to be quiet and only privately discuss my knowledge of Americans that were held back by the Vietnamese. After almost six years of silence, I decided to publicly disclose my first-hand knowledge of other Americans still in prison camps in Vietnam, in a December 4, 1984 article in the 'Wall Street Journal'. Much to my surprise, I received little attention from Congress as a result of this alarming disclosure that I had seen 60 to 70 other Americans between 1973 and 1978. On March 22, 1985, I held a news conference in Washington, D.C. and gave names, dates, and locations of the other Americans I knew who were still in Vietnam to Congressman Bill Hendon for transmittal to President Reagan. To date, I am given to understand that the President's advisors have refused to permit a meeting between the President and Congressman Hendon to discuss the live POWs I saw. I cannot understand why a President who has declared the POW/MIA problem to be this nation's highest national priority, would allow his advisors to stop information from reaching him that I saw several other Americans still held prisoners by Vietnam.

I met in a closed session with members of a House subcommittee on May 15, 1985, after what I understood was an intense lobbying effort by some of my friends to set up this meeting. I cannot understand what you are hiding! I was interrupted and instructed by Congressman Gilman, in an elevator full of congressmen, not to discuss openly my sightings of live American POWs held in Vietnam. I cannot understand why you want to keep it quiet that you left live Americans as POWs in Vietnam and have not taken steps to rescue them! I freely volunteered to come forward in open session and swear under oath that these Americans POWs I saw with my own eyes want to come home to America. They want to be rescued. You şimply cannot write these live Americans off as war casualties. I understand that congressmen Soloman and Solarz want to see me again in closed executive session on June 12, 1985.

Listen closely! The only reason I came forward six months ago with a public disclosure of my eyewitness accounts of U.S. POWs, was to help bring these Americans home. Not to be ignored, not to be hidden away in a back room and not to be told by congressmen to be quiet. It's my understanding, from other POWs as well, that we received better treatment when it was publicly known that we were important to the American public. It would be a betrayal of American values and the Constitution of the United States if you as congressmen were not doing everything in your power to bring these Americans that want to come home, home. It has been six months now since I came forward and pray, tell me,

1. What have you done to bring these Americans home?
2. Why you walked away and left us there? and
3. Why do you want to hide from the American public, the proof that we left live American prisoners of war still in Vietnam? Please tell me.

I am prepared to testify in open session where the American people can judge the truthfulness of my information. I am unable, at this time, to meet with you behind closed doors. I would like to receive a written, formal response to the three questions I have asked in this letter.

Thank you for your interest. Please bring home the live POWs!

Sincerely,
Robert R. Garwood

## MISSING IN ACTION

By Rep. Bob McEwen

Like many in our nation, I was skeptical of recent reports that Americans who served the United States in southeast Asia and listed as missing in action might still be alive and, in some cases, held against their will.

It seemed unlikely to me that 12 years after our involvement in Vietnam,

Americans trapped there could have survived. Further, there seemed to be little motive or advantage to the governments of the region to hold our servicemen.

Now, however, I'm not so sure. Having recently returned from a fact-finding mission to Vietnam and Laos and participating in many hours of hearings, some of them closed to the public, I fear that American soldiers still may be alive in Southeast Asia. While the evidence presented before our committee was not irrefutable, it was highly convincing.

What lends even more credibility to the live sighting reports is the fact that the governments of Vietnam and Laos have refused to allow any international body to investigate these reports. In fact, when I suggested to the Vietnam Foreign Minister Nguyen Co Thach that he could choose any international organization to investigate, whether the Red Cross, Amnesty International, United Nations, or anyone else, he simply responded, "Oh, no; we can't allow that. But we will allow you, Congressman, to come back and investigate."

While our delegation, which included Sens. Frank Murkowski, Dennis DeConcini and Rep. Michael Bilirakis, welcomes the opportunity to return and engage in further negotiations with the Vietnamese, it is unrealistic to expect us to conduct or possess the expertise necessary to investigate properly. That is best left to the experts who have the equipment and knowledge to resolve these unconfirmed reports.

The information referred to Congress in two full days of hearings cannot be dismissed summarily. For example, Army Lt. Col. Robert Howard, a 30-year veteran awarded the Medal of Honor in Vietnam, provided us with names, dates and places to substantiate reports of living MIAs.

During the hearing, he said, "Based on all intelligence reports which I have seen and my personal experiences in this matter, I am personally convinced that there are in fact live Americans in captivity and that there is an ongoing effort by the Defense Intelligence Agency to ignore such reports."

Two other witnesses, retired Army Maj. Smith and retired Army Sgt. Melvin McIntire, gave us detailed evidence of living American soldiers in Southeast Asia.

These are credible witnesses who have no reason to give false information. While we cannot and should not accept their testimony at face value, we owe it to the thousands of families of the missing in action to do all within our power to find out whether or not they are right.

All of this should be unnecessary. Congressional hearings and fact-finding missions should not be needed. If the U.S. had received the kind of cooperation from Hanoi that the dictates of humanity, and, indeed the clear provisions of the 1973 Paris agreements, gave us a right to expect, the issue of missing in action would have been resolved long ago. The questions of the families of those still unaccounted for would have been answered. But the U.S. has not received the kind of cooperation that compassionate members of the family of man expect.

Never in history has any nation engaged in bartering with the remains of soldiers who fought on their soil. Never before has a country, purely for political purposes, toyed with the hopes and grief of the families of these servicemen. It displays a level of barbarism perhaps unprecedented in the history of mankind.

The resolution of America's missing in action remains a matter of the highest national priority. Our congressional mission to Southeast Asia, which followed closely on the heels of a joint State and Defense Department delegation, demonstrated to the Vietnamese that Congress and the Administration are united on this issue.

## POWs: THE EVIDENCE IS THERE; NOW LET's ACT

By Bill Paul

Memo to Gen. Leonard H. Perroots Defense Intelligence Agency, The Pentagon:

It's time to see President Reagan and admit that your agency, in a December 1984 briefing for him, completely blew the analysis of the best live-sighting report ever received on American soldiers still being held prisoner in Vietnam.

You weren't DIA director at the time, but many members of your POW investigative staff are holdovers from that period. They described for the president a report by a Vietnamese refugee who had told the DIA that, in 1978 and again in 1982, he saw U.S. prisoners in a courtyard in the Ly Nam De military complex in the heart of Hanoi. This is the courtyard with the water cistern and the railroad tracks behind it.

This refugee had already passed two polygraph tests, which, experts say, means there is roughly a 93% probability he is telling the truth. Nevertheless, DIA staff members told Mr. Reagan this refugee had been shown to be a liar. They explained how he couldn't have seen some landmarks he claimed to have seen. The president accepted that explanation at face value.

But what you've never told Mr. Reagan is that you subsequently found out that the DIA's description of the courtyard was in error, and that the refugee apparently knew the landmarks better than the DIA did. Nor have you told the president that you've recently reopened the case based on new information.

Well, not exactly new. On Dec. 4, 1984, Robert Garwood, the former Marine convicted of collaborating with the enemy after being taken prisoner by the Vietnamese, said in this newspaper that he also had seen American prisoners in that same court-yard. Your agency initially claimed that he was lying-even before your people had debriefed Mr. Garwood. But after recently meeting with Mr. Garwood, you now deem his evidence sufficiently credible to reopen the Ly Nam De case.

But merely reopening that case isn't enough. The Pentagon's own POW Fact Book spells out what this country must have before the president will do whatever it takes to secure the release of any prisoners. I suggest the Ly Nam De case meets this litmus test and that it's your job to tell Mr. Reagan the U.S. has the proof needed to take "appropriate action," as the Fact Book puts it, "to ensure the return of those involved." Or, as Vice President Bush said last July, to do "whatever's necessary" to get the men home.

(Don't let any of the president's advisers, afraid of creating another Iran hostage crisis, tell you that the U.S., by recently sending an assistant secretary of defense and an assistant secretary of state to Hanoi, is already doing all it can.)

The Fact Book says the DIA want more than one source, and current data that can be backed up, it is hoped, by technical means (i.e., satellite photos). Further, these reports by sources should be specific in time, place and circumstance. And at least one source's credibility should be "enhanced" by polygraph tests.

Let's look at the facts. The refugee and Mr. Garwood saw several American prisoners in the courtyard with the cistern, which is across the road from the building where visiting military officials from Russia, East Germany and other communist countries meet Vietnam's military elite. Both sources saw the POWs in 1978, and the refugee passed two polygraph tests and Mr. Garwood has done even better.

I refer to the recent trip by several U.S. Congressmen to Hanoi. Using a map drawn by Mr. Garwood, they managed to get inside that courtyard. They are convinced that Mr. Garwood was telling the truth.

How much more evidence do you need? To your credit, you have recognized how inadequate the DIA's POW section was before you took over last year, and you appointed a special outside review panel to re-examine your agency's analyses of live sighting reports. The group is headed by retired Gen. Eugene Tighe, who has been very critical of the U.S.'s POW effort. Its oversight committee includes Texas businessman H. Ross Perot, whose frustration over the U.S.'s inability to resolve the POW issue is well known.

Further, your staff has indicated it intends to re-analyze many cases previously termed "fabrications"-including some where POWs were named by sources.

But now it's time to see Mr. Reagan and urge him to get out front on the issue the way he has on Nicaragua and Libya.

Mr. Paul, a reporter in the Journal's New York bureau, has written extensively on POW issues.

'The Wall Street Journal', Monday, April 21, 1986

The organization which must receive much credit for keeping the POW/MIA issue alive is the National League of Families, presently headed by Ann Mills Griffith. This league initially represented the families of the MIA, collected data and pressed our Government toward official actions to recover missing bodies and account for those suspected to be held as POW in Southeast Asia. Nothing said or written can take away from their original efforts. However, in recent years there have been serious splits in the leadership group of the League of Families. State coordinators are threatened when they do not tow the mark in accord with National League Policy and major groups such as the "Live POW Committee" have broken away feeling that Ann Mills is too autocratic and is influenced too much now by the very system the League fought for years. "She is a part of this administrations team", stated Congressman Salarz, POW/MIA TF Committee Chairman. Therefore, the Leagues Live POW Committee has split with the League to a great extent in doctrines. They feel the League is much to interested in the recovery of the dead, and not in the recovery of POW's, which The Live POW Committee have no doubt remain in Southeast Asia today. Some say Ann Mills Griffith has made a profession of the POW/MIA issue. Her salary is in excess of $50,000 a year plus expenses.

The official stand of the U.S. government is that on going government to government communication is the best way to account for the missing and to a great extent this is true; but, many POW activists feel that this and previous administrations have been weak in their approach and that Presidential influence has been lacking in the effort. Many feel that with our intelligence capabilities we should have been able to recover a POW if the effort was properly motivated. Certainly recent U.S. military actions against terrorists and terrorist nations would attest to this fact. A real good question to ask your Congressman. Have negotiations with Laos ever been opened to recover our POW? The fact is to date Laos, as a nation, has not been **negotiated** with for the release of POWs. We have made overtures and demands but not negotiated.

Throughout the years of POW/MIA questions the U.S. Defense Intelligence Agency, DIA, has been the principal U.S. entity to deal with the POW/MIA issue. In 1985 there were 18 full time employees dedicated to this project, to process and eliminate live sightings of American POW reports received mostly from Southeast Asian refugees. Over 800 such reports have been received throughout the years. To date the DIA has put aside all but a little over 100 of these reports as, unlikely, bogus, fraudulent, mercenary or false information, although many are duplicated and meet criteria for acceptable intelligence. Then the fact exist that over classification has clouded the issue, and lead to charges of a POW cover-up of some kind.

Also, one link of the Intelligence effort under fire is the Joint Casualty Resolution Center. This (JCRC) is located in Bangkok, Thailand until recently was directed by a Lt. Col. Mather. Mather had been in the job since 1973, an unheard of length of time for any service man to be in one position. Some of the criticism of JCRC is justified. They are under-manned. In 1986 only three U.S. field representatives were supposed to cover all of Southeast Asia from Korea, Japan, the Philippines, Taiwan, to Malaysia. They must question, record and "investigate" live sighting reports. Lt. Col. Mather has had success in recovering bodies only to have the families raise questions about proper identification. Another point often raised is that Lt. Col. Mather is married to a Vietnamese lady who is always welcome to travel to Vietnam at any time and return as she chooses.

There are some who openly state she is a suspected Vietnamese spy. This is an interesting statement since she can walk through the U.S. Embassy gates in Bangkok when ever she chooses. In an informal lunch with Lt. Col. Simons, she was quite open and insisted Vietnam should be paid the sum agreed on at the Paris Accord but in goods and trade credit instead of cash.

## POW/MIA NEWS BRIEFS

### McFarlane believes U.S. Prisoners of war are still alive:

In an October 15, 1985, article, WALL STREET JOURNAL staff reporter Bill Paul reports that Robert C. McFarlane, President Reagan's national security advisor told a private business group that he believes U.S. prisoners of war are still being held in Indochina and that the U.S. should step up efforts to gather conclusive information about any POW's there. The comments by Mr. McFarlane, which were made at a semi-annual forum for business executives and political consultants, leave a different impression from previous White House statements that the United States was using all applicable intelligence capabilities to determine what happened to the missing Americans. The sessions are held under ground rules that require that all remarks made at them by public officials are off the record. Former Congressman John LeBoutillier recorded the talk and made the tape available to the Wall Street Journal. Mr. LeBoutillier and another symposium participant, who is a vice president of a Wall Street investment banking firm, say they were not told the session was off the record. On the tape recording, Mr. McFarlane emphasized that he was expressing his personal feeling. "How I really feel about it," Mr. McFarlane told the group, "I think there have to be live Americans there." He acknowledged that there wasn't any conclusive proof that U.S. military or civilian personnel are being held by communist governments in the region but said, "There is quite a lot of evidence given by people who have no ulterior motives and no reason to lie, and they're telling things that they have seen." Mr. McFarlane was critical of U.S. efforts to find out what happened to nearly 2,500 Americans who remain unaccounted for. "What we need to do is to have better human intelligence in Vietnam," he said. "Now we don't. It takes time to get it. But I wouldn't pretend to you that we have done enough to even start. And that's bad. And that's failure." He did say that he believed that the Reagan administration had made progress by continuing to press the Vietnamese government for an accounting of the missing Americans. He also indicated that U.S. efforts to collect better intelligence on the subject would be stepped up. "We are doing more (but) there is more that we ought to be doing than we are. And I think we shall very soon."

Jerry Dennis is the brother of Mark Dennis who was reported KIA in 1968 and his alleged body was returned by the U.S. Navy. In 1971, Jerry exhumed Mark's alleged remains and found not only that it could not possibly be Mark, but found evidence that the body may have been tampered with to make it appear to be Mark. He presented evidence that several individuals listed as KIA in the same incident as Mark may have escaped and been captured.

Dr. Donald Parker, the nephew and legal guardian of James R. Fuller, was a crewmember of Spectre 17, a U.S. Air Force gunship shot down near Pakse, Laos, in December 1972. Dr. Parker presented 28 fragments of bone which have been positively identified as James R. Fuller by the U.S. Army Central Identification Laboratory, along with the report of an independent pathologist which says that the bone fragments cannot possibly be identified as the human remains of any individual.

Lieutenant Colonel Tom Hart was a crewmember of the Pakse aircraft. His wife reported that the 7 fragments of bone which have been positively identified by the Central Identification Laboratory as being those of Tom Hart cannot be so identified by any scientific basis. She further reported that information has been withheld from her by the Air Force regarding her husband, including an aerial photo taken 7 months after the crash which revealed 20 foot letters trampled or cut in the elephant grass which read "1973 (or 1953) TH". This was originally correlated with Tom Hart, but she was never notified or told of the existence of the photo or the photo analysis report.

Kathryn Fanning, reported that Major Hugh Fanning was shot down over North Vietnam in 1967, and that the alleged remains of her husband, which has been positively identified by the CIL, had been exhumed and examined by two forensic anthropologists who have concluded that it is impossible to identify them as being any individuals. She also said that she had been lied to by her U.S. Marine Corps "casualty assistance officer" for months after she requested it. She further stated that intelligence reports have been found which indicate that Hugh Fanning was alive and in captivity in Vietnam, but that, contrary to the stated policy of the Marine Corps, those reports were withheld from her.

Dr. Michael Charney, who is one of only 35 Board Certified Forensic Anthropologists in the United States has examined the purported remains of Hart, Fanning, and Fuller, and stated unequivocally that they cannot be scientifically identified. He also said that the reports presented by the Central Identification Laboratory reveals that the identifications are highly speculative and that, in fact, some of the reported data actually contradicts the conclusions drawn.

## SMITH/MCINTIRE LAWSUIT

**Compiled By:**

**Homecoming II Project**

On Jan. 29, Major Mark Smith, testifying before the Senate Veterans Affairs Committee, said that within the preceding five days he has "...viewed evidence which proves beyond any doubt that in excess of 30 Americans and other nationalities are presently being held as prisoners of war in Southeast Asia." Information has now been made public regarding the conclusive evidence viewed by Major Smith. This report provides all relevant facts which can be revealed and corrects some misunderstandings about the resultant controversy....

The intelligence service of a foreign power friendly to the United States showed Major Smith a four-hour, eight-minute videotape which had been produced from a 16mm film which was shot over a period of five days in the recent past. It was produced for the purpose of documenting certain facts which an unidentified organization in Southeast Asia wanted to make known to certain other political organizations worldwide.

Smith says the videotape shows (incidental to the purpose for which the film was produced) four segments which reveal the existence of Caucasian prisoners, many of whom are believed to be, and are reported by other sources to be, Americans. A portion of the film reveals a unique landmark which allows conclusive identification of the location in which it was made. A portion of the film reveals conclusively that the film was made in the recent past (two-three years at most). Through alternative means, it has been determined that it was probably produced in mid-late 1985.

The four segments which show Caucasians are as follows: (1) 20-40 individuals who appear to be Caucasians who are a part of a much larger group of prisoners of several nationalities; (2) 30-40 Caucasians panning gold and doing related hard labor. These men are in chains and shackles and under armed guard--guards are identifiable as to their political association by the uniforms they are wearing; (3) A close-up of an individual (not in a captive environment) thought to be American but not yet conclusively identified; (4) A segment in which "John Obassy" (one of the affiants in the Smith/McIntire lawsuit) is shown examining male Caucasians and administering medical treatment to them. Other portions of the film reveal information which can have profound International political consequences if it becomes publicly known.

Obassy showed an edited version of the tape to Major Smith, SFC McIntire and attorney Mark Waple in December, 1985. He refused to show an unedited copy of the tape because some information revealed in it could put lives in danger if that information fell into the wrong hands. (The reason he originally obtained the tape was to prove certain facts contained in his affidavit in the Smith/McIntire lawsuit. DIA had contended that he was lying about the existence of something in a certain region. The videotape proved that DIA was wrong!)

Not being able to obtain the videotape from Obassy, Maj. Smith initiated an effort to discover who else might have access to, or possession of, the unedited version. He discovered that the intelligence service of a nation friendly to the United States had a copy. Smith made contact with a member of that foreign intelligence service who was personally known to him. An opportunity was arranged for Smith to see the tape, with the caveat that he not reveal publicly the most sensitive portions thereof.

In the tape Smith saw that other evidence, which was even more conclusive than the tape itself, was in the possession of a particular anti-communist group. Smith knew that Obassy had contact with that group, and asked Obassy to investigate whether the other evidence might be obtained from that group.

After meeting with that group, Obassy returned with a list of items for which the group would trade the "other evidence". The list included food, clothing, medical supplies, arms and ammunition. Smith, McIntire and Waple attempted to estimate the cost of the listed items and arrived at a figure of $4.2 million.

Waple drafted a letter to President Reagan, hoping to obtain the assistance of the President in acquiring the needed material. Not wanting to confuse the issue in the initial communication by including the entire list of demanded items, Waple wrote, "...required to pay the sum of $4.2 million in cash and take receipt of the original of the film and other evidence of live Americans and other allied POWs still being held in Southeast Asia." This minor mis-statement of the facts for the purpose of simplicity would come back to haunt them later. Even though the whole truth was completely and exhaustively revealed to USG representatives in follow-up meetings, someone leaked the letter to the media (a possibility which should have been foreseen). The letter created the impression that someone was demanding $4.2 million in ransom for the tape. Actually, the real importance of the tape was that it would prove that the "other evidence" was in the hands of the group requesting the supplies.

Subsequently, the Vice President reportedly authorized Hendon, Smith and Waple to travel to Southeast Asia to acquire the tape and the "other evidence". Mr. Bush is said to have arranged to pay the travel costs and to have caused $4.2 million to be deposited in the Singapore Bank of America in the name of Bill Hendon. The three Americans met with Obassy and told him that they had the ability to supply the $4.2 million for the "other evidence" but that Hendon's authorization to proceed with negotiations was contingent upon his viewing the tape.

Obassy refused, saying that money was not and never had been the issue. It was the supplies themselves, and the ability to accumulate and deliver them, for which the involvement of the U.S. government was most needed. Further, because it had been revealed in the American press that Obassy was a Britain, some people in Southeast Asia had been able to determine his true identity. As a result, his life was in danger, and he had been denied authorization to show the unedited version of the tape to anyone, including

Bill Hendon. He did, however, show an edited version to Hendon, and Hendon was able to confirm many of the elements of Smith's report regarding the content of the videotape.

When questioned in closed session of the Senate Veterans' Affairs Committee by Chairman Frank Murkowski about the supplies being requested, Major Smith read the list compiled by Obassy. Murkowski interrupted, "I don't want to hear a laundry list, what's the bottom line---what will it cost us?" Major Smith responded that it appeared the cost of the material would be in the neighborhood of $4.2 million. After the closed-door meeting, someone told the media that Obassy was demanding $4.2 million in ransom for the tape.

One of the conditions required by Obassy for his cooperation was that his true identity be absolutely protected. Although never told by Smith and McIntire, U.S. intelligence officials believed that they had "figured out" who he was. (He is an individual long known to the intelligence community, but not known to them as "John Obassy"). U.S. Navy Commander Frank Brown, who is associated with U.S. intelligence in a manner which we have not yet determined, allegedly notified the Senate Veterans' Affairs Commitee staff that "Obassy" was one Robin Gregson. A member of the Committee staff then reportedly called "Washington Times" reporter Susan Katz and spilled the beans. Brown also called Katz. An unknown source in Southeast Asia informed an associate of former Congressman John LeBoutillier that Obassy and Gregson were one and the same. Katz was told to confirm the story with LeBoutillier. Another person whose identity we know but cannot reveal, was informed by Brown of the alleged identity of Obassy, and Katz obtained further confirmation from him. On April 2, "The Washington Times" published a story by Katz (entitled "Rumors Aplenty") in which Obassy was identified as Gregson. On May 1, in an open, public hearing, Chairman Murkowski identified Obassy as Gregson.

On May 6, Rep. Bill Hendon wrote Murkowski, "Mr. Chairman, your identifying this critical witness is the most reprehensible action I have ever witnessed in my five-and-one-half year effort to help return U.S. military personnel from communist prisons in Southeast Asia...here we have what appears to be the ultimate in dirty tricks: you subpoena Major Mark Smith to produce the Obassy videotape-and then in the same breath you virtually ensure that he cannot produce it when you divulge his source's true identity in open session. Had you asked me, I could have told you that divulging this mans identity would jeopardize not only Obassy's life but the lives of U.S. prisoners of war whom I am convinced he has direct access to."

Murkowski then wrote Hendon on May 8, defending himself by saying: (1) "Mr. Gregson's identity was revealed some time ago (3 days before the hearing) in an internationally available publication..." (An article entitled "Rumors Aplenty" hardly provides conclusive identification. Publication of a rumor article did not release Murkowski from his obligation to guard sensitive information. Murkowski had been told that efforts to obtain further cooperation and assistance from Gregson would be seriously damaged if his identity became publicly known. What did Murkowski hope to gain by confirming Katz' story?); (2) "Former Congressman John LeBoutillier, in a letter to CIA Director William Casey, also revealed Mr. Gregson's identity." (The fact that the Director of CIA knows something shouldn't automatically make that information public!); (3) "...Mr. Obassy's true identity is contained in an unclassified document given to me by the Office of the Secretary of Defense prior to the May 1 hearing." (The "unclassified document" was reportedly a memorandum authored by Frank Brown. Why is it in the interest of the Department of Defense and/or the U.S. Government to reveal this man's name? Are they so desirous of defending themselves from the various allegations about their bad faith in pursuing live POW information that they're willing to throw away any assistance he may be able to provide?); (4) "..identity was not 'divulged' against the wishes of the Defense Department.." (True, it was divulged over the objections of DIA Director General Leonard Perroots who has privately stated that he believes Smith and McIntire.

Fortunately, Gregson was in Southeast Asia and did not know that his identity had been compromised. Following a series of discussions between Smith, Waple and Gregson, Gregson brought a copy of the edited version of the tape to Washington, D.C. on June 25th with the intention of taking it to the White House. Being convinced that he would never "get within 100 yards of the White House" he agreed to show it in closed session to the Senate Veterans Affairs Committee on the next day. Upon arriving in Washington, however, he discovered that his true identity had been revealed in a session at the Senate Committee by Chairman Murkowski. He was furious!

After several hours of unsuccessful attempts by Smith, McIntire and Waple to convince him to show the tape anyway, or at least some still frames from it, Gregson took it and left town.

Smith was scheduled to testify before the Committee on the next day. A subpoena had been issued by the Committee demanding his presence, but upon his promise to appear, the Committee decided not to serve the subpoena. Smith, McIntire and Waple knew that the subpoena demanded evidence which they had earlier claimed to have, but exactly which of the evidence was in demand was unknown to them. Smith knew that if he went with no videotape, no Gregson, and no documentary evidence, the Committee would serve him with the subpoena demanding information which he did not want to turn over to them. In a last minute meeting, Smith decided not to identify, so those involved could have time to decide what to do next. When Waple called the Committee to tell them Smith would not be appearing, three Committee staffers rushed to National Airport with the subpoena and an AP photographer and a newspaper reporter in tow. Smith, unwilling to participate in a media event, ducked out and returned to North Carolina. Eight days later, Waple invited US Marshals to his law office where Smith accepted the subpoena.

The subpoena, as written, demanded all evidence in Smith's possession. However, in a cover letter authored by Committee Counsel Tony Principi, specific references were made to closed session testimony of Smith in which certain evidence had been mentioned. These references were to pictures of Americans left behind in 1975, and specific locations where American prisoners have been held. Unwilling to provide all evidence to the Committee, Smith chose to supply only that which was specifically demanded in the cover letter, as that information was not particularly sensitive. If the Committee were to demand additional material, he was prepared to refuse, be charged with contempt of Congress, and go to jail if necessary. When asked by the Committee why he had presented only such insubstantial material, Smith responded, "I brought exactly what you asked for." The Committee did not pursue the matter.

The reason that Smith is willing to pay such a price to keep information out of the hands of the Committee and its staff is that it is extremely sensitive in several ways, and the Committee had already shown that it cannot be trusted with sensitive information--on three occasions, critically sensitive information has been "leaked". Some of it could endanger the life of Gregson, and his assistance is much needed, not only in acquiring various kinds of information about identities and locations of American prisoners but in obtaining the cooperation of foreign organizations which can be very helpful in implementing any kind of extraction plan. Some of it, if revealed publicly could endanger and/or alienate foreign organizations which have already been helpful in some ways and which can be even more helpful in the future.

Smith has also become convinced that the Committee does not intend to do anything useful with any evidence he provides to them. The Chairman has refused to pursue several available avenues to the truth, and besides the Chairman, only Senator DeConcini has made himself available for all of the hearings to hear the testimony and cross-examine witnesses.

Perhaps the most compelling evidence that the Chairman is not interested in a good faith pursuit of the truth is his denial of Congressman Hendon's request to sit on the panel where Hendon would have the opportunity to cross-examine government witnesses if and when they are "less than accurate" in their statements. It is interesting that the Chairman would deny participation to the man widely known to be the most knowledgeable on Capitol Hill regarding the evidence presently in the possession of DIA.

After having been twice refused a seat on the panel, Hendon wrote Murkowski in the May 6 letter, "if you want to see overwhelming evidence of U.S. prisoners of war being held in Southeast Asia, why don't you direct Defense Intelligence to let me and several of my colleagues show you and your Committee some of the evidence DIA already has in its possession? We don't want to show your personal staff or your Committee staff, we want to show you and your Committee along with 'Interagency Intelligence Senior Review Panel' which is now investigating the work of DIA...If you really want to get to the bottom of this, I challenge you to arrange such a session immediately."

Murkowski wrote back in his May 8 letter, "...my earlier invitation to you to testify still stands" - No comment on whether he thought it would be useful to have DIA analysts bring intelligence files and explain them in the presence of someone knowledgeable enough to make sure they keep their story straight!

Another problem with providing to the Committee all evidence in their possession, according to Smith and McIntire, is that certain of it proves their allegation that individuals within USG have destroyed files which contain evidence of living American POWs. If Smith and McIntire were to provide proof of that allegation to the Committee, it could be given to the government so that destroyed files could be "reconstituted". Additionally, it is clear that the Justice Department attorneys are much in need of advance knowledge of the evidence which they intend to produce in court, as that will give Justice the greatest opportunity to take actions and formulate plans to off-set the impact of that evidence. Smith and McIntire believe that the Senate Committee could be a conduit of information to the Justice Department.

Additionally, revealing all the evidence might damage the lawsuit in another way. Judge Boyle has made it clear that his case is not going to be "tried in the media". While the priority must remain bringing prisoners home, the lawsuit is important in itself because it will provide an opportunity to obtain information, in two ways, which can never be acquired outside of court: (1) Many individuals have notified Smith, McIntire and Waple that if subpoenaed and placed under oath, they will provide information that they cannot supply in any other form. These include individuals presently employed in the U.S. intelligence community, active duty military personnel and officials of foreign governments; (2) If the court allows and the litigants agree upon terms which will allow "discovery", Waple will be granted access to information not otherwise accessible. "Discovery" is the process through which the two sides can agree to provide all their evidence to each other before the case is tried. It gives both sides the opportunity to put the adversary's evidence to the harshest test, and evaluate their own chances to win in court. If the Justice Department is able to determine from the Senate exactly what Smith and McIntire have, they will argue against discovery in order to deny Waple access to important Live POW information now in USG files.

Publicly revealing conclusive evidence of the existence of Live POWs could accomplish one important objective: cause the American People to DEMAND their return. However, those same revelations could destroy the best opportunity to bring some of the men home quickly, and Smith and McIntire won't throw away those opportunities unless they give up hope that necessary USG cooperation can be obtained to implement actions with the greatest hope for success.

On June 19, 1986, U.S. District Court Judge Terrence Boyle announced his decision on the U.S. Justice Department motion to dismiss the lawsuit. In rendering his decision, Judge Boyle issued an order denying defendants motion to dismiss the case. A portion of the suit, the mandamus action, was dismissed on the grounds that such was a question of foreign policy and therefore under the exclusive authority of the Executive Branch.

On the declaratory judgement action, the court ruled that whether or not

American Prisoners of War exist is a question of fact for decision by the court. Judge Boyle wrote:

"The government claims that the court is barred by political question considerations from entertaining any inquiry into the existence of the alleged group of persons. If there is a contested issue of fact over the existence of such persons, then the government finds itself claiming dual power. It claims the executive power to exclusively administer and execute the government and laws of the United States. This is a legitimate claim. It also claims the exclusive power to determine the facts that it will use in administering the government and executing the law as it applies to this class of persons. This claim of power is in excess of the government's legitimate executive authority...the court is mindful of its obligation to accept the exercise of judicial power under the United States Constitution where parties seek relief and have the right to the exercise of the judicial power of the United States."

"For the reasons outlined in this opinion, the defendants motion to dismiss the plaintiffs claim for mandamus relief under the Hostage Act...for lack of subject matter jurisdiction is ALLOWED. The defendants motion to dismiss the plaintiffs action for declaratory judgement..is DENIED." Plaintiffs Smith and McIntire were dismissed from the case on the grounds that they have no legally recognized representative capacity regarding the rights of American POWs who may still be alive. According to attorney Waple, "...this is an inconsequential development in the case..they stand ready as material and relevant witnesses on the ultimate issue."

Twenty-five POW/MIA family members who have joined the suit as plaintiffs have been allowed to continue to seek declaratory judgment as to the existence of living American POWs. This is an important victory for the plaintiffs. The case may now proceed to the critical process of discovery. There is a possibility that the Justice Department may attempt an appeal. It is an open question whether that right exists, and even if the court should rule that appeal is permissible, then the appeal itself would have to be argued on its own merits. Whether the defendants intend to appeal will likely not be known until the time limitations approach expiration.

Whatever the outcome of the case, it is already clear that the U.S. Government is feeling the pressure as a result of the victories already won by the plaintiffs. The clearest evidence of this is presented by the outlandish attacks on the integrity of Smith and McIntire themselves. Interestingly, and wisely, the defamers have left Lt. Col. Howard alone. America's most highly decorated soldier says Smith and McIntire are telling the truth. Do you believe him?

## SAM DUNLAP

## TESTIMONY FOR U.S. HOUSE ARMED SERVICES COMMITTEE

## SUBCOMMITTEE ON SPECIAL INVESTIGATIONS

Chairman Bill Nichols, members of the Committee and staff: My name is Sam Dunlap. I was hired by the Department of the Army last November and began employment as a physical anthropologist at the Central Identifications Laboratory, Hawaii on January 6, 1986. It was clear to me, virtually from the beginning of my employment, that two important areas of my job description were not adhered to at the Lab: 1) "Prepares comprehensive Certificates of Identity and Anthropological reports...and concluding with a concise decision in a format that is scientifically sound for presentation in any court of law"; 2) "Develops new or advanced identification techniques..."

Also from the beginning, it was clear that management, supervision and evaluation was being carried out by individuals without professional scientific credentials or experience. Moreover, the chain of command above the lab included no individuals with professional, scientific backgrounds, credentials or experience.

As evidence accrued from the press, professional colleagues, the December 1985 Kerley, Maples and Levine report on the lab, Mr. Fleshman's report on the lab and my own personal observations, that the Department of the Army had no sincere intention of upgrading the lab or listening to my legitimate suggestions for proper scientific procedures and protocols.

I was ultimately placed in a position in which I had little choice but to resign on August 8, 1986. In spite of lab personnel claims to the contrary, the serious scientific issues remain unaddressed surrounding past and present lab identification techniques. My efforts to elicit documentation from lab personnel regarding their scientific data supporting their use of morphological approximation, superimposition, and handedness determination were completely unsuccessful. However, abundant and legitimate scientific data exists rendering these techniques useless for skeletal identification.

I did not spend years acquiring my doctorate to be subjected to the kind of treatment I have received from the Department of the Army. As an anthropologist, my first responsibility is to my clients or those I study--in this case, the dead, and by direct extension, their immediate next-of-kin. This responsibility is not and should not be inconsistent with the principles in the Department of Army Code of Conduct.

Much of my previous correspondence to this Committee substantiates today's comments. However, should you wish further clarification, I will be happy to answer questions.

## STATEMENT OF WILLIAM T. FLESHMAN

### September 10, 1986

Mr. Chairman, in March 1986 you directed that I look into the activities of the Central Identification Laboratory (CIL), Hawaii. The investigation was predicated on receipt of information alleging that remains of U.S. Servicemen listed as Missing in Action from the Vietnam Conflict were being misidentified by the laboratory. Mr. Chairman, I have completed that investigation and would like to submit a copy for the record and summarize my findings in this statement.

The Central Identification Laboratory is a field element of the U.S. Army Personnel Center. It was moved to Honolulu in 1976 from Thailand, and its mission was expanded to include as its primary mission: -- Conduct search and recovery operations in the Pacific area for World War I, Korean War, and Vietnam War dead. -- Apply anthropological and other scientific techniques in the processing of remains to establish POSITIVE identification. -- Accumulate and catalog information on American and allied personnel listed as Missing in Action (MIA) and those declared dead but body not recovered (BNR).

With the cooperation of host countries, the CIL maintains a search and recovery capability to conduct searches and examinations at crash and burial sites to recover remains and personal effects. Upon receipt of the remains by the CIL the process of identification begins.

The allegations of misidentification first arose earlier this year out of the identification of the remains of the crew involved in the crash of an Air Force AC-130 shot down near Pakse, Laos in December 1972. With the cooperation of the Laotian Government, the CIL excavated this crash site in February 1985 and recovered a large number of severely commingled and fragmented remains and personal effects. Because of the lack of whole bones with scientifically accepted identification landmarks, the laboratory used a technique developed by Mr. Tadao Furue, the Senior Anthropologist on staff, referred to as "Morphologic Approximation". Based upon this technique all manifested crew members aboard this aircraft were identified without equivocation and remains submitted to the next of kin for burial. One of the families (Ann Hart), skeptical of the identification, sought a second opinion from an independent forensic anthropologist, Dr. Michael Charney. This Anthropologist concluded after examination that positive identification of these fragmented remains was impossible.

Dr. Charney, after reviewing the labs record of identification, concluded that the age could not be determined within five years, the race and sex cannot be determined, and the stature determination to a plus or minus 1.6 inches is "an intentional deception". He stated "the entire report of the CIL, HI is loaded with a brave attitude of exactness of traits as to sex, race, age, height. This cannot be supported by the evidence from the fragments. Such sureness of results can only be meant to impress the uninitiate, the person not familiar with forensic anthropology."

In another example, Dr. John Lundy, before he joined the staff of the CIL, examined the remains of Sgt. James Fuller, whose remains were identified from the Pakse crash site. He concluded that "The remains are in such a condition that one can state that for the most part they are identifiable as being human in origin...However...No statement can be made regarding the individuality of the person or persons represented and hence, it is impossible to positively identify these remains as belonging to any one person."

The Forensic Anthropologist I have talked with generally agree that somewhere between two and four individuals could have been positively identified. This is based on dental evidence. The rest of the fragments are unidentifiable, and there is no technique known to science that could identify individuals based on the evidence available. The problem is further exacerbated by the fact that not only can the lab not determine the identity of all individuals on the manifest of that AC-130, but the CIL cannot say with certainty that all persons aboard the aircraft were in fact killed in this crash. Independent anthropologists state that individual fragments should not have been turned over to the next of kin, but a recommendation for mass burial should have been made.

After a period of discussion and correspondence between the military services and the Hart family, the CIL eventually rescinded its identification of Lt. Col. Thomas Hart. What is still not known, however, is what the status of this individual is at the present time--is he now listed as an MIA, killed in action, body not recovered, or some other category?

As you will remember, Mr. Chairman, you wrote to the Secretary of the Army twice in March of this year. On March 11 you cited the results of an inspection visit to the CIL in December 1985 by Doctors Kerley, Maples, and Levine. One of their recommendations was "A Nationally or Internationally known forensic anthropologist who would bring his or her credibility to the CILHI Laboratory should be appointed in a supervisory capacity to assume responsibility for the accuracy and reliability of the identifications and reports of the anthropology team." You strongly urged the Secretary to consider placing this anthropologist at the CIL.

Mr. Chairman, this has not been done. Instead, Dr. Kerley, one of the consultants hired to inspect this lab, has been retained to review the product of the laboratory. He is located in Washington, D.C.

The laboratory is suffering from a serious credibility problem at present. It is commanded by a Quartermaster Officer, and until very recently a mortician served as Chief of the Lab. Some witnesses will say he is still overseeing the Lab. Mr. Furue, who has served the U.S. Government admirably for over 30 years, is the Senior Anthropologist on staff, overseeing the work of a number of Ph.D. Anthropologists. His technique of Morphological Approximation, however, is at the center of the problem. I fail to see how placing the person responsible for the questionable identifications in charge of the laboratory will resolve any problems. I do not question his devotion to duty, but I must concur with the recommendation of the review team and your strong recommendation that a Senior Forensic

Anthropologist with the highest credentials be placed on staff at the CIL. I believe this would help alleviate the Labs credibility problem and resolve some of the internal dissension within the laboratory.

The Secretary of the Army also responded to your letters saying that Morphologic Approximation would no longer be used as a basis for identification until Mr. Furue's technique is accepted as a scientifically valid technique. At least two anthropologist in the laboratory maintain it as still being used. Regardless, one of the most recent identifications shows that the CIL still uses questionable techniques and procedures. In this case, referred to as Savannakhat, while fragments were not individually identified and turned over to the next of kin, the laboratory identified all crew members on the manifest as having perished in this particular crash in Laos. However, dental identification could be made for only nine individuals. How do they know the five other crew members perished? It was not determined scientifically. A mass burial should have been recommended for those individuals who were positively identified.

I examined several other allegations about the operations of the laboratory, Mr. Chairman. The most serious of these include:

1. Anthropological reports are altered by CIL administrative personnel.
2. Why is the CIL located in Hawaii?

Concerning the first allegation, I found that reports had, in fact, been altered by administrative personnel. The explanation I received from one of the administrators was that he believes part of his responsibility is to assure that the narrative portion of the lab report "Flows" so that the reviewing authority, the Armed Services Graves Registration Office (ASGRO) Board, which consists of non-anthropologists, will be able to fully comprehend a technical report. Other changes in identification reports include the deletion by administrative personnel of standard errors of measurement. For example, one chart reported the "Estimated Height" as exactly 65.9 inches. No scientific methodology known could provide this measurement based on the evidence with such exactness. All anthropologists I interviewed believe that these lab reports need more detailed technical justification and explanation, not less. It is not only unacceptable to change generally recognized scientific practices and explanatory methodology in order to make them more readable, but also it is intentionally deceptive.

Concerning the location of the CIL, I have been told that it is necessary to have it located in Hawaii so that it is closer to the area of operations and excavations of crash sites.

The staff questions the need for the location of the CIL in Hawaii. It would seem more prudent and cost effective to locate this lab at or near the Armed Forces Institute of Pathology (AFIP) so that the AFIP could play a larger role in reviewing CIL reports. The search and rescue team could be located in Hawaii if necessary, but the actual examination and forensic work would seem to be more suitably located.

RECOMMENDATIONS

1. The CIL should discontinue the use of the "Morphological Approximation" technique for identification of remains until it has been examined,

approved, and formally accepted by the forensic anthropological community.

2. Tadao Furue's technique should be submitted to proper civilian authorities for study and authentication. Mr. Furue's 35 years experience with fragmented and commingled remains is without equal. He should be encouraged to share his techniques and scientific skills with the general forensic anthropological community.

3. The identification of the remains in the Pakse crash and any future identifications should be based on currently accepted and proven scientific techniques. Remains which cannot be identified with such techniques should be designated "within all reasonable scientific certainty" or "very favorable comparison".

4. Anthropological reports should be fully supported by documentation, and alterations which change the meaning of the narrative or technical sections of the report should not be made by persons other than anthropologists.

5. The staff STRONGLY recommends that a senior forensic anthropologist be placed in charge of CIL. The CIL is an anthropological lab and should be headed by an anthropologist.

6. The Army should conduct a study to determine the necessity of continued location of the CIL in Hawaii. The study should address cost savings and moving costs associated with relocation near the AFIP or other suitable location.

## GEORGE W. GILL

## STATEMENT REGARDING THE CILHI

## SKELETAL IDENTIFICATIONS OF POWs

This statement has been prepared for the September 10, 1986, hearing of the Investigation Subcommittee, U.S. House of Representatives Armed Services Committee.

I have become involved in the CILHI identification controversy since taking office as Secretary of the Physical Anthropology Section, American Academy of Forensic Sciences. I am also on the Board of Directors, American Board of Forensic Anthropology. My close involvement in particular CILHI cases, however, results even more from my recent professional contacts with Dr. Michael Charney, Emeritus Anthropologist, Colorado State University, who lives nearby. Dr. Charney has been quite closely involved with the re-examination of skeletal remains for family members of certain of the MIAs. He and some family members of the MIAs have invited my participation in reviewing several of the CILHI cases, and I have examined the actual physical remains attributed to CMSgt. James R. Fuller, Maj. Hugh M. Fanning and Capt. Milton J. Vescelius, Jr.

Before making my statement to this investigating committee I do wish to make it clear that I am speaking as an individual forensic anthropologist, and my views do not necessarily represent a consensus of those from either the American Board of Forensic Anthropology or the American Academy of Forensic Sciences.

First I wish to state that as one of the few forensic anthropologists who has examined a significant number of the actual skeletal remains of CILHI cases and compared these to the statements of the corresponding CILHI reports, I am deeply concerned about the discrepancies that exist. The problems with these reports are much more serious than would be thought from a review of the records alone. It is clear to me that the differences in perception between the team of forensic scientists who visited CILHI in December 1985, and Dr. Charney, regarding the gravity of the problems, relate in a large way to the kinds of evidence examined. The Team investigation included records only, while Dr. Charney's investigation has in many instances included the actual bones. I too have studied the actual bones and can therefore corroborate much of what Dr. Charney has stated.

In two of the cases in particular (Fuller, Vescelius) a comparison of the bones with certain statements made about them in the CILHI reports reveals such alarming discrepancies as to cast doubt on the honesty and integrity of those making them. In the Fuller report the statement is made that age was in part determined by "...a portion of the left pubic symphysis (most accurate method of aging)." In reality there is absolutely no symphysis on the fragment described, and it probably is not even a human pubic bone at all. When I confronted the CILHI anthropologists involved in that case, following a special meeting held at the 1986 American Academy of Forensic Sciences meeting, I received a candid and revealing response. I asked the investigator if she recognized the bone held in her hand (purported Fuller pubic bone) and she said yes, that she remembered well that fragment and never did see anything that resembled symphysis on it. I then showed her their own signed statement about aging from the symphysis, and reference to the value of the public symphysis in aging, and I asked where that had come from. The answer (which I immediately recorded in my notes) was "well, our first report did not state this, but it was bounced back to us twice with requests to add more specifics. That's when those statements were added." Realizing the possible bearing of this information on the CILHI investigations I recorded this immediately and later sent copies to the anthropologists on the investigating team (Kerley, Maples).

An even more suggestive set of findings come from the Vescelius case in which age is supposedly determined in part from portions of bones which are simply not present, and sex is corroborated by the innominates. It is stated in an addendum to the CILHI report, "...in this case both greater sciatic notches were present and had narrow angles, again a male characteristic." In fact, the sciatic notches are so wide that I have only seen one confirmed male with such wide sciatic notches. They are well into the female range and actually support femaleness more than maleness. Could such misassessments be made by accident? It would seem to be nearly impossible for anyone to do so who has had experience in osteology.

It is clear from the bones that the problems in the CILHI reports result either from extreme carelessness, incompetence, fabrication of data, or some combination of these things. It is probably not necessary to establish which factor or factors are primarily responsible for the errors since the solution should be the same in any case. The simple and clear solution has been stated in the recommendation of both the forensic team (Kerley, Maples, Levine) in their report to the Dept. of the Army, and the report of the investigations subcommittee staff following their separate investigation. I support the team in their statement, "A forensic anthropologist of national or international reputation and unquestioned credibility must be employed by means of proper search...This person must be superior to all anthropological personnel at CILHI, and must be the anthropology section supervisor" (Part II, page 3). I also concur with the subcommittee report that "by placing a senior forensic anthropologist in charge of CIL and by making...procedural changes...much of the credibility of the laboratory would be restored" (page 6). I also wish to reiterate one of the six staff recommendations. They state that "The staff strongly recommends that a senior forensic anthropologist be placed in charge of CIL. The CIL is an anthropological lab and should be headed by an anthropologist" (page 7).

In sum, I concur wholeheartedly with the recommendations of the Team and the Subcommittee Staff. From my own review of much of the CILHI work, I believe it is important to have an on-site forensic anthropology supervisor of national reputation inspecting and/or directing the anthropological work conducted there. This single, simple change will do a great deal to prevent problems in the future similar to those of the past.

**George W. Gill, Ph.D., D-ABFA**
**Professor and Forensic Anthropologist**

## WRITTEN TESTIMONY OF THOMAS V. ASHWORTH

My name is Thomas V. Ashworth and I'm from Fort Smith, Arkansas. I served my country as a Marine Corps Officer and as a helicopter pilot in Vietnam. I also flew secret missions inside Laos - the records of which were falsified to protect the secrecy of the operation. I was released from active duty as a Captain of Marines.

For more than nine years following Operation Homecoming, I believed there were no living Americans held by the Indochinese Communists. The few live sighting reports I heard while listening to news broadcasts were not impressive. I was certain that if there were captive Americans held in Southeast Asia our intelligence services would be aware of the matter and our political leadership would effectively act as legally required to gain the freedom of any hostages the Communists might be holding.

I began to question what would prove to be my uninformed and naive presuppositions in the fall of 1982. By that time, I had spent over 6,000 hours working with, assisting in some way, or just being with Hmong people. It was only after this six year association that I first heard of live American prisoners being held in Laos after 1973.

My first information was received in the fall of 1982 from a Hmong friend who I casually asked if he had ever heard of Americans being held in Laos. I asked the question shortly after hearing a radio news broadcast about a live sighting report. To my surprise my friend replied, "Oh yes, a friend of mine saw over one-hundred Americans in Sam Neua in 1975 before he escaped." I was given the general description of the sighting report. I was also advised that the Hmong who had seen the Americans was living in California under an assumed name. I would later be given an eyewitness report that the man had attempted to tell the resident CIA operative at the Ban Vinai refugee camp about the sighting. The CIA agent, Jerry Daniels, had told them to keep quiet and said, "Don't talk to me about the American prisoners. It gives me a headache. Don't ever talk to me about them again." This was in early 1976 when the House Select Committee on Missing Persons in Southeast Asia was conducting hearings on the MIAs.

I also have another first hand account of Jerry Daniels telling a person who claims to have seen live Americans to forget the information. Because of "Jerry's attitude, few Hmong have been willing to speak of their knowledge of live Americans. Unfortunately, persistent rumors in the Hmong refugee camps warn the refugees that they will receive severe retribution if they talk about U.S. prisoners held in Laos or any other sensitive matter. Consequently few are willing to talk to official Americans about live sighting reports.

A second report I received from a friend and employee who fought in Laos until 1979. After his resistance group surrendered to the Communists, his group was told by a North Vietnamese soldier that they should not try to run away or they would be put in prison and kept "forever" just as the Americans were being held. The North Vietnamese soldier also bragged that he personally had recently been a guard at a prisoner of war camp which held Americans. These statements were made by the Vietnamese soldier in early 1979. A third Hmong told me that he had personally seen two "whites" being held captive in Xiengkhouang Province during 1979. This man, a former officer in the CIA's Special Guerrilla Units (SGUs) was supposedly captured in 1975 and held until he escaped in about early 1979. Besides the first-hand information he also had second-hand information. I felt somewhat comfortable with the essence of this man's information because I had a friend who lived in a resistence village which became the home of the escapee. According to Tu Kue, who was a resistance fighter until 1979 and the son of my best Hmong friend, the escapee came to his village and told of seeing Americans and of being the object of medical experiments. He later told the same stories in Thailand and in the United States.

I passed the substance of the above information to the League of Families in about January 1983. I was told that DIA would contact me. About six weeks later I was called by a Mr. Lloyd Nash. I eventually had two conversations that day with DIA analyst - Nash and a Michael Burns. These men supposedly were concerned about their lack of knowledge of the refugees from whom they were supposedly eliciting information. A few examples include:

(1) One or both officers claimed to have no knowledge of the fact that a significant percentage of the Hmong refugees had gained entrance to the United States by in some way falsifying information. I estimate that at least 30 percent of my friends have falsified information which they gave to U.S. immigration officials in Thailand. How can polygraph information be valid when the person with sighting information often has to hide personal information?

(2) There was no Hmong interpreter to work with the Hmong people. The Hmong are a naturally suspicious and secretive people. They seldom trust outsiders especially ethnic Lao, who are often ethnically prejudiced against the people they call the "dirty Meo" - a term analogous to saying "dirty nigger." (It is my understanding that DIA later hired a full-time ethnic Lao interpreter to work with the Hmong and other Laotians).

(3) The analysts also seemed unaware of the great stress experienced by the average Hmong refugee, their tremendous fear of authority figures, and the fact that scores of Hmong refugees had died suddenly in their sleep for no apparent reason. I had always thought that you needed to understand and be knowledgeable of people one dealt with professionally. I was surprised that the intelligence officers felt they could work effectively, openly and successfully with people about whom they seemed to have so little knowledge.

In short, my first contact ended in an unsatisfactory manner. One of the agents said that it sounded as if the Hmong "are just blowing smoke up your ass", and there seemed to be nothing to the three reports I had given them. I protested that the man who had supposedly seen the "100 Americans" lived in California and could be found although it would be "difficult" and would require effort. The DIA analyst was not impressed. He did not want to follow-up with either of the second-hand informants. He did agree that the one man should be interviewed. By the end of May 1983, a Hmong friend who was a high ranking intelligence officer had informed me of the substantial information in the possession of the CIA which concerned a large number of sighting reports of an estimated 200 to 300 Americans who were held at a place called Nakay (also called Sam Neua Caves, Ban Nakay, Ban Kakay Neua and Ban Nakay Teu). He claimed that this was the only permanent holding facility for Americans in Laos although small numbers of Americans were held temporarily at other locations. He claimed that their information had been very substantial -especially during the 1960's, but had decreased in volume and scope during the early 1970's after they had been forced to abandon a nearby safe site from which an intelligence team, a Controlled American Asset or CAS Team had worked from 1966-1970.

According to this man the information was so substantial that the CIA had began planning a raid to free the Americans by the late 1960's. Van Pao, he said, was offered $5 million in reward money if his men pulled off a successful raid. Commandos were suppposedly trained at Pha Khao. While the men were not aware of the object of their training, the officer in charge had been advised that he was preparing his men for an operation designed to free the Americans.

Live sighting reports on the American prisoners held at Nakay supposedly came from these sources:

(1) Captured enemy personnel who had seen the Americans.

(2) Enemy personnel who had seen the Americans and had "rallied" to the Royal Lao Government side.

(3) Civilian refugees from the area who had seen the Americans.

(4) One or more soldiers (Hmong) who had been captured, held near Nakay, and later escaped after seeing the Americans.

(5) A spy who had inserted in the area during the mid 1960s and who later provided information on the prison camp where the Americans were held. According to his man who supposedly had close contact with prison officials, the majority of the prisoners had been captured in Vietnam, the next largest group was from Laos, and one or two had been captured in Cambodia.

Overall information indicated that the Communists were making an attempt to keep the Americans alive. There was no significant number of executions. Furthermore hospital facilities were located very near the prison. There was no reason for the prisoners to die because of the lack of medical care. Treatment of the prisoners, however, was sometimes extremely brutal. On the other hand, prisoners were allowed to exercise or play various sports in the large prison compound which surrounded the cave entrance.

My informant stated that the existence of the camp was confirmed by aerial photograph and active steps were taken to ensure that the American POW compound was not bombed in order to protect the Americans. The information concerning the bombing practices was later confirmed by a DIA analyst.

The cave which housed the Americans was a very large cave. Huts were constructed inside the cave to house the prisoners. Spring water ran through the cave, and there were electric lights. Long term surviveability was a definite possibility. General Eugene Tighe, a former director of DIA, has told me that an aerial photo of Nakay showed people with "caucasian features" playing volleyball or soccer at the prison camp. DIA analyst, however, disputes General Tighes opinion. According to one analyst, the photo was "Non-specific" in relation to race of the individuals. Retired General John Singlaub, former Commander of SOG operations and other secret activities in Laos, has read a fifteen page description I wrote of the Hmong intelligence operation and the Nakay prison camp. He has stated in writing that my material conforms to his knowledge of that area of Laos and intelligence activities in that area.

Shortly after hearing of Nakay I was again contacted by Defense Intelligence Agency personnel. They apparently had waited approximately one month to contact the man who supposedly had seen two Americans in 1979. Unfortunately he had moved and they could not find him. They asked me to try to find his new address and telephone number. This I easily did using my contacts. The man was interviewed approximately three months later and again during 1984. I later asked him how the interviews went. He told me he was treated as an enemy, the interpreter was not trustworthy and that a DIA analyst had told him that I was a Communist. I would later discover that this was normal procedure for the DIA. I can provide substantial information on DIA tactics if anyone is interested.

During June 1983, I had numerous conversations with various intelligence personnel concerning Nakay. I felt that the DIA should attempt to check the veracity of the information. They eventually asked a contact of mine, General Vang Pao's chief intelligence officer, to write a letter describing his knowledge of Nakay. This enraged me. The man has ten years of knowledge about Nakay and can barely write English. Again typical mishandling by the DIA. I contacted Ann Griffiths and told her of my frustrations and she said she would go to her contact in the White House. Ms. Griffiths later asked me to cooperate with DIA and to speak to Col. Mark Richards who headed the DIA's POW-MIA Division.

I called Richards and he informed me that DIA would follow-up on the Nakay information in six weeks or so. This is top National priority?

I called Ann Griffiths back to explain my frustration. She told me that she more than understood my feelings. But, she said, DIA was preparing for the League of Families' annual meeting and should have more time in six to eight weeks to follow-up on the Nakay information. She did say that she would once again speak to her contact in the White House.

Because of the seriousness of the matter, I decided to follow-up myself.

I was determined to talk to Vang Pao's former chief of intelligence; a man who had worked on a daily basis with American CIA operatives for fifteen years during the 1960s and 1970s. He was a close relative of some of my best Hmong friends. Nevertheless he refused to talk to me over the phone about American prisoners held in Laos. He said that the matter was too sensitive and that he would talk to me only in person or he would talk to American intelligence officers. Since the DIA was dragging its feet on the matter and I had come to doubt the sincerity of their effort, I decided to go see this man. (DIA later made an appointment to meet with this man and several others. Without explanation all interviews were later cancelled) I traveled to Providence, Rhode Island and spoke for several hours with the man. He confirmed the information I had received earlier concerning Nakay. I was deeply concerned and expressed my concern to Ann Griffiths. I told her that I could not understand how this could have happened, "Why", I asked, "didn't the CIA pass the information to our leadership." Ms. Griffiths replied, "No, that's not what happened. A person who was a top administration official at one time, told me that a high level decision was made to leave the Americans held in Laos." I was dumbfounded.

While in the Northeast, I turned down a personal invitation from Col. Mark Richards for me to be the recipient of a "grand tour" of DIA. I returned to Arkansas, made an additional contact with a Hmong intelligence officer who also confirmed my previous information on Nakay and other related matters. I later wrote a memo to Col. Richards outlining my information on Nakay..

Ann Griffiths then wrote me and explained, in effect, that it wasn't appropriate for me to send that kind of information to DIA. They needed current information, she stated.

By that time I was attempting to get "current" information. I had traveled to California to see my old acquaintance General Vang Pao, I informed him that George Brooks had assured me that the MIA problem had become the Nation's highest priority. General Vang Pao laughed at me. He told me that he had told American intelligence officers many times about the Americans but nothing was ever done. I told him that I had been assured everything had changed. He was not impressed but agreed to cooperate with DIA if they would contact him. He told me that he did not at that time, July 1983, know an exact location. He did, however, state that he knew a general location of an active POW camp for Americans, and he drew the area out on a map for me. He claimed to have last known of an exact location of a POW camp for American prisoners in June of 1982, and before that, in May 1981.

I returned to Arkansas and relayed the information to Carol Bates who works for DIA. I asked them to contact General Vang Pao. She was noncommittal. Moreover she seemed unimpressed with General Vang Pao, but did ask if he claimed to know a specific camp location. I told her he claimed to know "a general location."

Other than attempting to establish contact between Vang Pao and the DIA, I was not to be involved in the matter. I was not going to work with Vang Pao and I was not going to work with the DIA. I was just trying to get the DIA to pay attention to a man with important contacts in Thailand,

Laos and other critical areas. I later called Vang Pao at his home to see if DIA had followed up with him. They had made no contact with him. I bitterly complained to Ann Griffiths about DIA's failure in this regard. She checked the situation out and wrote the following to me in an October 11, 1983 letter:

As of utilization of Vang Pao, his political contacts and involvement as well as residence in the U.S. rather than on the scene are all problems which need not be faced when there are numerous individuals with as great or better contacts in the nationalist Lao community. Should Vang Pao wish to be helpful, he definitely knows who to contact in Washington, D.C.

So much for follow up with Vang Pao. Col. Mark Richards later responded to my criticism by stating that the DIA checked out "even the thinnest" of leads. Speaking of me, he went on to say, "Any time we had any type of report we had unlimited resources and were doing everything we could to check them out." Richards then stated that many of my leads turned out to be "false stories."

This is a most interesting situation. DIA supposedly had checked out "even the thinnest" of my leads without talking to the people involved. People whose names DIA did not even have in several cases. For certain, someone is telling "false stories".

By October 1983, I had developed information concerning disaffected Pathet Lao officials who might work on securing information on the American prisoners held in Laos, and more importantly, on the supposed exact location of an active POW camp in Laos which held a large number of Americans. The information was based, in part, on a recent live sighting. Other, more sensitive information tended to confirm the validity of the existence and location of the camp. By this time I had little confidence in the DIA, but was determined to play it straight and hope against hope for the best. My cautious optimism, however, would prove unfounded.

On the first Monday in October 1983, I called Carol Bates to tell her of a current location of a POW camp holding a lot of Americans in Laos, and of potential contacts with "the Communists." She wanted me to write her a letter about this sensitive information. I agreed. I was not to be involved except to write the letters and possibly to verbally encourage cooperation between my contacts and the DIA. But it should be noted that one of my contacts, who had been a long-time, school trained CIA asset, was skeptical of the intentions of our intelligence people, as were his contacts in Thailand. Their first choice was to work with two CIA agents whom they considered personal friends. Unfortunately one of the men was dead and the other was supposedly severely injured. This was the reason I was contacted concerning this current live sighting report. Being a very close friend of relatives of the man, I was trusted. He was relying on me to make the contacts with our intelligence people. I had hoped that he would become comfortable with the DIA people once he met them and I could get on with my life without having to worry about my comrades who had been left behind so many years ago.

In dealing with my contacts, I always attempted to inform them of my every step. I believe that close and exact communication is a requirement if sensitive and potentially complicated human relationships are to be successfully conducted. Consequently I attempted to contact my two informants concerning the two letters I was to write the DIA, and to inform them of my every move. Two days later I had been unable to contact my most important source of information, the one who knew the exact location. I then decided to call Carol Bates to tell her that I was having trouble with the one contact and would send the letter as soon as possible. I wanted them to know that I wasn't playing games, that I was doing the best I could. The call, however, was never completed. The operator was briskly told that the DIA would not accept calls from me. Again I was shocked. I called my Congressman's office and complained about the DIA refusing to follow-up on a current location of a POW camp in Laos - a camp which held live Americans. My congressman's aide, a Mr. Reed, replied that I shouldn't be doing things that gave "false hopes" to the families of the missing.

I later called my Hmong source to tell him that no one at the DIA would talk to me. I asked him if he would work directly with the DIA. He said, "no". I did not contact the DIA for the next two years and they never contacted me.

I believe that his potentially significant opportunity to gain critical information on living American prisoners of war, then currently held in Laos, was intentionally mishandled by DIA. I can see no other possible explanation although I was told by one DIA official that the reason they didn't follow-up was my fault - that I had not sent the letter and they therefore had no obligation to follow-up the then current information on an active POW camp holding Americans.

Today Brian Bonnet of your staff informed me that he had heard that the DIA did not follow-up on my information because I was trying to insert myself in the process. This is not true. I can prove by taped conversations that (1) I told Carol Bates that I was not asking for money and (2) that I asked my most important contact to work directly with the DIA without my being involved. To briefly recap: Past or present DIA officials have claimed that:

1. They followed-up on my information but they were "false stories".

2. They did not follow-up because I did not send them a letter and that, in essence, following up on the live sighting report was my responsibility not theirs.

3. They did not follow-up because they did not like for me to butt-in on their business.

Concerning Vang Pao:

1. I was told by a DIA official late last winter that they did follow-up on the information by contacting Vang Pao's sources who they knew without having to consult with Vang Pao.

2. The above explanation is only slightly at variance with Ms. Griffiths contentions that the DIA had better sources than Vang Pao in Thailand.

Interestingly, Vang Pao now works in Thailand with Thai intelligence -according to various knowledgeable sources. Additionally, Vang Pao, according to a recent AP story was offered $1 million to work on a project supporting the Contras in Honduras.

On October 21, 1983, I wrote Ann Griffiths in an attempt to gain her assistance in getting someone to follow-up on the current information. A little less than six weeks later she replied and stated that she was "unaware" of my having spoken to the DIA about "the precise location of a POW camp." She also questioned me about what I intended to do concerning the possible contacts with "the Pathet Lao leadership." And, in response to my criticism of the DIA and it's handling of live POW information, she wrote, "There is little question that what you are reporting about the DIA was valid at one time." What was not said was that what was once true is still true.

Just before I received Ms. Griffiths' December 1, 1983 letter, an active duty Air Force Lt. Col. attempted to check out my information. He listened to me for awhile, told me that I sounded very convincing but that he knew there was "only one chance in a thousand" that there was anything to what I was saying. He was about to hit a long shot.

On or about December 5, 1983, this Lt. Col. had two telephone conversations with Colonel Mark Richards, the OIC of the DIA's 'POW/MIA" Division. Briefly stated, the first call consisted primarily of Col. Richards informing the Lt. Colonel that, while he did not question my integrity or intentions, I was "nuts." Col. Richards asked the Lt. Colonel for the telephone number of the informant who had told me of the exact POW camp location. I followed the Lt. Colonel into a nearby room where earlier he had written the telephone number on a "chalk board." I strongly objected to the Lt. Colonel giving the telephone number to Col. Richards. The Lt. Colonel stated that Colonel Richards had maintained that they had followed-up on everything I had ever passed to the DIA, but there was nothing to any of it. I said, "If they followed-up on everything then why are you giving them (the man's) telephone number?" Obviously, if they had followed-up with my sources then they would already have their telephone numbers. I then mentioned the DIA's failure to follow-up with Vang Pao and Ms. Griffiths' explanation of why there was no follow-up. I also offered to play my tapes of my conversations with the DIA. The Lt. Colonel then informed Colonel Richards that the telephone number had been misplaced and that he would call him back in a few minutes.

We then discussed the matter in some detail. The Lt. Colonel seemed to accept my point of view and called Richards back to tell him that the telephone number had been misplaced. What ensued was an approximately ten minute conversation. I heard about nine minutes of one side of the conversation. I purposely left the room for approximately one minute in order to let the two officers speak in private if they so desired. I had done the same thing during the earlier conversation. When the conversation was concluded, the Lt. Colonel seemed stunned. He then began to tell me in detail what was said. I would return home within the hour and write detailed notes of the conversation. The following information is from those notes.

Richards stated that he probably should not have said that I was nuts, but that I was really "red, white and blue", but in over my head. He then said that he shouldn't be talking but he nearly had his thirty years in and what were they going to do to him? I had the feeling from what was being said that Colonel Richards was planning on retiring before too long. Richards went on to say that he has a "SI" clearance and was cleared to work with the President on the matter. He did not, to my knowledge, say that he had ever worked with the President - only that he was cleared to work with him.

Richards then began to tell of sensitive information about Laos. According to Richards, they knew where the American POWs were being held in Sam Neua. He claimed that the camp was being monitored both by a ground team and a satellite. He said that, while the ground personnel had not personally seen the Americans, they did know the POWs were there. The satellite photos of the prison camp were "almost good enough to read a newspaper from them."

Nevertheless, I was told, the American prisoners could never be brought home publicly. Past government mistakes precluded openly bringing the men home. I interrupted the Lt. Colonel and said, "Did Richards say that?" "Yes" was the reply. I was once again dumbfounded.

Richards, however, did say that the Government was concerned about the men and that no expense was being spared. I was told that the prisoners would "be taken care of." At the time, I totally rejected what I heard next. I was told that some of the prisoners would be brought home secretly, paid off and kept from talking. I told the Lt. Colonel that I did not believe this would be possible. He stated that it would. I asked how everyone - mothers, fathers, brothers, sisters, old buddies, etc. - would be kept quiet. I then dropped the matter.

I later said, "What you're telling me then is that I'm in jeopardy." He said, "No, you're one of the good guys." "Good guys, hell," I thought. I replied, if the POWs can't be permitted to talk because of the trouble that it would cause for the country, then they would have to somehow keep me quiet. The Lt. Colonel then said that they would say that I was nuts to everyone I talked to and no one would believe me. The Lt. Colonel then said that they would never work with the old Hmong leadership. He stated that the Hmong were Communists and could not be trusted. I said, "Then what I've been telling you is all true." He replied, "Yes." He mentioned again that no one was questioning my motives or honesty. The Government's fallback position, he said, is that I'm a nut if I pursue the matter. I understood this to mean that I would somehow be discredited if I pursued the matter. The same policy applies to anyone who gets too close to the truth.

**END OF WRITTEN TESTIMONY**

The latest instructions I received from Senator Murkowski on August 4, 1986, requested that the testimony I am submitting "Be limited to specific information pertaining to missing Americans reported to be in captivity as a result of our military involvement in Southeast Asia. I have attempted to adhere religiously to these instructions by submitting information which deals with specific live sightings as noted below:

1. The Hmong information on Nakay is based on numerous live sightings.

2. My original three informants gave me specific information based on live sighting reports.

3. General Vang Pao's information was based on a live sighting report.

4. The information on the current location of a POW camp for Americans in the fall of 1983 was based on a live sighting report.

5. The information from Col. Mark Richards is based in large measure on live sighting reports - the satellite photos.

**Respectfully Submitted,**
**Thomas V. Ashworth**

In a letter from Michael Charney, Ph.D. to Bill Nichols dated September 2, 1986 the following was stated:

I am grateful for the invitation to appear at the forthcoming hearing of your committee on 10 September. The following is a synopsis in some detail of my views on the issue at hand:

The U.S. Army Central Identification Laboratory, Hawaii.

This facility, entrusted with the analysis of mostly skeletonized remains of our servicemen and women in the identification process, is guilty of unscientific, unprofessional work. The administrative and technical personnel have engaged knowingly in deliberate distortion of details deduced from the bones to give credibility to otherwise impossible identifications.

**SUPPORT DATA**

The skeletal fragments collected at the C-130 crash site, Pak Se in Laos, were divided into thirteen piles with positive, individual identification for all thirteen. The anthropological reports on all thirteen are shot through with untenable and indefensible analysis. The following six cases serve to illustrate:

**CMSgt. James R. Fuller - CILHI 0048--85**

Twenty-eight fragments with no possible clue as to their belonging to one individual. The largest fragment 2.5 inches with all others from one inch to less. Details of sex, race, age, height not possible. Age determined from a fragment labeled "pubis" has to be a deliberate fabrication as no symphyseal face, necessary for aging, is present. The fragment is actually from the skull.

**Col. Paul O. Meder - CILHU 0044-85**

Seventeen fragments again with no clue as to their collective personal sameness. Again, age determined from a fragment labeled "pubis". The fragment is a split section of the conjoined ramii of the ischium and the pubis - the connecting section of the two bones. The symphyseal face is not a part of this. To say one got the age from such a fragment is also a fabrication. Estimate of height from fragments of 1.25 inches by "morphological approximation" do not hold up under independent study of some 100 complete bones. The question of morphological approximation as a working tool of any dependency will be discussed later.

**Lt. Col. Thomas T. Hart, III - CILHI 0050-85**

Seven fragments with, again, no connective validity. Age of 30 to 40 said to be based on juncture line of head of femur to the neck. This joining will occur at approximately 14 years of age for most with an end date, when even the late-comers join, at 19 years. There is nothing in the literature about determining age past this date from the appearance of the line. It would seem that Mr. Furue fabricated data when such is necessary. Height was estimated from a fragment of a humerus. Again, Furue calls into play his own technique of "morphological approximation." This method has no relationship to that found in the literature for fragmented bone; work of Muller (1935) and Steele (1969). In a letter to Mrs. Hart dated 5 September, 1985, Lt. Col. Webb details Furue's technique for the humeral fragment; how he, Furue, was able to arrive at exactly how long the intact bone would have been, thus going into the stature reconstruction tables of Trotter and Gleser for the stature. This enabled a testing of the technique. I, and two of my colleagues, have measured some 100 humerii and femora (Meder case). Both instances, humerus and femur, show no relationship whatever of the details on the bones as used by Furue to estimate total length of the fragments. Details as to sex and especially race cannot be validated.

**Capt. George D. MacDonald - CILHI 0042-85**

The assignment of the bone fragments to this case is again arbitrary. Of significance here is the stating of height to and exact 70.0 inches which so happens to be that of Capt. MacDonald. The bones used to establish total length (from fragments) and thus the height, could not give so exact an answer even were the bones truly whole. The tables of Trotter and Gleser demand a plus-or-minus figure in all cases and the tables are based on the lengths of complete, intact bones not fragments.

The other details as to sex, race, age and dental description are without foundation.

**MSgt. Charles F. Fenter - CILHI 0046-85**

This case consists of just two fragmented remnants of teeth; a partial root (tooth #4) and a partial, split crown (tooth #17). Both are devoid of any enamel. From these two fragments the anthropologial reports the age, sex and race. More, the report also reads that "recovered dentition perfectly matches antemortem radiographs and records of this individual". The antemortem dental record of Fenter shows that neither of these two teeth had any restorations or anomalies. A most remarkable identification.

**MSgt. Rollie K. Reaid - CILHI 0049-85**

There is but one fragment here, the head of a humerus. Furue said that the line of epiphyseal union with the neck and shaft of the bone is evident, hence it represents a person of near 19 or 20 years. Only two of the crew answer to that age, Reaid and Fenter. (It must be stated that an end date for the end of growth of this segment is 23 years. There are two other members of the crew who would thus fit: Elliott and MacDonald at 24 years). Furue stated at the New Orleans meeting that the decision to assign this fragment to Reaid rather than Fenter was that the fragment was a small one, indicative of a slightly-build person. That Fenter was 200 pounds and Reaid only 115 pounds. He did not explain what a man of only 115 pounds was doing in the armed forces! In actuality, Reaid was 175 pounds (from his medical record). It is not possible to distinguish size of such a bone between these two weights. If this not be a fabrication then I know not what. It has been rumored that the Pakse material is to be understood in the light of a political decision; that the "identification" were known by the personnel of the CILHI to be of no value, but that such identification had to be made (emphasis mine) to impress the Laotian government. If this be true then it only explains what happened, it does not justify or excuse it. For whatever reason, any scientists, any scholar, any intellectual who submits to such chicanery has lost all credibility. The families of the POW-MIAs deserve better. They only ask for the truth. As they believe in the truth so must we all. One can confuse the truth but the world believes in the truth. To twist it as have Furue and others at the CILHI is to offend the moral rectitude of the world. There can be no forgiveness for such actions.

## OTHERS CASES

**Major Hugh Michael Fanning, USMC - CILHI 0013-84**

Details as to sex and height can be accepted, but again, no plus-or-minus figure is given for the height. Furue totally disregards the standard procedure followed by all physical anthropologists with no explanation for his actions.

Details as to race, age and handedness are not to be accepted. The bones and portions of bones for these traits are not at hand. Furue has used the comparative muscle-markings on the lower arm bones, the radii, for his estimation of handedness. Such analysis will not be found in the literature due to too many exceptions. Even more, were one to accept this technique, in this case, the markings on the right radius are heavier, larger than that of the left. Hence, this individual would thus be called right-handed and not left-handed as claimed.

It is now claimed that a positive identification is possible on the basis of "exclusionary evidence". Such evidence is permissable where the control of evidence is unquestioned. I do not know if this can be said to hold here. That is for others to say. It is passing strange that no justification for the biological analysis of the skeletal remains by the CILHI is defended. Were Furue's analysis correct, why is it not so defended? Why the turn to exclusionary?

**Captain Milton J. Vescelius, Jr., USN - CILHI 0080-85**

Two separate analysis were made on these remains, 22 October 1985 and 1 May 1986. Both are "bad anthropology" with the second report by far the worst.

No bones are intact and yet the height is again given to an exact 70.0 inches -no plus-or-minus, on the first report. The second list this error factor as though the whole, complete bones are at hand. More, of two sets of femur and tibia, right and left, Furue used the worst two, that on the right which were badly broken and his "morphological approximation" called on to fill the missing gaps. The two bones of the left, better in all regards, gave a height some two inches less than that of Vescelius. It makes one wonder. Age was based on many factors not even present and one, that of cranial suture closure which is not accurate or employed as a rule.

Yet here, the sutures were all open and could not be aged at more than 20 years. Certainly not the 33 years when Vescelius was shot down.

The clavicles were used by Furue as an aging device. But, the part of the bone that serves this function was not present on either of the two clavicles. Both sternal ends were missing. The second report, that of 1 May 1986, has a puzzling analysis of race. Furue gives a racial trait, straight femoral shaft, as indicative of a caucasoid when in all the literature this is recognized as a black trait. In the determination of sex Furue lists the degree of the angling of the Greater Sciatic Notches, right and left as "narrow", a male trait. He does not give the actual value of the angles. Sixty-seven degrees is the dividing value; less is that for males and more indicated female. The two angles measure 72 and 90 degrees respectively. This is hardly a "narrow" angling. It does not mean that these notches of the pelvic bone make this specimen a female as there are far too many exceptions. It does point out, however, the willingness of Furue to fabricate his results whensoever he chooses.

These remains assigned to Cap. Vescelius were independently examined by Dr. George Gill of the University of Wyoming. In the first report, 22 October 1985, Furue claimed to have reconstructed the face. All the facial bones are missing from this specimen. He reported that "the morphology matches antemortem photographic physiognomy of Vescelius, Milton J. Jr." One can only wonder just what nasal bones he constructed? The curvature of these nasali will make for decided differences in the final appearance. Were these nasal bones those of a Paul Newman? Jimmy Durante? Bob Hope? The second report makes no mention of this. Col. Webb and Mr. Furue have been quoted in the press as demanding to see "concrete evidence". They call to mind the story of the farmer who goes to a circus for the first time and looking up at a camel, says, "there ain't no such animal." I have been citing instance after instance of such concrete evidence of their fabrications since 10 July 1985 when I saw the skeletal remains of my first case, that of Lt. Col. Hart. They, Webb and Furue, do not see for they do not want to see.

Lt. Col. Webb's credibility does not fare well - as well. He has admitted to Mr. Fleshman that he made substantive changes in the anthropological reports so that the narrative would "flow", as he put it, for the members of the ASGRO board, this body being charged with the final decision of any identifications. At the same time he said, when defending the identifications from my attacks, that not only were all cases identified (250 at that time), but that the "bottom line was that not one of their identifications had been turned down by ASGRO". One might well ask just how Webb wants his ASGRO? On one hand they are too uninformed, too ignorant about matters anthropological so that such reports have to "flow", to be simplified. On the other, they are the very wisest, the court of last resort.

**Summation and Recommendation**

The CILHI in their skeletal analyses have shown itself to be shoddy in their workmanship and guilty of lying outrageously. The evidence is overwhelming. The army has used under-educated and inexperienced technicians for far too long. Given the wealth of first-rate physical anthropologist on the American scene it is difficult to understand just why lesser have been and still are being used. More, such technicians rather than scientists are still in charge.

Nonscientists such as Lt. Col. Webb and Mr. Sorensen, a mortician, the civilian administrator, have assumed for themselves the authority to judge the work of skeletal analysis and more, to interfere to the point of changing the reports. This is intolerable and must cease.

The laboratory in Hawaii is poorly equipped, has no library and very little comparative skeletal material so essential in skeletal identification.

I recommend that:

(1) A physical anthropologist with his doctorate, a Ph.D. and certified by the American Board of Forensic Anthropology be hired as a full-time head and administrator of the CIL.

(2) That the laboratory be moved to Washington, D.C. and that the task of skeletal analysis be given to the Department of Anthropology of the Smithsonian. This department has some twelve physical anthropologists on the faculty with three and probably more certified as Diplomats of the Board of Forensic Anthropology. They have one of the finest collection of skeletal remains of any museum in the world. Their library holdings are second to none. The Library of Congress and that of the Armed Forces Institute of Pathology are close at hand. Perhaps a working union in the task of identification should be these two to the Quartermaster Corps of the U.S. Army.

The families of our servicemen and women, some of whom have been waiting for twenty years for word of their missing, whether they be among the quick or the dead, these waiting ones deserve the very finest of the scientific community, scientists and scholars, not just technicians.

**RECENT NOTES:**

BO GRITZ AFFIDAVIT ADDS DETAIL TO THE GROWING "BIG PICTURE" ABOUT USG INVOLVEMENT IN COVERT MISSIONS IN SEARCH OF POWS:

Based on information coming to light as a result of the Smith and McIntire litigation, a better picture on early covert actions to recover POWs is emerging. In a recent affidavit filed in the litigation, Bo Gritz detailed four separate missions to recover or photograph POWs in Laos.

The four missions were code named "Velvet Hammer," "Grand Eagle," "Operation Lazarus," and "Brokenwing."

While all were nominally private operations, according to Gritz, the first two were US military-supported and the third was CIA-supported. The fourth was a private operation mounted by Gritz after the others were shut down. The first operation was allegedly cancelled in favor of a Delta Force operation. The second was allegedly cancelled due to US intra-agency infighting. The third was allegedly compromised by a team member and the fourth was intercepted while crossing the MeKong River in December, 1985. In his affidavit, Gritz also states that the existence of live POWs was discussed at the highest levels of the US Government and that his last mission involved facts basically identical to Smith and McIntire's widely reported attempt to recover three POWs in 1984.

Gritz's affidavit is interesting in light of the following items: a 1985 Washington Post discovery that a secret DOD intelligence group had supported Bo Gritz's operations, locations of POWs in Gritz's affidavit which correspond to locations mentioned in Schwab's correspondence to Ann Mills Griffiths in 1980, 1981 press reports that indicate that Ms. Griffiths was "sharing" intelligence information with a private cross-border group training in Florida, a Larry O'Daniel affidavit that states that Ms. Griffiths and he discussed the Gritz operation in detail, and the enclosed Bill Paul article, which suggests that President Reagan, around this same time period, was briefed on the live POW matter and asked the CIA to investigate "alternatives" to the ransom demanded by the Vietnamese.

## WESTMORELAND CALLS FOR REPLACEMENT OF ALL INVOLVED IN POW/MIA ISSUE

The Committee has learned that General Westmoreland, recently speaking at Stony Brook College in New York, called for the replacement of all USG officials involved in the POW/MIA issue. Gen. Westmoreland apparently did not spare the military from his suggested reassignments. Based on the information presently available, Westmoreland made his recommendation after concluding that the issue had been mishandled by everyone involved. Later he softened his statements saying he did not mean Pentagon Officials--?

**Article From The Fayetteville Observer, Oct. 16, 1986**

## TEXAS BILLIONAIRE CONVINCED POWS IN SOUTHEAST ASIA

Texas billionaire H. Ross Perot, asked by President Reagan to investigate whether American prisoners of war remain in Southeast Asia, has answered that he is "absolutely convinced" they exist.

But Perot, who would be named to head a special congressional commission to investigate the POW/MIA issue in a resolution co-sponsored by 275 members of the House, said he had no answer to the question, "How do we get 'em back?"

It is a question asked appropriately of Perot, whose sponsorship of a mission to rescue Americans held in Iran was depicted in the recent television movie "On Wings of Eagles".

Perot said it is not feasible to stage military raids in Southeast Asia because 25 or 30 would have to be simultaneous in all suspected POW areas and the Vietnamese or Laotians would kill or move all the prisoners in that case.

A House panel on Asian affairs, voted 4-4, failed to approve the resolution to form a congressional commission or a more permanent presidential commission. The measure cannot get to the floor until the subcommittee finds a way to break the tie.

Perot attended a meeting of the subcommittee to hear the testimony of retired Lt. Gen. Eugene Tighe, former head of the Defense Intelligence Agency. Tighe headed a panel that issued a report-most of it still classified-saying there is a high possibility some Americans are being held against their will in Laos, Vietnam or Cambodia.

Tighe said there was unanimity on the part of his panel of experts that some Americans are left in Southeast Asia, but some of them might be men who voluntarily stayed behind with their Asian wives or were military deserters.

Perot said he has been "working seven days a week" on the project and is confident there are still American POWs in the region.

"I'm absolutely convinced (there are)," he said.

Perot said his research into the experience of France convinced him the Vietnamese are using the live Americans and remains of the dead as economic bargaining tokens. He said economically troubled Vietnam seeks diplomatic recognition and "reparations" from the United States. (Although the writer has never been able to confirm, information has been passed throughout the World Intelligence Community that 22 French soldiers, captives of Vietnam as a result of the French-Indochina War, were ransomed sometime in the late 60's, early 70's, for the sum of $1 million per man. Possibly this is what the general is referring to.)

The Vietnamese relationship with the Soviets, Perot noted to United Press International, has been disastrous. He described the Soviets' 99-year lease on the former U.S. base at Cam Ranh Bay as "Guantanamo East," a reference to the isolated U.S. naval base in Cuba.

Perot also told UPI he has put a requested $4 million in an escrow bank account to try to get a mysterious film, which reportedly shows American prisoners in a jungle labor camp. The Texas billionaire said he has not gotten any response from the people who said they have the film.

## THE RETURN (cont.)

Next morning still in Hawaii:

The way current regulations are written, a retiree has little chance except to be on hand. I made one contact for the Philippines that I'd be able to use later, and one in Guam. I wondered if I would ever get there. I had not been able to get myself upgraded to category B-2 from category 4, by speaking to an important Air Force official. The cost of waiting was not great but it was hard to live in the terminal. The reason no space-available travelers had been able to get quarters on base for several weeks was because of Marcos, ex-president of the Philippines. He was on base, and the officers club and area were closed to the rest of us. There are rumors that Marcos had contributed to the election fund of Reagan--$6.7 million was mentioned. I found myself wondering what really happened and why he was allowed to use our base when I could not. I was not alone in my criticism.

In addition to lack of aircraft, the terminal was filled with soldiers going to Korea on operation "Team Spirit", a twenty-one-day exercise to reinforce South Korean defenses in case of invasion from the north. Other space-available people kept arriving and none were leaving.

I had been on a plane the night before and it could not fly. That's four C-5s in a row grounded. Impossible? But it was a pleasant day's wait with Steve and Alice, also waiting. We ran out of things to talk about, but Steve is Air Force intelligence and "guessed" I was on a mission. The terminal was beautiful, with an open-air atmosphere. Plants and trees were everywhere. The next morning the space-available situation was looking better, but deteriorated as the C-5A did not come up to flight status. I was beginning to see these aircraft have a problem. Six failures in a row is enough to make me wonder if the plane would stay up. Then things started to change. At 1200, I was on a flight to Cubi Point, Philippines. I thought, "Let's see if it takes off." I had explained my mission to "Boss Rabbit" and finally got a position at the top of category 2. Alice of Guam told me her husband will meet me at the airport, so I lent her $10 to eat on for a couple of days until she could get on a plane. We left the terminal and waited on buses to board the plane. It was not ready, so the buses withdrew 100 yards and a questionable engine was tested. We loaded and began the long taxi to the end of the runway. I might have guessed after one hour of starts and stops and revving of engines that we were again parked. The return ride to the terminal was quiet and a low murmur was audible above the din of normal airfield noise. Some "small mechanical problem" had returned us. For the seventh time a C-5 had failed. I met a young Sergeant named P.C., a relief to a bad day, and we had coffee. Surprisingly within the hour we were again boarding and to the great relief of all took off for Guam. This had been the worst week I could remember, but I had to wait for a stand-by aircraft. At this point money was of great importance to the mission. I had the time. A commercial flight was out of the question.

As we left I thought about Boss Rabbit who looked more like a Hollywood character than an airport commander. At least the beard was Hollywood, but he spoke with the authority of a full colonel. He was famous for "shanghai-ing" drifters who were using the terminal as a flophouse. He had them put on some aircraft for somewhere.

He was one to remember. I checked back with Boss Rabbit later. He also felt deeply about the POW situation.

With the C-5 airborne, my stay in Hawaii was over and, although unpleasant because of my circumstances, I was learning to live as a military traveler. Eight hours later we landed in Guam, 65 degrees longitude to the west of Hawaii. There was a time difference of four hours, and I had lost Friday since we crossed the international date line. In Guam I was befriended by J.D., a USAF police officer and former customs agent. It did seem strange that I was meeting only people in the police or intelligence business. There was Lisa 470MI, Steve of USAF intelligence, and now J.D. Of course I was suspicious of someone tracking my trip, but who and why?

J.D. had a nice bachelor house with another US type and was kind enough to give me a couch and the benefit of a hot shower. He opened a bottle of Jack Daniels. All this for a stranger.

I asked about living in Guam and in the Philippines and it seems things had not changed much since the 60's, beer up about fifteen cents a bottle, small apartment fifty to a hundred dollars a month, house girls thirty-five a month and food. Liquor and cigarettes were at a premium and of course are blackmarket items. One retiree I met in the Guam airport told me in the Philippines he could get no privileges on base except hospital. A "status of force agreement" was responsible, an agreement with Marcos.

In Guam living was easy and not too expensive, according to J.D. Cars were cheap, gas less than U.S. prices, and liquor about one third. J.D. was thinking of private investigation work after he left service in four or five years and I told him that insurance and arson investigation was the most lucrative. I gave him one of my cards. He had several letters of commendation on the living room wall and I felt he was a superior E-5. The USAF here in Guam seemed to have good people.

Again on the plane, I met a Guam hospital official. She described crime in Guam as very bad, male rapes, murder. Some place for a vacation. Yet Guam was developing into a "little Reno". But oddly enough this is the number-one spot for Japanese honeymooners. She was on her way to Japan and Korea. She seemed a nice person and had over sixteen years in service. Yet another strange thing happened, for one of the girls with her asked if I was working for Reagan. Now that was a surprise. I was thinking about clearing customs in the Philippines. Would I have more trouble with Philippines customs or US officers? I wanted to put my pistols in U.S. security at Cubi Point and hoped to get them back. Also, hoped for no restriction on an exit to Bangkok. I would have to ask about Singapore. All questions seemed to be unanswered because "No one knows". I hoped I would not be deported because of my weapons, but felt the guns were necessary in Thailand. Hoped the chief of police in Bangkok agreed that an import/export buyer needs a weapon. If not I would lose them. We arrived in the Philippines about three in the afternoon, Philippine time, another thirty degrees to the west of Guam. For each fifteen degrees there is one hour change of time. Arrival was on time. Customs was touch-and-go. I placed myself near the end of the line and moved bags rapidly, open to view. I declared the guns as per instructions. Maybe the Philippine agent could not read my writing, but in a minute I got clearance and moved past. I had told the American agent I had the guns. He only shook his head when I passed Phillipines customs. I asked him to find me a secure storage place for the weapons. After calling all over the base he could find no one who would accept my guns. It was all well, because I found I would have to leave from Clark for Bangkok, and so I called Steve, the Master Sergeant I'd met in Hickam. He asked me to stay a few days with him at Clark. I went to Navy operations and waited for the bus to Clark. When it came, the driver had already picked up a load. We waited about two hours until the Air Force captain got it straightened out and another bus was produced. After a checkout at the gate by a sharp Marine we were off to Clark. Again no problem. I was aware my luck had returned.

I did not recognize anything along the road to Clark. Everything had changed in the past eighteen years. On the bus I talked to a farmer, a retired military man who ran a farm of 2,000 acres. He stated he'd lost almost $1,000,000 since sugar prices had dropped and expected to lose the land soon. He admitted having sixty-five M-16 rifles and men who could use them. I was amazed to find that many of the landholders had private armies. Things had not gone well and it seemed everywhere you met people that were just waiting to see if Mrs. Aquino could bring it together. The country was still on the verge of revolution. The farmer was paying thirty cents a day for labor and gave five kilos of rice to each family every two weeks. He claimed to have four hundred men with families-that was 2,800 people to feed.

After I arrived at Clark AFB Steve and I went to the NCO club for a sandwich and beer. Steve knew I was beat so we left early for his quarters. Clark is one of the largest bases in the world, and one of the nicest. At 0400 I was awake and worked on arranging clothes and seeing if I could lighten the load. I tried, but found I had not brought many things with me I didn't want. I could send home a few items--flight jacket, etc.

Next day, Sunday, was slow. I bought our breakfast and some soda and beer. Steve took me around the base on his motorcycle, a Honda 400. It took a little time to relax again on a bike, but soon I was able to lean into a corner. I looked over luggage in the PX, and went by the base operation and terminal.

The space-available desk was busy, nothing going to Bangkok. Later I called the terminal and there were forty-two category (4) personnel ahead of me. There were twelve catergory (2) ahead of me, and one or two duty personnel. I was going to fly commercial in a few days, I decided. I was not going to stay around Clark waiting, as at Hickam in Hawaii. I was within $200 air fare of Bangkok.

We went to town and bought a beautiful pair of snake boots for Monika. I'd been ten days on the road. I went to see if Sergeant Pedding or Captain Berry at the terminal would get me on a plane. But when I approached Pedding he seemed uninterested, distant to the idea of helping with a catergory change. I was referred to the base commander, a colonel who turned out to care even less, afraid to make a move in any direction without backup. I decided it was time to become an import/export buyer. I spent the next few days establishing myself as a buyer and kept all cards.

While staying at Steve's house I worked daily as a buyer and learned about shipping, got three boxes ready for mail, some of my clothes and some items for Monika. According to Steve, most of the beautiful Philippine girls in Angeles City had V.D., so it was easy to stay on base and get ready for entry into Thailand.

One antique shop had items from $50 to $1.5 million. It was the strangest shop I had ever seen, in the middle of Luzon. He had $25,000 worth of things on the street and claimed never to have lost an item. I guess that size of antique had no practical value to a thief. To get into his shop you rang a bell, waited, and upon identification several doors were unlocked.

The visit with Steve brought many feelings. The military service is not all good, not all bad. But when we leave it, it should be left behind. As I knew it, the U.S. military does not exist today. But it still is a good job.

In reality I'm not sure Steve was not on assignment, as he helped me at Clark. Maybe someday I would know. He was Air Force intelligence all the way. I discussed with him his feeling about the project I was on and he felt as I did, that within our intelligence effort there had been slippage.

On Friday, I got an insight to how the United States Government was taking care of retirees. With twenty or thirty years of active duty, a retiree in the Philippines was denied postal privileges. U.S. stamps were not sold over the counter in the post office. No packages may be sent, and a machine must be used if a twenty-two-cent stamp was required. The reason was given that the Marcos government objected to retirees using U.S. mail. Of course, U.S. taxes are taken out of the retirees' checks, but in the Philippines they are denied postal use. Some officials at Clark also should be fired. The base commander first then anyone else having a part of this fiasco. I did not think I ever really felt like a second-class citizen anywhere before and I'm not proud of the U.S. government. I thought that something must be done but I would put it on the back burner.

The night before I left the Philippines I was able to get a call home to Monika. Mark was on active duty with the Navy and I wanted to let them know all was going well. Monika told me my permit to bring weapons to Thailand had been approved and I would have to leave the weapons with the customs and then see the police chief for the permit to carry. Things started to look up. I had a major general in Thailand to talk to, and one contact was all I needed.

I spent most of the day in final preparation for the bus trip to Manila and onward, by Air France, to Bangkok.

Sunday morning I arrived at the place to board the bus for Manila International Airport. The time of the bus passed and it became evident something was amiss. A general strike had been called. This strike was meant principally to affect the base. We waited over an hour after the bus arrived for it to depart for Manila. But the driver was afraid to drive off the base. He did agree to take us to the main gate of Clark. As we passed the other gates we noticed signs of striking workers and a few picketers, but all seemed calm. The time was now about 0830. We were met at the main gate by a mob. I had convinced some of the group in the bus to take a jeepney to the Manila airport. One of the passengers was afraid, but I noted everyone in the picketing group was smiling and seemed to be having a good time. We passed through the mob without incident and within five minutes we had struck up a deal with a jeepney owner. None of us was in much of a bargaining position since we all had nonrefundable tickets. The price was fixed at $50 for seven of us and that included a lot of baggage. That might seem a bit high but the bus fare was $5.50 each so it was the best deal in town. It turned out to be quite an interesting ride.

The highway had greatly improved since 1971, my last visit. Bridges were in good repair and a toll road established. But the countryside had not changed, with rice and cane fields still worked with carabao, a large water buffalo, common throughout the Far East, used as oxen were used a hundred years ago in the U.S. We approached Manila and the streets became more congested as we passed poorer areas. Like many places in the world the Philippines is a country of "haves and have nots" and the gulf is great.

The older two of our jeepney party were let off at their hotel and in five more minutes we had arrived at the airport. I have seen masses of people before, but there was no way to imagine this crowd on a Sunday morning at Manila airport. One of the ladies had been appointed as banker and the jeepney driver was paid. The five remaining passengers, including one Urasian beauty of French-German-Korean mixture disappeared in the mob scene surrounding the airport. By a stroke of luck, I entered the door where there was no security equipment. I was worried that my metal-boxed guns might cause a real problem traveling on the civilian French airliner. I could have saved the heartburn. Airport security lacked full coverage, and my bags were checked without a hitch. The next security check before entering the gate area was a magnetometer in the hands of a young lady. She was good and the dogtag in my wallet set off the machine. We were soon loaded on the Air France 747, served a French-style snack, and landed in Bangkok before the three-hour flight was really noticed.

I was pushed through customs and even though I'd declared the Rossi and Jennings pistols I was not asked to show them. I understood the chief of police had left a permit number for me at the airport. I'd try to see him tomorrow. I thought, "I suppose he'll be disturbed his customs officers failed to hold the pistols, but maybe not and that would save me a long trip back to the airfield." The airport is twenty miles from downtown. It took an hour for the minibus to bring us to the hotel I had selected from a list at the airport. The Malaysia Hotel cost $12 a night. It wasn't much but had bath, bed, and a bar downstairs. I'd stay a couple of nights and try to leave for the northern border areas where information would be available, if there was any. It would only take one contact. That night I met a young Canadian who might travel with me.

Next morning I was up at 4:30 a.m. to think about the mission and enormity of the task. At 0800 I went down to the hotel snack bar they called a restaurant and had a good breakfast-steak and eggs with tomato juice, potatoes, small pot of coffee, for $2.10. I always tried to miss lunch. I found a three-wheel motorcycle and made a deal with the driver. The trip to police headquarters was like a Keystone Cop movie. The driver would run ninety klm into a traffic jam. We were almost killed three times. At the police headquarters I found I was in the wrong building, in fact the wrong area of town, and after a lieutenant colonel called the general's office to find its location I found other transportation. The cab cost $2 for twelve miles. There I met the general who explained that I had made a great mistake passing customs with the guns and he must have a customs receipt to provide me a pistol permit. He felt I had made a right decision in bringing the guns, but probably would be sorry for the paperwork in Thailand. I wondered if the embassy would support me in an attempt for a license. I doubted it. I had to return to the airport with a captain of police. At the airport we found the duty officer was off duty. Well, you don't win all the time, and considering my luck with customs in the Philippines I was not going to complain.

Tuesday I was up at 0600, twelve hours and one day from El Retiro, my estate on the Tippecanoe River in Indiana. In the hotel restaurant I'd made a contact with a blond Canadian entertainer who was unusually wise for her age and felt she might be good for the mission since she had been in Asia six or seven months. I might try to enlist her for the trip. I'd start by the end of the week. When I first spoke to her, her words were, "I'm not a prostitute, I'm just having dinner." I had assured her I was not in the market, and we talked for about an hour.

Early Wednesday on the way to see about my guns and license I reflected on yesterday's events. The blond Canadian who might have traveled with me backed out and was thinking of returning home. I had received some good advice from the VFW Commander of Thailand, Dick Valera. The POW issue in Bangkok was at a standstill. There was not much information. I spoke to the XO of JUSMAG Thailand, Lieutenant Colonel Turner USAF who was attentive but noncommittal and of no help. I was referred to the mailroom and then to the Army attache, Colonel Avery. I went to see him at the embassy. He turned out to be a man of icewater blood, who seemed remote from the POW issue and tried to send me to the Joint Casualty Resolution Center, JCRC, commanded by Lieutenant Colonel Mather, a long-time resident of Bangkok. At this time I had no real reason to see him, since he could be one of the people involved in a coverup, if there was one. Why set myself up? I made my intentions to investigate on the Lao-Thai border known to Avery and left the embassy. I thought, "He may be of future value, but probably not." I made a confidential note for Congress, if he ever went up for general.

Off to customs for the guns. The taxi driver was Lao and drove at least eighty miles an hour, but if I got everything straight today I'd leave for Chiang Mai tonight or the following day.

The redtape was serious, and I had to post a $200 bond. I hoped I never had to use the guns. It was a problem, but once I had gone this far the challenge to fight the system was great. I had no delusions that I'd get the $200 back. All morning was spent trying to get customs to work around their mistake without admitting it. I felt they were doing well until they dropped another tax on me, and the paperwork continued.

I had not used the letter of credit or even deposited it. The cost for staying in Bangkok would not go over $100. The trip had cost $400 to date, but I was not upcountry yet.

Finally the guns were produced and I was off on an overnight bus to Chiang Mai near the Burma border. I thought I would start in the northwest on the Lao border and travel southeast until I came to the Mekong River then I would go south along the river. This plan would let me walk and, take buses and small boats so that I might get to places Americans usually did not travel. Chiang Mai was a pleasant change from Bangkok. In Bangkok I had found absolutely nothing to help the mission. No information about live POWs sighted in Laos. Yet I had some leads.

I bought a bottle of whiskey and three or four sodas, had breakfast, and asked a lot of questions of travelers. I got nothing, not even a flicker of concern from most people I talked to, about the possibility of Americans across the border.

That day I caught sight of two young American travelers and even though they wore local clothes I felt they were more than they appeared. One was carrying a bag and briefcase. They smelled of agency or embassy.

Monday: Still don't know if the two men are tracking me, they seem interested in everything else, they took separate rooms. I presume to play games with local girls. I wonder what their orders were. Was I a target? I hoped I didn't have to kill them-they seem like good enough types. I don't like the feeling of being the hunted. It is becoming more obvious to me I must move to the border towns. I will reduce my load once again, send more clothes to U.S. tomorrow. So far I've not been sick. What's that? There is some shooting near. I wonder what the hell is going on, well it's about 2 blocks away. I'd better mind my own business. I've been drinking a lot of soda water at twenty-five cents a bottle, not bad really and it assures good health. Americans really should not drink the water in most of the Far East.

Chiang Mai has a night market reminiscence of the Casbah, the Indian traders and small cafes where agents and tourists mix and can't tell one from the other. I enjoyed searching the area for items of interest for some of my backers in Indiana. One couple, avid "Buckskinners", had ask me to look for items of interest. They are Trader and Blue Star. This husband-and-wife team are in real life a firechief and well known Indian artist and beadwork expert. I used their "want list" to further my cover as an import/export dealer.

I will say this cover was accepted by Thailand officials only in part. They allowed it, but always let me know they believed I was in Thailand about the POW issue. I had not been able to be a trader and ask the necessary questions. They did accept me as a writer, and investigator and I got all the support from the Thai Government I might have expected. I got nothing from the U.S. Government.

One restaurant where European and Asian agents met to exchange information was the Bierstube, a good German restaurant by any standard. It was owned and operated by a twenty-one-year-old Thai beauty named Tip. She was helpful in giving me leads and pointing out some foreigners of interest from Hong Kong, Vietnam, Laos, China, Malaysia, Burma and other Asian countries. I had enough contacts along the border, and using Chiang Mai as a center of operation I spent a week or two on two-day trips to the northern border area.

The weather did not seem really hot in Chiang Mai because of altitude.

The nights were pleasant. I guess it would be a good place for a vacation. I would like to return to this area someday.

I went about my business as an export dealer and sometimes asked questions as a writer. Tiger teeth are high like hell, and claws go for $20 to $25. I knew the prices will be better out of the tourist area. Chiang Mai has a lot of European visitors. I must mail a package and leave here soon. I'll first go north to the Golden Triangle area then head south along the border. The time in Chiang Mai was a good reintroduction to Southeast Asia for me. I was always in the small villages near the border and talked to everyone from business owners to whores about rumors of Americans in Laos, but information was non-existent.

It seems that some American was swimming the MeKong river and was picked up by Lao troops and taken to Vientiane. But when I got it sorted out he was living in Thailand and often swam the river. Then one day he was sunbathing a little too far on their side. After questioning and a large fine he was released.

One smuggler said he had heard of Americans, but didn't know firsthand of any. I'm too far west and north. The Vietnam and Lao governments would not keep POWs this far west, in my opinion, but I had to make sure. What a strange country. I had just finished a German lunch, Thai-style, it wasn't bad, cost $3 with a beer. I had three hours to kill before buying a ticket at the bus station and heading for the northern border area known as the Golden Triangle, a place between Laos, Burma and Thailand. I have a contact there and may do better than Chiang Mai. I had a leather strap put on my leather briefcase. I really don't know how the U.S. men ever got away from carrying a leather pouch or shoulder bag. All of our frontiersmen used one. I guess that's one change that was made I don't feel is a step forward. Well, here all foreigners carry one. I also feel the shoulder bag meets the part of their law which requires me to carry my pistols in a bag. I guess I'll know if arrested. But I've got as good a weapon license as is possible in the short time I worked on it in Bangkok. It normally takes three months to get the regular carrying permit.

Watching the tourists go by I noticed I had seen one man too many times. I'm still expecting somewhere to be confronted by our people. Hopefully they won't be ordered to terminate my visit. With several hours on my hands and having seen as much of Chiang Mai as I wanted, I decided to return to the hotel and drink a few beers. Beer is $1 a bottle and a nice room is $6 a night and I'm told a Thai girl is $12 additional; it's an interesting country. The small bamboo restaurant at the Guest House Villa was pleasant enough and the rotating fans made it very Asian.

As I looked around I wondered just who is tracking me. It could be anyone--the two young Americans, the big silent older man (I've not heard him say a word in four days). Well, it doesn't matter. I'd passed the word I was leaving for Udorn. I'll be damned if I wanted to make it easy on anyone if I was being followed.

The Thai are a friendly people in general and many times an American will misinterpret them, thinking a friendly girl is a whore or a pleasant young man a little gay. Of course, in some cases, both are true.

The area to the north of Chiang Mai is jungle and elephant country. It's possible for a tourist to take a vacation trek of several days along the Burma border by foot and on elephant. My business precluded thoughts of this kind, but it might be of interest to would-be travelers.

The next weeks were spent walking the border north to south and meeting with many people of the Hmung tribes. I found interpreters hard to come by, but in one village I was presented to a young woman who would travel south with me a few days. Most of our communication was through a Lao-Thai dictionary I carried and she proved valuable in seeing to it I met border crossers. It's rather easy to cross the Lao border in this area, but the lack of information was prevalent. Some of the trails wound around so much I really didn't know if I was in Laos or Thailand and the people are all the same. Generally I felt less threatened with these people than I had felt in Chiang Mai. There were some villages so remote I'm sure a white man had never visited. Everywhere I was given the best treatment possible. They gave me what they could. They just didn't have much. I tried to pay my way...sometimes I could not.

During this part of the trip very little happened except one day the second week we entered a small village which seemed to have more activity than usual. My guide, over several minutes and many questions, explained to me a child had been carried away by a large cat, possibly a tiger. I was under the impression most tigers had left this area or were killed out years ago. The local law was some miles away and the village chief or leader ask if I had been a soldier. I answered yes, through the girl, and the chief then asked me to hunt the tiger. I suspect my interpreter told him I'd also been a hunter. I really was not here for this, but after seeing the distraught mother and finding that the only hunter in the village was down with a broken leg, I told the village leader I would hunt the cat, but that I had no weapon for this kind of game.

He came to me an hour later with an old single-barrel twenty-gauge shotgun and five rounds of questionable-vintage ammunition. This was not going to be just another hunt. A big jungle cat can weigh 300-500 lbs. and be eight-feet long. After looking over the old shotgun shells I decided to take one apart to determine what shot was inside and if I wanted to hunt a large cat with them. But time was important. The cat would move on and strike again in another village. I had to act that night.

Early that morning I had seen an old truck wrecked and in a gulley along the trail. I asked the village leader to recover the battery. When it was brought to me we broke it open and pounded some large heavy slugs out of the old lead. The process did not take long and soon I had three heavily-loaded shells for the old twenty-gauge. I put extra powder from the other two shells in those I selected to reload. I fashioned the loading tool out of junk I found around this village.

Early that night I got a goat and staked it out as bait. It was too much to expect the cat would return, but then there is no counting for hunter's luck.

The night jungle sounds again became familier to me. I could have been on a night ambush in Vietnam. I thought about that and decided I was in more danger here hunting a tiger with this old 20 gauge shotgun I would not have hunted rabbits with back in Indiana. Besides I was alone. Well it was at least one to one. God, what a thought, could there be two tigers-not likely. I let my mind drift for awhile. The night was hot. I was trying to stay alert, but the hours passed slowly. I found myself overwhelmingly compelled to think back to my time in Vietnam.

# CHAPTER 4

## Hue Nhon District

My transition into the Vietnam War was rather slow after the Laos adventure of 1960. Back in the United States, assigned to the First Division, I had assignments as company commander, Brigade S-3, and Division G-3 operations and training officer. After two years I received an assignment that took me back to the Far East. I had expected Vietnam. However, I was assigned duty in the Philippines.

At that time I knew little about the U.S. Army Security Agency (USASA) except that it was all top secret and the unit to which I was assigned was based at Clark AFB on the island in Luzon. I was assigned to command the ninth USASA company. There was also a section of this unit in Vietnam. The Vietnam section was at Phu Bi a town near the demilitarized zone. This unit had the mission of monitoring electronic transmissions throughout North Vietnam. Besides commanding the company at Clark AFB, my job was to keep in touch with this unit in Vietnam and over the next year I made several trips.

My initiation into the Vietnam War, after Laos, was to enter the country as a courier and stay as long as possible. I worked on some of their security problems. I am not sure I did them any good but I believe that this transition, however slow gave me some idea of how things were going in Vietnam during these years of '64 and '65.

In 1965 I was promoted to major and assigned to Fort Bragg TDY (temporary duty) as Senior District Advisor in the Military Advisory Command, duty. Vietnam, (MAC V). Duty at Ft. Bragg gave me the skills an adviser needs and I had a chance to study the language of Vietnam. I also needed to understand the Vietnam War. Another of the objectives of training was to learn what the Vietnamese people were like, how they were trying to conduct their war. It was their war in fact, was it not? Also, we were supposed to learn as much as possible about the Vietnamese culture and about the fitness of South Vietnamese soldiers.

The average Vietnamese is a small person compared to Americans. But he can walk farther, eat less, and carry more in the field than any soldier I have ever seen. My opinion of South Vietnamese soldiers is different from that of our troops who only saw them guarding bridges and check points. These duties made them look like they were conducting a passive war.

The Regional and Popular Forces of Vietnam were good soldiers and with leadership regardless of how things eventually came out when the U.S. withdrew, these soldiers were adequate and equal to any I have seen. Their reputation was bad because of poor leadership. Strangely most U.S. advisors were not in good enough shape to keep up with these soldiers. Granted I was a good deal older than the average American soldier. During the six weeks of training at Fort Bragg we received an extensive physical training program that got most of us into reasonable shape.

It was in November 1966 that I boarded a flight to Saigon for my second official tour in the Vietnam War. We arrived at Tonsonhut airport in the late afternoon after an uneventful flight that only stopped overnight in Hawaii and less time in the Philippines. It was almost a direct flight. I did get out on the town in Hawaii, but Wakiki Beach seemed like a dull prelude to something ahead and for some reason I didn't enjoy myself.

Arrival was late, and processing at the airport routine. We were told that if we had any personal weapons we had to register them. It was the normal military orientation. Was this a war?

The bus, standing by, took us to a downtown Saigon hotel. The trip downtown was also uneventful and exceptionally quiet. Most of us were taking in what sights we could see through the bars on the bus windows.

Saigon was quite different from Western cities. The streets were full of motorcycles and fumes from these motorcycles hung fifteen feet above the traffic. At a stoplight you felt like you did not want to breathe. This was the way of the people of Saigon. If a man was successful he owned a small Honda. On the handlebars rode one child, his wife would sit sidesaddle on the back with another one, or you might see a young couple dressed up and going out to dinner. The military had all the jeeps and sedans, but there were many civilian trucks and a few fancy French or German cars.

We looked over the three-wheel Japanese imports, and many open shops and open air markets. The hotel was nice with a large dining room. Most of us were traveling light, with only duty uniforms and two sets of jungle fatigues issued at Fort Bragg. We would receive combat gear and weapons within the next few days. Most officers coming from Bragg at this time carried a personal weapon and I can say it gave me confidence to know that I was not a sitting duck in the middle of Saigon. There were many attacks and bombings acknowledged by the Saigon Command but, these events were not important enough to reach the 7 o'clock TV news. The Vietcong also tried to kill U.S. troops.

Strangely, except for military police there were rules against anyone carrying a weapon except on travel status coming into or leaving Saigon. As for activities within Saigon, you were supposed to move throughout the city unarmed. I could not believe that any provost marshal or any command group could ever come up with such a ridiculous order. But that is exactly what the situation was like until the Vietcong TET offensive of 1968.

As history proved, the enemy was everywhere. Those in power in Saigon with authority to tell officers and senior enlisted people of the U.S. Army that they should not carry a weapon in Saigon were the same officers who had armed guards and traveled with machine-gun jeeps in front and behind. They were able to move about Saigon without personal weapons. Along with many officers I refused to obey this rule. We did have to appear to obey it, so personal weapons, the 45's, 38's and 9mm, were carried under our jackets. We were liable for court martial if found with these weapons. An officer found himself officially unarmed in a combat zone. I am sure that if we had made a point of this we might have gotten something done. But the army did not work like a union. Orders came down and usually were obeyed. At that point in time, most of us would rather have been caught with a weapon than caught without it.

We worked our way around this situation by ignoring the rules and overlooking the fact that our subordinates often carried canceled weapons. I am sure the military police and some of the higher ranking officers also realized that any sane, thinking officer or NCO had a weapon. But in the TET attack we lost officers who were on their way to work at MAC V headquarters. There the security was good, but officers on the bus were not allowed to be armed. Hopefully the lesson was learned.

Next day by bus we headed toward Long Ben about twenty miles north of Saigon. We still had little baggage. Long Ben seemed to be a much larger complex than I had remembered from a visit two years before. There had been a buildup. This area had many house trailers for senior officers, but there were fairly good quarters for almost everyone. There also were not many weapons in sight at this headquarters and Long Ben could be mortared or attacked anytime. However it must be said we did have several American combat units surrounding Long Ben at that time. At Long Ben we received weapons officially. We received more uniforms, jungle boots, and equipment you would normally carry in the field. Everything would fit in a duffle bag. We had the rest of the day for orientation and one more night in Long Ben.

Next morning, bright and early, I was at the airfield waiting for a C-130 that would take me to DaNang. When we embarked there were about six or seven seats alongside the fuselage. The Air Force and Army did not change things much, and just put the same seats in bigger, newer aircraft. The seats were up front. Most of the advisers were heading in different directions, once we arrived. DaNang was headquarters of the I Corps area. Behind us they loaded about three hundred Vietnamese troops. I did not know where they were going but they were going, all standing up. It was the most crowded aircraft I have ever seen. They were packed so close that only the retaining lines and straps held everybody in place. None could sit down, but no one could fall either.

Within an hour we landed at DaNang (I Corp) and I got my first look at the Marine Corps in Vietnam. I noted a great many helicopters on the airfield. The Army also had a small adviser contingent near the airfield. Corps headquarters for the Marines was in central DaNang with a three-star general running the show. It was clear at that time, the Marines commanded the corps but had no real operational control over MAC V teams. We had our chain of command outside that of the Marines except at corps headquarters which was intergrated. this was to lead to many problems. But, as I look back, it is the only way that Army personnel could have survived within the area. The officers club was a combination of Air Force, Army, Navy and Marine Corps and was nice, but not at all plush, a common-type building, near the temporary quarters we received.

Obviously on our way to war, the feeling existed that you were more closely controlled than was required.

You could go anywhere in DaNang in the daytime that you wished, without MPs bothering you. Houses of pleasure were as numerous as bars.

DaNang was not like Saigon, but there was enough traffic that you could not cross the street without looking. After a day of orientation that led nowhere, I was taken by helicopter to Hoi An, a small-town province headquarters that was located near a large river about 25 miles south of DaNang. This Province Headquarters compound was the area in which I would live for the next weeks.

The compound was in the middle of town, unfortunate because you have few good fields of fire in a town. If you shoot down the street you are shooting into Vietnamese houses or businesses. There are a great many problems trying to defend such a location. But that was where team headquarters was and I was not going to have much to say about it.

I was assigned as senior adviser to the Hue Nhon district, three miles southeast, toward the river and the ocean.

The first day as district senior adviser was very interesting. I met the team members and took the short drive from province headquarters to district headquarters. I had a chance to look over the district compound and noticed the poor bunker and perimeter defenses. I would have to see what I was up against-lack of supplies and materials, time, knowledge, troop labor. I had no ideas except that the compound defense would need work. I got a chance to meet the district commander and we had a good meeting.

The district headquarters was on the outskirts of Hue Nhon. The Vietnamese district chief, Captain Trun, had been district chief about twelve years. His family lived with him at headquarters. Quickly I discovered he was much feared by the Vietcong. I also found that this man was inexperienced in organized military operations, even though he had been in the war for twenty years. It was easy for me as an army major coming in from the outside to see the problems in this. But I was going to have to approach the captain in such a way as not to offend him, to gain his cooperation and gain respect of his staff and troops. I knew my job was going to be tremendous, because of lack of communication, logistics, and fire support planes. The district chief had not learned to use these military tools.

We returned to province headquarters and I met the province senior adviser. He was nice enough for a boss and his guidance was general. That was the best kind if you know what to do.

I spent time in the province headquarters bar that evening getting acquainted and reflecting on events to date. What was I in for this time? At 3:00 a.m., two hours after I had gone to bed, I found out. There was a mortar or rocket attack, I didn't know or care which at the time. Only three rounds hit the town close to the province compound, but close enough to send us all to the bunkers. I thought I could hear other mortar rounds going off several miles south and wondered if district headquarters had also been attacked.

The alert was called off in about thirty minutes and I returned to bed. Fifteen minutes later my interpreter was shaking my shoulder. "Major, the outpost at Kim Kam across the small river, Lig, has been hit hard. The district commander wants to take a relief force and asked me to come for you." I rolled out, dressed, quickly picked up extra ammunition and hurried to the waiting jeep. Two of my sergeants were also ready. Twenty minutes later the chief and I were leading a column along the road to a small village opposite Kim Kam outpost. It would not be light for an hour. Kim Kam was quiet, too quiet. The district chief started across a bridge of sorts. I followed, not knowing if the bridge would support my weight. We were alone until about halfway across when the others started over. "This is the dumbest thing I've ever done", I kept thinking. If there is one Vietcong on the other side they surely will kill us as we cross. Somehow I would not let this happen again. We crossed without a shot and Kim Kam post was suddenly all about us. The smell of death was everywhere. The few survivors were bringing the dead together in one place for a count. The district chief's brother was among the dead. He played no favorites. His younger brother was assigned this dangerous outpost duty along with thirty-three other men of his regional force. The feeling I got that first night on relief patrol will stay with me a long time. I would never go on another until they knew how to conduct a relief mission. They would know how to get and use all the combat support possible. It was a good initiation and set the tone of my attitude and future actions. I am glad I went that first night.

My team consisted of one master sergeant, or team sergeant, who handled the team, captain as team second-in-command, and four other NCO's. Master Sergeant Jameson, the team sergeant, from the first had my deepest respect as a soldier and gentleman. He took care of the needs of the team, along with Sergeant Parker who handled supply. Parker, incidentally, proved to be one of the finest scroungers in the country. He also was considered a weapons and communications expert. We had a good medic and a heavy weapons expert to handle training of the troops.

A few weeks of traveling back and forth from province headquarters to the district headquaters convinced me to set up a team house at district. I determined that living at province headquarters and commuting daily was an extremely dangerous approach to advising. We went down the same road each day to district headquarters for operations and returned many nights to province headquarters. This was a predictable pattern. The Vietcong would catch on and we would become history. I knew it was possible for the Vietcong to ambush us anytime. There was no alternative routes or reason to tempt fate. So after three weeks I made the decision to move the team to Hue Hon. A U.S. team had never lived at the district headquarters and I felt it would give confidence to Vietnamese troops and the district chief. Also the move would expose us less to ambush.

The fact that the Vietcong did not go out of their way to ambush U.S. advisers at this time has always been a mystery to me. Maybe they felt that if they killed us, the U.S. would send twice as many. The Vietcong would rather find out about each of our personalities, our advisory techniques, and operate accordingly. Although at this time the advisers were not principal subjects of attack, it was always a possibility and one I did not want to risk. Vehicles moved two hundred yards apart. The killing zone for an ambush then is stretched out to where it is difficult to get two vehicles. The

Vietcong had to attack all vehicles in a column at once because soldiers in other vehicles will immediately attack the ambush.

I inquired of the district chief where he wanted us to live. He said he would build a house next to the one where he lived and we could move into his old house. There were many reasons for his recommendation. He could rent us his old house and augment his income. I decided to go along with it.

The district forces built him a bamboo house and within a few days had put on a nice thatched roof and laid a concrete floor. Within a week my team had moved into this old sturdy French-style building, stuccoed outside, with wood ceilings and tile floors. We proceeded to make ourselves at home. Requisitions for a stove and a kerosene refrigerator were filled. Our lights were kerosene. My chief scrounger would go to DaNang with a truck borrowed from district headquarters and bring back all sorts of goodies -steak, bread, chicken, beer. At that time the Air Force and Navy had these items. But Army advisers had access to captured weapons, Vietcong flags, and other souvenirs, and it was easy to make a deal. Once Parker brought back an extra machine gun, claymore mines and barbed wire that otherwise was not obtainable without paperwork and a long delay. However, things unavailable officially always seemed to be available to Sgt. Parker.

Obviously the compound would have to be extended to encompass both our team house and the district chief's house. This might seem to be a minor task, but without equipment, without wire, without cement and without troops for labor it was a major undertaking. At this time the district chief had under his command only regional forces and popular forces, part-time soldiers similar to a home guard. They did not get paid much and were not required to be on duty all the time. Most were making a living by farming. Somehow this district chief arranged for most of his troops to be available most of the time. How did he do it? I did not ask. I suspect he was paying them with scrounged food and clothing. How else did he make it possible for a man who makes $8 and $10 a week to be on duty most of the time? For awhile we were going to be living outside the perimeter of the compound. I knew this in advance but the move had to be made. We just couldn't go on trying to run the district operation from province headquarters. Besides district operations were never good without full time advisors.

In Hue Nhon district there were many outposts. Some were across the river, which made them hard to defend. I never agreed with the old French outpost idea. But, since I inherited this situation, it would take time to change it. There were ways to protect the compound and the town without outposts.

The French outpost system put twenty to thirty soldiers in a small defensive location to give early warning of a Vietcong attack. But it was not effective and it only gave a "present" to the Vietcong. Anytime they wanted to take a small outpost they would throw a 200-man unit into the attack and overrun it. This outpost problem was something we wanted to work on immediately and so I set up a system with Marine Corps artillery, which was located down the road four or five miles. Until I could get rid of these outposts I wanted to be able to defend them with artillery. Still, the ill-trained troops were not skilled enough to use a forward observer to call artillery. We had to come up with something that would be easy for them to use and yet sure enough to get artillery when they wanted it and without an American adviser. Our job as advisers was to teach them how to win the war. A good adviser should work himself out of a job. It was going to be a long time before these South Vietnamese Soldiers would be prepared to run their own war.

We made compound sketches, circular cards with numbers of the clock. If there was a large tree inside the compound, we would draw in the tree. The soldier would look at the card, align it toward the tree, and on the radio ask us for fire at 1-2-3-4-10 o'clock and at what range. Their estimate of range was good. One of the NCO's would go to the outpost to act as a forward observer for the artillery and "fire in" concentrations around these outposts. Each concentration received a number and these numbers would be transposed at our Headquarters to Marine artillery coordinates. Details of fire direction were reduced in order that outposts could get immediate support. When we finally got the concentrations fired in and outpost were attacked, the Marine Corps could immediately fire for effect on the Vietcong. All requests for fire would go through district headquarters or my team. Within the next few weeks we managed to get a real Vietcong body count of 200-300.

## CHAPTER 5

## ADVISING THE CHIEF

District headquarters was functioning. We were working fairly well with the Marine Corps, which is a difficult task at best. Marine commanders had little respect for Vietnamese forces, and seemed to have little respect for the U.S. Army advisers. If you talked to the average Marine officer, he told you Vietnamese forces were poor and Army advisers worse. This attitude made a tough job even harder.

In addition every Marine Corp unit in my area took us under fire at some time. Individually each Marine is a fine person, but collectively, they were difficult to deal with.

The Marine colonel in our area was a 24 year Marine and should have been able to see our problems. I do not believe I ever liked him, even a little bit. But, his staff, and company commanders, were good people and gave me a lot of cooperation. The average enlisted Marine, of course, is a good man. You could always tell when the U.S. Marines were shooting at you. They put out a lot of fire. I found out that you could never get in front of a Marine unit. If we did they would always take us under fire. My troops were much more afraid of the Marine Corps than the Vietcong. To say coordination was possible but difficult is an understatement. But they could shoot artillery better than any unit I have seen.

At Hoi An, I found the district chief, was aggressive and a natural leader. He lacked military education, and some basic skills of a military leader but not bravery. The first scheduled patrol we conducted after I arrived at district headquarters was a notable experience. We had been on patrol for an hour, when I mentioned to the district chief that I thought the point had gone too far ahead. You might wonder what the district chief and district adviser were doing on patrol. This was the way it was done if you really wanted the patrol to go where directed. The district chief and district adviser led the patrol or you were never sure where the unit would patrol. They might go out of sight and sit down and come back three hours later. The chief knew this as well as I did. That was the way of young men in a war where there seemed to be no end. They were born in the war; they grew up in war, and were going to live as many years as possible. They avoided as much enemy contact as they could. Many times we called patrols "a walk in the sun".

When I told the chief I thought we were getting a little bit behind the point man, he had an amused look on his face. I had a translator and anytime he did not understand the language or I did not understand his Vietnamese the translator would try to get us together. The captain had muttered something. The translator turned around and said, "Captain said, we are the point". I called a halt to the patrol, and the captain and I had a long discussion about patrol tactics. I explained that if leaders are the point and they get involved in action they cannot maneuver the patrol against the enemy. His rationale was simple--he was the leader, and should be in front.

This is what I mean when I say he lacked tactical education. He would listen and seemed to like me. How he had lived this long in this area of Vietnam I will never know. After talking to him we took a shorter way back to the compound, on a different route. This also was a new idea for him. I did not change his methods drastically that day, because that would have been a "loss of face". I found later that in a hot combat situation he would react quickly to advice.

The next morning he was in the team house with a drawing board and a sketch of the way he thought a patrol should be run. I noticed he had two point men out in front and also some flack security. Apparently he had gone back to study that night or maybe he had talked to some of my team sergeants. Maybe he knew what to do but had forgotten. I'm not sure what 15 years of everyday war will do to a man. He explained to his staff that morning how the next patrol would be run, and the district chief and adviser would be along with the center of the group somewhere so that we could control the action, if in fact there was contact with the Vietcong.

With the captain you never know when you were going to run into the enemy. Sometimes I felt we were patroling where the enemy was not. However, once he pulled the slide back on his carbine and put a bullet in the chamber you could bet within the next few minutes we were going to be in contact. He had a sixth sense about the enemy. I do not know whether he could smell them, but it seemed like it. Always within two to three minutes of his loading the carbine we were engaged.

Our radio operator was a young fellow. Usually I kept the Vietnamese radio operator with me and one of my sergeants carried a radio. With Sergeant Parker carrying a PRC/25, I always knew I would have communication. The Vietnamese used their PRO/10 radios well, but with the PRO/10 sometimes you had communication, sometimes you did not. A lot depended on the operator. Usually the Vietnamese operator would also stay close to the district chief. In the field, radio antennas can be seen from long distances. Radio operators become targets. The leader was also immediately recognized when he reached for the radio. Field radios are used to keep contact with air observers, who can contact Air Force fighter cover. You also must be able to keep contact with adjacent units, and to call for artillery you must be tied in to the fire direction centers. Coordination with headquarters is always required and we tried to let the Marines know where we were. It generally did no good. We still got shot at.

Theoretically, along the route of the patrol you will have recorded check points and plotted artillery registration points designated for easy reference on the map. Coordination was not one of the captain's strong points. I hoped he would pick up on the advantage of good coordination if he saw us do it.

We started being fairly successful on patrols, often making contact and it became obvious that this captain and his unit, with proper support, was capable of handling the Vietcong every time they engaged a comparable size unit. The first patrol we made was unsatisfactory, the next one was a bit better, the next better. Operations now could be farther away from headquarters. I will say that after I first arrived if we wanted to fight we only had to move 1,000 meters in a southerly direction. That is not far, a little over half a mile. As patrols got more support the Vietcong kept a better distance.

One time we crossed the river in small wooden boats. These dugout canoes are called san pans. Crossing the river in the san pans was a dangerous experience for the American advisers because usually these boats were built for little people. A san pan might have 200-300 pounds in each boat, four Vietnamese and equipment. Once one of the advisers got into a san pan, with a Vietnamese in each end to paddle, we wound up with two inches of free-board. A tilt right or left by anyone would sink the boat. Rivers were swift and we were loaded with ammo, weapons, radios, and extra batteries for the radios. It was dangerous in other ways. You were exposed to enemy fire during the 5-10 minutes it took. If Charlie was, in fact, on the other side, you were in trouble.

Once across the river we were looking for the fortified village of Khung Tau. We had spotted Khung Tau by air photographs. The aircraft that carried mini guns in those days were C-47's and referred to in I Corp as "Snap the Magic Dragon". Snap had been over these villages and shot them up; but every time we took air photographs the people were back and the village working on more fortification.

The day of that river crossing I had decided to carry a M-1 sniper's rifle. We were getting into areas with long fields and rice paddies. I would be able to return fire if we were fired on at long range. Because of the lack of marksmanship on the part of the territorial forces I was the only one in the unit who had the capability of making long range shots. We had crossed the river and slipped through the jungle for about an hour when I called for the Air Force spotter plane I had set up the previous day. The Air Force 0-1 light aircraft was flown by an experienced combat pilot. He flew very low and slowly over the troops to keep contact. In some cases I think they tried to draw enemy fire so we would not be surprised. We had an excellent pilot that day. I was again asking the captain, "How far are the other platoons?" The captain had told me this was a company operation. We knew the area we were going into had at least one Vietcong battalion and I suspected two more companies. We were always told what units of the enemy were in front of us, but for some reason we kept capturing enemy from different units, which led me to believe there were two or three battalions in our area where only one battalion was designated by G-2. The captain looked at me, answering, "They're right here to the left and right." But as I talked to the 0-1 pilot I asked him if he saw any units to the right and left. I told him, "I've got about forty men with me." He said, "I see about forty people down there moving and I see you with the radio operator, but I don't see anything to the right and left of you." Once again my heart in my throat I stopped the unit for a quick break. This operation, to destroy the fortified village, was likely to get us all killed. When I asked the district chief, "How many soldiers do we have today?", he thought for a minute and answered, about forty-three. So the captain considered forty men a company while I have always considered a company to be 175. I began to realize some of the deep-rooted problems of the Vietnam government. We were at least six miles into enemy-controlled territory and here I was with 42-43 regional forces with a possible opposition of 300-400 Vietcong. I cannot complain about the captain's bravery or the fact that his soldiers would follow him anywhere. But here I was again in deep trouble, and the tour had just started and again this incident brought to my attention what a large job was cut out for me. Was I going to make a commander out of this district chief? I really wondered.

We were too close to the fortified village not to go ahead at this point. But I knew we did not have enough fire-power to take a fortified village if they wanted to defend it with a real force. I told the 0-1 pilot to be ready to react immediately if I called for air support. It would be our only chance to break contact if we hit a full battalion force. In the area there were two villages, 1,000 meters apart. As we approached the village it became apparent the fortifications had been maintained. We had to avoid large numbers of booby traps and pungie pits. A pungie pit is a pit dug in the ground with sharpened bamboo stakes at the bottom and sides. Once you step or fall into one of these traps you are wounded badly, if not killed, and you cannot climb out. As the pungie-pit traps became more evident we had to slow down and make sure the path into town was not mined. The approach wound up being very slow, down a single path. This tactic would scare the hell out of my infantry officer of the U.S. Army. If you approach a village on one path your channelized. I stopped the district chief for another discussion. He explained that this was the way the farmers came and went. The Vietcong usually did not mine the main roads in and out of villages. That was something I had to think about. After all he had managed to get by here for fifteen years. So we continued on into this little village and I began to see exactly how the Vietcong had prepared the village for a fight. Why had they decided not to fight? The village was deserted. Some huts were 30-40 feet long, 15-20 feet high, with straw over thick earth and rock roofs. Walls were earth about 10 feet thick. These were bunkers, which looked like large village houses from the air, and appeared easily to house 40-50 men each. They were not defendible; they were only bunkers in which to hide from bombs or the fire of the gun-ships. At the end of each bunker was a tunnel leading somewhere. I did not send anybody into the tunnels since the Vietcong were known in this area to trap tunnels which poisonous snakes tied from the ceiling. Besides we did not have the time or equipment. I wanted to get back to the river before the Vietcong found out we only had 43 men. We were going to have another long discussion, the District Chief and I.

The search of the fortified village was quickly over. We found several mines left in town to cause casualties. Everywhere you stepped was hazardous. They had buried 105 mm. projectiles in the ground with just the tips or fuses above ground, or sometimes covered with a layer of sand. If one is stepped on, it would kill 2-3 soldiers and hurt many others. It became obvious there was not going to be a fight in this town. We did not have the explosives with us to blow these bunkers. It would have taken several tons.

They could take a direct hit from some of our larger bombs and everyone inside would survive. I noticed the roofs of the bunkers had been shot to pieces with the mini guns from Snap or our gunships. To my consternation we started down the same path that we entered. This was a shaky situation. Again I had to take the district chief aside and stress that this was madness and we would likely get ambushed going back the same route and that our air cover would not see the ambushers since they had seen our spotter plane all day. He nodded and we left the village in another direction. Again we did not go through the rice paddies but on the rice paddie dikes, and again he took his time and explained to me that in most cases the farmers and people walked on these dikes. The Marines went across rice paddies, the rice paddies were mined and the farmers were notified accordingly.

As additional protection against mines, one of the older soldiers had his young son with us that day. Now you wonder how an adviser could allow a child of ten or eleven to be on that mission. I must remind the reader that this was their war and their country. They had been at it a long time and I was new in the area and I was making my corrections as diplomatically as I could. I was amazed to see this teamwork. The young man was right out on point with his nose about a foot from the ground. When and if there was a mine or grenade wire stretched across the path he would reach back, grab the old man by the pants leg, and the unit would stop until it was disarmed. He was the most effective mine detector I have ever seen. He and his old man had worked as a team for many operations. I am not sure I would have interfered with this situation even if I had authority to do it. We were moving very rapidly. Faster than any unit I had worked with.

We arrived at the river, made the crossing just after dark, and returned to our compound about 9:30 p.m.

At every opportunity I was urging the district chief to confuse the enemy, by taking a different route each operation. I did not want to make it easy for the Vietcong. But for the Vietnamese soldier, officer or leader, the war got tiresome. Everyday was the same. You leave your house, usually you turn right or left on the street in front of quarters. Your choices are not many, and if you turn right it is a little farther than if you turn left. Usually you turn left. In a combat area when you form a habit you invite ambush. In the combat area the adviser must be on the alert or he will be dead. As a team we discussed security. We knew we were susceptible to ambush. So did the district chief, but he got tired of always being on the alert. The advisers were only there one year at a time. He had to be there year after year. It was his war.

We later got photographs of another village to the south which seemed to have larger bunkers and seemed to be another highly fortified village. This time we decided we would send a spy. The district chief and I selected a beautiful young lady to enter the area and come back with information. Spying in Vietnam was not uncommon. This girl was good at her business.

After four days she came back with the information plus a fine poster picture of myself, complete with a reward noted at the bottom. The local Vietcong battalion Commander in that area had placed a reward on my head. Naturally, I had to find out who he was and get a picture of him. I then put up 100,000 P's reward for him, had the posters made and dropped 1,000 of these posters over the nearby Vietcong held territory.

The real information we sent her for was also interesting. The bunkers of concern were bunkers built to raise and house ducks. We had considered asking for a B-52 strike, we had considered destroying the area, and as it turned out these were duck bunkers. Only duck bunkers. I decided I might use that agent again. She had saved the U.S. Government hundreds of thousands of tax dollars.

## THE SPOTTER PLANE ATTACK

The days I spent in an Air Force spotter plane were never my best, although some were better than others. Across the DucTo River I had a strange experience, over which I had little or no control. As I recall, I was only a passenger for this adventure. I felt like the victim.

The Vietcong had been moving supplies on the river's backwaters. We were trying to set up some kind of an interdiction effort and I was making an "air recon" when we were fired on. Suddenly we had air bursts all around us at 1,500 feet. The closest I had ever come to flak was watching "12 O'Clock High" when I was a high school student.

I am not sure what the pilot did, but the aircraft fell out from under me, then caught up too quick. We were out of the air bursts and within seconds there was an air strike on the point of land from where the fire had come.

My pilot was on his third tour. The other two were as a flight pilot. I will say one thing. They act fast. My stomach was not the same for days. Had my soldier's Buddha worked again? Maybe this time the fighter pilot had the luck. I was just his guest.

## THE WATER BUFFALO

One of my favorite Vietnam "war" stories happened within the first month or two I was in the district. We had known there was a small Vietcong terror unit in the area. Because it was a small unit, we had been unable to make contact. But one morning about 3:00 we heard some shooting several hundred meters down the road, possibly a mile. About 8:00 that morning a young man, I would say twelve years old, came to district headquarters, not crying but angry and making a real loud complaint. I had to ask my interpreter what was going on, since I could understand nothing. He was talking to fast. The interpreter told me a Vietcong squad had come down a trail from the hills and surrounded his house. At gunpoint they had taken the family's water buffalo, slaughtered it, and taken the hind quarters into the jungle to feed a larger unit.

The water buffalo in Vietnam is the family workhorse. It was the only thing a farm family owned that was of any value. It pulled the cart, the plow, and turned the stile to grind the rice. When these Vietcong killed the family buffalo they did something we would consider extremely unkind. In the mind of this child it was a heinous crime. It took away the one thing that separated his family from common workers. It had been the young mans job to care for this animal each day and ride it to the field, since he was six years old.

In a few minutes it became evident that this young man had not come to the district headquarters to just complain. He was asking for a rifle and ammunition. I tried to pass it off, saying to the district chief that I thought he was a little young. The chief turned to me and said bluntly, "This man hates the Vietcong, he will make an excellent soldier". They found him an M-1 rifle, which is 43" long, and I think this young man was 44" tall. They took him and the rifle with two bandoleers of ammo out to the compound berm, sat up some tincan targets, and let him shoot all day under supervision of an NCO. The M-1 rifle kicks like a 12-gauge shotgun. This young man was beat around the rest of the afternoon. I wondered what he was thinking as he practiced firing. He hit some tin cans and missed a few, but in general he learned how the rifle functioned.

By the end of the afternoon, he had shot two hundred rounds. They gave him another bandoleer, about 160 rounds in eight round clips. The boy and rifle disappeared down the road. I asked the chief to explain to me what he had done. "You've armed a young man and sent him out alone to kill Vietcong." I said. "Is this really the way this war should go?" He said, "Maybe not, but this is the way it is. He now hates the enemy. That's something you Americans don't have. You don't hate. Because you don't hate the Vietcong, this war may never be won. We hate, we hate the Vietcong. They've killed our families. I understand the way the young man feels. He told me he will hunt down this Vietcong squad."

I said, "OK, fine." I did not want to ruin my rapport with the chief by arguing about this so I let it go. It was his district, his people, and his war. I changed the conversation to plans for other missions.

For three weeks we were busy carrying the war to the enemy. I had forgotten about the water buffalo. Then one morning about 4:30 I heard firing down the road. The M-1 shots (a 30-0-6 round) is distinctive and cannot be mistaken in the middle of the night. Someone was in a fire fight. What was this? I counted about forty to fifty rounds. I thought one of our guards was shooting at shadows again. It was not uncommon. I went back to sleep. This had been one of the few nights I had been able to sleep without being disturbed to call artillery. At 8:00 a.m. I looked out my window toward the compound and saw a small shape coming down the road. It was our young friend who lost the water buffalo. Over his shoulder he had four Vietcong rifles and was dragging a couple more. I found the chief and we went out to greet him. He again started yelling in Vietnamese. He was beyond himself. Again I could not understand him but my interpreter told me he had ambushed and killed the terror squad, the same squad that had come into his village and butchered his water buffalo.

We got a patrol together to go to his farm and police the area. Within ten minutes we were on the road and within thirty we had come close to the ambush site.

We entered his farmhouse area and continued on the trail toward heavy jungle to the north. This young man had been sitting on this trail every night, all night, for three weeks. Shortly we came on the site. We found five dead and three dying Vietcong. I think he got them all. There was fifty rounds of expended M-1 ammunition near the boy's place of concealment.

It was a real mess, but a pleasant change policing up enemy bodies rather than ours.

The boy was put in a Local Forces platoon, made a corporal, and presented a medal. He would be a soldier now. I could only shake my head and try to remember this war was theirs.

## THE RIVER VILLAGE

On patrol to a village three miles across the Cau Do River South of Hoian we came across a situation that might be called a typical adviser's problem.

There had been reports of a Vietcong unit that operated from the village of PacNu. The chief asked if I would take a patrol to the area. He had been given another task by the province commander. When we got into the area of the village I went forward to make a reconnaissance. As I did, I passed a small hut, a rather nice hut, empty, of course, by the time we got there. The people in Vietcong-controlled country will move out before the fight. They were possibly hiding in their bunker. Each family had a bunker, and the bunkers were never molested by our troops. No one ever threw a hand grenade into one of them. You would pass these family bunkers. When I first got to I Corps I often wondered if this was where the enemy was hiding, but on patrol the chief paid absolutely no attention to these family bunkers. None of our troops ever felt they were being used for anything but family protection.

The people were not in the house. To move around a little bit easier I laid my pack on the porch. As I got to the edge of a small river I could see the enemy moving on the other side. They were all dressed in black and carried K-47's. It was a hundred yards across the river, maybe not that far. The rumor was true; the Vietcong was using this town as a headquarters. I called in the spotter plane to mark both ends of the town with white smoke and immediately called for the air strike. Suddenly I realized I had made a mistake. I did not specify the ordnance.

The spotter plane knew where we were, and surely the Air Forces would come in with CPU's, small anti-personnel bombs or possibly with a rocket attack and then burn it with napalm. This village would no longer be a headquarters. But I was wrong. To my surprise the first plane dropped a 750-pound bomb, which came down on the edge of the river right across from me. I was virtually in the middle of the explosion. I remember looking at my radio operator who had wrapped his arms around a palm tree to hold himself down to the ground. The shrapnel from this bomb cut palm leaves and dropped them on us. I looked around; the Vietnamese forces with me had disappeared into the jungle. I could not blame them. I would have liked to disappear myself. But Parker who was on the radio, and one Vietnamese soldier, stayed with me. Parker had contact with the spotter and asked the Air Force to take the strike to the other edge of town. They would catch some of the Vietcong leaving town in that direction.

The next run was a rocket run and a few rockets strayed out of position and hit the river in front of us. I decided we had better move back behind the house and the family bunker we'd seen. As we got up to move, the young Vietnamese soldier who stayed with us was moving about ten feet ahead of me and I saw him hit a mine. His left leg was taken off above the knee. It apparently was a homemade claymore mine placed on the side of a tree. He tried to get up. Of course he could not. I reached for my first aid packet where I kept a line used for a tourniquet. The leg was not bleeding much, because in a traumatic amputation the blood vessels are seared closed. But I was worried about him bleeding to death. The look on his face will be with me forever as he reached around and picked up his boot which had a piece of bone sticking out of it. He threw the boot aside, reached into his jacket pocket, pulled out a grenade, quickly pulled the pin and rolled over on it. It happened quickly, but I managed to roll him over, get the grenade, and throw it in the river thirty feet away. He was attempting to kill himself. But, I was not about to let him take me with him.

In a few minutes we called for a "Dust Off". These medical helicopters landed in the front-line areas. There was a place a hundred yards behind us in the jungle. We managed to carry the young man to the helicopter. Within twenty minutes after he was hit, the young soldier was off the ground and in thirty more he was in DaNang at the hospital. In this sort of action a doctor came in with the medical chopper. These heroic pilots, doctors, and crew took our casualties right out of the battle area.

As the air attack ended, two of our Vietnamese swam across to enter the town. It took real guts. I had not ordered this crossing, but the chief had ordered it and these young soldiers went without hesitation. They came back to report that the Vietcong had left. We found a crossing site and took a patrol in to see what we had done with the strike. Large holes where the 750-pound bombs had hit were everywhere and there was evidence that a few of the Vietcong had been hit. There were K-47 Russian assault rifles lying around. Usually they did not leave these rifles. There were human parts and pieces here and there. The air strike had been successful. Before we left town people started reappearing. We had killed no civilians. When the operation was over I went to the hospital. I had caught a piece of the mine with my hand.

# CHAPTER 6

# COMBAT

The next mission was an attack on a river island. The river was a half mile wide. Vietcong attack groups would use the island as they come north to hit our outposts, harass the outer edges of Hoi An, and attack transportation and communication lines. The district chief decided to clean out the island.

I remember that we approached the island in assault boats. I do not remember where the boats came from. I guess we borrowed them from some engineer unit, but we had assault boats with 25-horsepower Johnson engines. The engines were blue, brand-new, and worked beautifully. These little assault boats were 18-20 feet long and we could get twenty-five Vietnamese soldiers in them. Everyone seemed to be able to get down below the water line except me. I was just too big, which became important later that morning.

We made an assault landing, and had a spotter plane overhead that reported a few Vietnamese had left the other side of the island in a small san pan as we landed. The spotter noticed they were armed and called in an Air Force attack plane. The rocket attack had taken care of the san pan. Much to my surprise, the village came out to greet us. But, within a few minutes the Vietnamese S-2 came up with a prisoner, an old man of about sixty. He had a little girl with him, three or four years old, maybe five, it was hard to tell. She was carrying his Chinese-style hat. Our S-2 already had this man's hands bound behind him with barbed wire. He had found him in one of the huts at the other end of the village.

Usually our troops treated prisoners fairly and I did not have much doubt that this old man would be treated well. But the turn of events in the next few minutes made me wonder about the S-2 lieutenant. He was not a good actor. He forced the old man to kneel down for questioning. His granddaughter was still standing there, holding that Chinese hat for him, tears running down her face. As they searched him they found a Vietcong pass. He had been friendly enough with the Vietcong that they had given him passes to go up and down the river. I had never considered these passes to be much of a problem, but the South Vietnamese considered Vietcong supporters as much their enemy as Vietcong soldiers. I always felt these were farmers and villagers who had to use the river and if it took a Vietcong pass to get there, they would get a Vietcong pass.

The questioning went along fairly reasonably, but for some reason the lieutenant suddenly, kicked the old man down, pulled out his bayonet, put it to his neck and yelled at him in words I did not understand. I started to get my interpreter to tell me what he was saying but the interpreter was ahead of me and said, "He is going to kill him if he doesn't tell him what he wants to know". I said, "Not with me here he's not", and at that second I hit the lieutenant beside the head with my carbine butt and the knife that was already in the old man's throat was released. The lieutenant never quite understood what happened to him. He also never forgave me, I am sure, but it did not make much difference in the long run. I noticed the troops around me, surprisingly, were pleased with my actions. I explained we did not kill prisoners and they were not going to kill prisoners in front of me, and that this was part of their training. Later the district chief agreed. I found I was supported. Every Vietnamese soldier present understood the lieutenant was not going to kill the old man in front of his grandchild or me. The lieutenant got up. He was not hurt badly, I did not hit him hard enough and as he got up he said a lot of things in Vietnamese and reached for his pistol. My interpreter said to him, "You'd best leave the major alone. Troops don't like what you do either". The lieutenant got his hand off his pistol quickly enough. The fact that I had a carbine pointed at him had something to do with that. At the end of the mission we took the old man to the prisoner compound. The following week he and his granddaughter were released to go back to their island.

As we started to leave the island I noticed we had a small squad of soldiers out on a sand spit two hundred yards from the island and five hundred yards from shore. Many times the Vietcong would hide underwater. They might have been hiding on the other side of this sand spit. We could not see the blind side, so the squad had gone out to take a look. About the time I spotted them they were taken under fire from the mainland. I knew the U.S. Marines were on an operation in that area and without any doubt in my mind this was Marine fire. My troops on the sand spit were getting into position to shoot back and if the Marines received fire eventually they would call their artillery in on that place and we would take casualties. Sergeant Jameson, the team "old man", saw what was happening and with total disregard for himself took off over that two hundred yards of open water. The water was knee-deep and he was running in sand. As he crossed the two hundred yards of open water, bullets dropping around him like rain, I thought he'd go down, but he managed to make the sand spit and get our troops down so they could not be hit. In the meantime I was on the radio to the Marine captain trying to get him to call off his fire. The firing finally stopped and Jameson brought the squad back. It was not his squad but he had a deep feeling for these people and this was a real act of bravery. He had crossed two hundred yards of open water and knew he would be the target of at least 10-20 Marines firing at him. Machine-gun fire had also started to rake the spit. He was a man among men. No one noticed he was black.

After we got the Marines fire called off and started to leave the island in the same boats we had used to get there. As usual almost everybody was down below the water line except me. Our boat driver was doing well crossing the open water when a Marine amtrack a thousand yards down river took us under fire. An Amtrack is like a tank that can float. I do not understand how this happens, but the Marines are apparently taught to shoot at anything that is in their area. Again I was on the radio trying to get this Marine captain to straighten out communications with this Amtrack. The bullets were bouncing everywhere across the water. All six machine guns on this Amtrack had us under fire, but at extreme range they were ricocheting before going through the boat. One bounced off the motor and got me in the knee. More like a burn than a hit. I was the only one who got hit out of five boats. I got a hold of the captain on the radio but that Marine Amtrack did not stop shooting until we pulled ashore in the captain's area. I guess he decided he better get the fire off us. I think that if he had not been standing in the middle of a whole two hundred man company of Marines I might have shot him. Luckily, I was the only one hurt in the operation but that was the second time that month.

A week later this same captain had his unit working in coordination with my tiger platoon. The latter was one of our finest platoons and led by one of the best platoon leaders. The district chief had taken all the aggressive young men he could find and placed them in one strike-force platoon. I am not sure this was a good idea but it had been done before I got there. The leader was Corporal Woo, a lieutenant at one time, who had gotten into a bar room fight with another lieutenant over a girl and killed him. In Vietnam leadership of quality was rare. If you had a fine leader you did not put him in jail and you certainly didn't have him executed. What the government did was make him a corporal in the army forever. He was never going to be anything more than a corporal. But he was always going to be a platoon leader.

Corporal Woo always carried a two to three day growth of beard and looked extremely unmilitary. But, I noticed his men treated him with greatest respect. When I went to the field one day with the tiger platoon I watched Woo accent his commands with carbine bullets. He would give an order and if somebody did not move fast enough he would fire his carbine within two to three feet to get the desired response. Although the inspector general would not agree with his methods of leadership, it was effective. His men not only gave him the greatest respect, but loved him and followed him without hesitation. He kept them all alive.

I remember that Corporal Woo, on this particular day was charged with clearing a mangro swamp near Hoi An. I had gone along to furnish communications and liaison to the Marine Corps. They were to be the blocking force at the other end of the swamp and the corporal was to go through and clear the area. But when we got there the Marine colonel argued that since we only had thirty-two men in that platoon, he would send a company through and let the Vietnamese platoon block. I spoke to the corporal. He shrugged his shoulders. "If they want to send their Marines through that swamp, let them," he said. The Marines moved out smartly and looked good. They went through that area maintaining almost shoulder to shoulder contact. At the end of the swamp, six hundred meters long, they all came out wet, hot, and dirty. There had not been a shot fired and the colonel took delight in telling me, "Yes, this is another one of these god damn adviser's fuckups. You guys don't know anything about what the hell you're doing and you're working in my area." I informed him that I felt he was operating in my district. We never did get along too well.

We had seen an enemy platoon enter the swamp the night before. I felt there was 35-40 Vietcong in the swamp. We had it outposted during the night. The observers reported the Vietcong had not left. So as far as I knew the Vietcong were still there.

That day I said, "OK, colonel, why don't you give this platoon a chance. You didn't find the Vietcong in there; I think they're still there." He said, "No, goddammit, they're not in there." I asked, "Well, how about putting some Marines down at the other end of the mangro swamp, to block and we'll see?" He answered, "All right, all right, it's already ten in the morning so we've wasted half a day anyway." I told Corporal Woo to take his tiger platoon through the swamp. I have never heard anything quite like what happened next. As they progressed through the swamp each man was shouting at the other. I was to hear this battle cry again during Vietcong attacks. It sounds like the old Indian attacks you see in the movies or on television. The Marine colonel was laughing until the firing started. You would hear thump-thump as the rifles were fired with muzzles under water. This firing lasted about thirty minutes. Then they started bringing out the bodies and weapons. The Vietcong had been under water breathing through reeds and waiting for the U.S. troops to pass. Corporal Woo and his troops knew their brothers. American Marines were looking for Vietcong, not the pieces of reed that might be a little out of place.

That day Corporal Woo brought out thirty-five bodies and twenty-nine weapons. They apparently lost a few weapons in the swamp and maybe a few Vietcong got away. As Woo laid out the dead Vietcong on the dike that separated the mangro swamp from the rice paddies, the colonel stormed all over the company commander, but said no more to me. The captain was a good man. (He had won the Navy Cross in a fight a few months before. Just before he was to finish his tour several months later he was to step on a 105-mm mine and lose both his legs.) Still fuming, the colonel got back in his jeep and returned to base. It was several more weeks before he would talk to me again.

We returned to our compound. The Vietcong bodies were turned over to the local villagers. They were laid out near the cemetery. The Vietcong bury their own and they took them away that night. The weapons were turned in, except for those rat-holed by Parker to trade in DaNang for food.

Basic leadership was hard to find. In a U.S. Unit if the squad leader was killed the assistant squad leader took over and continued the mission. That might not happen in the small Vietnamese Unit.

The South Vietnamese leader had a better knowledge of Vietcong tactics, but then could not coordinate operations well enough to take advantage of it.

In general the troops of my district commander were able to get on an objective without casualties, then why couldn't they get rid of the old French outposts, the poor bunkers, passive patrolling, all of which made them susceptible to ambush and surprise attack. It was the advisers job that often seemed unsurmantable. Later there would be a term "Vietnamazation". This meant turning the war over to Vietnam. It was going to take time. I wondered even in 1967 if the U.S. people would give us the years it would take.

## THE FLAG

Before I knew it, it was TET of 1967. The TET celebration was traditionally a time of peace and friendship. TET of 1967 was different from the following year, when the Vietcong made their offensive. I had never been in Vietnam during a celebration and I did not know what to expect. As TET approached I noticed the war was slowing. District headquarters and provance capitals were not being mortared. I noticed a different attitude around district headquarters. I cannot say "gala" attitude but definitely an attitude of celebration. I started noticing some strange things in Hoi An. Sometimes as I would pass the bars, I saw several K-47's leaning against the outside wall alongside our M-1 carbines and M-1 Garands. I asked my interpreter, "What the hell's going on here? Are there Vietcong in town?" He said, "Oh, yes, some come home for TET. This will last for a week or two and we'll have celebrations and everyone will go to bars and drink and argue and there may be a few fist fights, but there won't be any real trouble in town. They also won't shoot at the American advisers during this time." I could not believe this was happening but the local Vietcong were coming home to visit their families. Some brothers were on our side, others with the Vietcong. The district chief did not plan any operations and did not expect any. The advisers would learn a little about Vietnamese culture.

In the smaller villages the adviser teams never went to bars. We had our compound bars. We did not go to town much at night, nor did we get involved with local girls. That was taboo. There was no way to keep the respect of the Vietnamese troops if you were competing for their women.

One morning during the TET interlude I walked across the compound, enjoying this peaceful time. I noticed no guard on the compound gate. When I entered my office, I found a large Vietcong flag on my desk. It measured six by four feet, new and made for a purpose. This was a garrison-size flag. When I started inquiring about my flag, I found it had been presented to me by troops of the outpost Kam Ho.

The Kam Ho outpost was across the river, south of Hoi An, and about thirty-five to fifty men strong. They had set up a nice defensive perimeter. I visited the area about a week before. I did not like the fact that the outpost was across the river. I did not feel it was reinforceable. I had been the last adviser to go into that area to visit and look over their defenses, talk to them and set up an artillery defense.

After my visit, during TET of 1967, a Vietcong platoon came unarmed to Kam Ho's defense perimeter and started throwing political insults toward the defenders. Soon personal insults were being exchanged and soldiers of my outpost were invited to go downriver a mile or two to a Vietcong village where Vietcong battalion weapons were laid out in display. "We are going to show you what we're going to use against you after TET and maybe you'll decide our side is the right one." Well, as hard as it is to believe, our outpost laid down their weapons and walked to this Vietcong village where Vietcong weapons were laid out in parade style around the town square.

Apparently a political argument got underway and it was decided that since this was TET there would be no fight but there would be a volleyball game. I do not know if it was the best two out of three or how they did it, but apparently my outpost won the game. The stakes were simple. It was the flag over that town or the flag over my outpost. My team won. I got the flag, since I had been the last American visitor. This was a strange war.

The week after TET an entire Vietcong battalion, over three hundred men, overran Kam Ho outpost and killed all but two men, who escaped by swimming the river. After this disaster I was able to have the outpost removed. We would cover that area using mobile patrols instead of giving the Vietcong a target.

In the weeks that followed activities were going along well. Our compound was consolidated. The district chief's new house was beautiful. The thatched roof was pleasant. Bamboo floors were five feet off the ground, so dirt could fall through the cracks. It was a clean little house. We had rice wine with the district chief and his wife every night or two and he would often visit our team house. His children would go back and forth to the team house as if we were one family. We got along fine and I was learning more Vietnamese and he was getting pretty good with English. We developed a close relationship. The adviser hasn't made it with the person he's advising until he can walk up to him and say, "goddamnit, that's just not the way to do it and here is why", and have the person your advising listen to you and admit your way would be better. When you get to this point of rapport you have the job under control. Up until that time its a very difficult situation.

Day to day we existed in a strange situation. We knew we had North Vietnamese in our units. Maybe half the unit was North Vietnamese; some of them were Vietcong. A lot of the North Vietnamese men and women who came south joined the army. How many were loyal to the South was the real question.

As time went on, because of Vietcong spies, I was able to understand how the district chief had to operate. He would tell his staff he was going in one direction and as soon as we hit the road he would turn in another. In mornings we went out on daily patrol to present a high profile for himself and his adviser and also to find out in each area of his district what was happening. He talked to the people. He let them know who was boss and that he was not afraid to go to these areas. The Vietcong had a tough time setting up a real ambush against us. It was hard to describe what our life was like, knowing day to day that you did not have support of a U.S. unit and that you were subject to attack from anyplace at any time. At best it was not a pleasant situation. The lack of security my advisers lived with daily was noticeable. It was nothing like the security an American unit enjoyed. I had five Americans usually operating with thirty to fifty Vietnamese troops. In my South Vietnamese unit the American soldiers could really only depend on each other.

You can imagine the difference between the attitude and concern of the adviser versus the feelings of a solider operating with an American battalion of five hundred or six hundred men. The despair of facing the Vietcong enemy virtually alone is something that is impossible to describe. I am sure my NCO advisers often wondered how their country could put them in this position and expect them to function well for a year. There were many American teams in virtually the same position. Each district team and each Military Adviser Team worked in the remotest of areas with Vietnamese troops mostly some distance from American units. Special forces also did this type of work, but they were much better trained and experienced in independent operational missions.

You have heard about the tiger platoon and mangro swamp. I want to say a few more words about the Tiger Platoon. I spent many days with them on various operations and only one time did I wind up being the star. Most of the time the corporal platoon leader was absolutely superb. One day when we were being fired on by a sniper, however, I did excel. The sniper exposed himself in a rice paddy at about three hundred yards. The platoon all fired at him as he ran. There were no hits. I reached over to my radio operation who carried a M-79 grenade launcher, popped in a high explosive grenade, held the sight over him twenty-five feet and twenty-five yards ahead of him and fired. You can see an M-79 round in the air and he looked like he was running to meet it. By a stroke of luck the round hit him directly on the butt and ended his sniping career. I popped open the M-79, blew the smoke out of the barrel, handed it back to my radio operator, never again to pick up an M-79 in front of this group. That was my one and only M-79 combat shot in 1967. The word spread through the district about that shot and I was not going to spoil the myth.

## CHAPTER 7

## THE CHINA DOLL

The district chief and I had been walking a lot each day for about a month. He had been particularly security-conscience. So sometimes he would announce at headquarters, "We're going to village Kim Nang". But he would go to village Kim Kong, which was on the opposite side of the road. One day he had pulled one of these maneuvers and we headed down the road with a thirty man security patrol. When we came to the road on which we were suppose to turn right, we turned left, and walked into a little village about two miles off the main road. I remember distinctly as we approached the main square of the village. It was about 9:30 a.m., about the time the women finish the market. The daily market was usually held around the town square. Most of the farmers would bring in their goods and the people would buy and barter.

The road was muddy that day; it had been raining most of the night. As we walked into this town I noticed at a great distance, maybe 200 meters, a tall, slim, good-looking woman. At least she was a beauty from the back. She wore the traditional black pants with a white blouse and I particularly remembered her long jet-black hair. She stood above the rest of the people of the village, by a foot. I was looking her over and as we came to the market place I saw the old lady beside her nudge her with an elbow, as if they were joking. But, as we approached to about thirty feet from where she stood, she turned suddenly, leveled a K-47 rifle at us, and pulled the trigger.

Fate has a funny way of stepping into my life, and that day I was wearing my soldier's Buddah. I have never forgotten the look in her eyes. This "China Doll" had me cold, but the hammer of that K-47 fell on a bad cartridge. Her weapon had misfired. She realized that by the time she cocked the weapon again, thrown the bad cartridge on the ground, I could have shot her.

She made no attempt to reload the weapon. The barrel started moving down very slowly toward the ground. She'd caught us by surprise. For some time I think I had the only weapon pointed at her. When the district chief saw her weapon going down and that I had not fired; he yelled to his other troops not to shoot. She stood there with her K-47 pointed toward the ground. There was no fear, only hate, on her face and in her black eyes. What a beautiful woman!

Then something strange happened. Tring N, my interpreter, decided to be brave. Ordinarily, when shooting started, this young man could run under a dining room table at full speed. In fact, I rarely could find him after the shooting started. He was not normally known for his bravery. But for some reason, that day, he got brave and made a great mistake. He walked up to the China Doll, snatched the K-47 out of her hands with his right hand, and with his left hand backhanded her across the face. Her face turned to one side but she had not even been phased by his blow. To our surprise she hit him from about knee level with an uppercut that knocked him off the ground. She had hit him on the point of the chin. His feet left the ground at least two feet. He landed on his back in the mud and the grudge and lettuce leaves left from the early market. Unconscious for about ten seconds, he finally realized what had happened to him and reached for his .45 pistol. But with a quick step the district chief stepped on Tring's hand and forced the weapon into the mud, saying, "We're not going to shoot this one."

That day our visit to Qung Nu Village was short. The China Doll was a Vietcong soldier who had come home to visit for a few hours and then return to her unit in the field. We took her back to the compound and as usual I left the interrogation of the prisoner for the Vietnamese. I usually did not interfere. We could not do much better than they could, and they would treat their own people much rougher than we ever would. Almost always the information required was forthcoming. They rarely killed a prisoner, but techniques were more brutal than ours.

I understand they used several tricks on her. A telephone ringer with the diode in one location and the other wire clipped on the breast nipple throws about 200 volts, But, apparently they got nowhere because when I asked the district chief later, "What did you find out?", he said, "Well, she told us she was a Vietcong sergeant, a squad leader, her name is Won-Nitu, and her serial number, and if we wanted to know anything else we could go to hell."

I asked, "What are you going to do with her?"

"I don't know", he said, "I think I'll put her in charge of the prisoner compound." He did just that.

In the compound were about seventy to eighty men prisoners and a few women. Two hours later as we were going by the prisoner compound, the China Doll had them all out in a column of two's. She was going down the entire length of the two ranks using her finger to pound on each one of their chests as she talked to them individually. She had been put in charge of the prisoner compound and she was in charge...at least the prisoners had no doubt.

I looked over at the district chief and asked, "Captain what have we got here, a squad leader or a battalion commander?"

He said, "You know I don't know, I don't know, we'll see."

In the three weeks that followed we found that she was extremely useful. This woman was big and strong, besides being beautiful. It was obvious she was not just in charge, but in command of the prisoners.

We were building bunkers at two corners of our team house and the prisoners were used on sand-bag detail. She would look back along the line of prisoners who were carrying sand bags and if one of the men was not carrying two, as she was, one on each shoulder, she would drop one, walk back, and beat him to the ground with the other. Two sand bags per prisoner were carried a couple hundred yards and placed neatly in position. For this extra work she got a couple of packs of cigarettes every few days. The China Doll was an aggressive woman and would talk freely to my team about the virtues of her communist leaders and the Vietcong cause, and she promised us all a quick death because we were so kind to her. I found myself wishing she was on our side.

I was not surprised when in about three weeks I awoke one morning to the sound of excitement around the compound. When I asked what the commotion was about, I found the China Doll had killed two of our guards and escaped. She took no other prisoners with her. She had put a barbed wire loop around each one of their necks and snapped it so hard she almost cut off their heads. I had that old sinking feeling we had not heard the last of the China Doll.

The communications systems at our headquarters were becoming extremely effective. We had been giving immediate Marine artillery support to outposts and patrols. There was no doubt that our headquarters, with the many radio antennas, was the coordination center responsible for increased security of the district. Our defenses were coming along pretty good, but in those days defensive construction materials were not always available. We had built the bunkers with overhead cover. We had our fire plans, but the barbed wire was not all in place. The compound, at any one time, only had thirty-two to thirty-five defenders besides the five Americans.

The night of March 13, 1967 was tough and I am sure a night my team members, each one in his own way, will always remember. I had been coordinating operations and had not had much sleep the previous three or four nights. I finally sent an outguard unit a thousand meters behind our compound and tried to relax. At least I had stretched out on the bunk, taking off my three-day-old uniform. I just got to sleep about twelve that night, when the S-2 was shaking me saying there was a big problem. Our Tiger Platoon was observing a large enemy unit, in a temporary position a thousand meters behind the compound. I went to the radio and contacted the Marines, asking them if their artillery was ready to fire. We had fired in concentrations in that area with good results. They could adjust from these concentrations and fire for effect. The S-2 was on one radio with the Tiger Platoon and gave me the enemy coordinates. As I was talking to the Marine corporal relating these coordinates, I got a wrong signal. I asked the Marines to wait, walked over to the operations map, and noticed a strange thing. The coordinates were almost exactly where I had noted a Marine ambush was going into location that afternoon. I realized that my Tiger Platoon was probably observing the Marine ambush. But the Tiger Platoon was reporting a large enemy unit. Sometimes Marine ambushers were thirty to a hundred men. I was never surprised when this sort of thing happens. Advisors learn that you often get a "snafu", a real screw-up.

On the radio to the Marines I said, "Hold it, don't fire, don't fire, check your board and see if you have a Marine ambush in that area."

I got a shout back real quick, "Yes, it's the Marines you're looking at, they're at those exact coordinates."

I said, "all right, you contact your commander and have the Marine unit pull back a couple hundred meters. I'll contact our Platoon and tell them to move back five hundred meters and we'll defuse this situation. Nobody shoot."

My S-2, as I learned later, gave the orders to the Tiger Platoon, "withdraw to the compound." He was speaking in Vietnamese which I did not pick up, and my interpreter was not on hand. They withdrew to their compound about a mile down the road from ours. That night we had thirty-two regional forces at the compound. We were on one hundred percent alert. But, my outguard had been withdrawn without my knowledge.

Fortunately or unfortunately, depending on the viewpoint, two Marines had been sent from DaNang on a deal my supply Sergeant made to help us construct partitions in the house, so I had two extra men. Before that night was over both of those Marines were to win the Navy Cross.

We knew our S-2 was North Vietnamese, but I had no idea he was actually Vietcong. When the S-2 gave the word to the Tiger Platoon, he left us entirely exposed. The Tiger Platoon had been correct--they had seen a large enemy unit. But with the S-2 giving them the word to move back, they responded immediately. The district compound was exposed. It was a well planned betrayal. Of course, at the time I had no idea I had been betrayed. I went back to sleep about 1:30.

At 3:00 a.m. we were under a full-scale Vietcong battalion attack. They came through the wire with bangalore torpedoes during the mortar attack. They used the classic Vietcong attack. As the mortars were shifted the Vietcong were already in the compound. Against the seven Americans and thirty-two RF/PF, the Vietcong had chosen to use a battalion attack. They meant business. They meant to kill us all. Three companies in attack, one across the compound, one directly at my headquarters, and the other attacking from the east. A platoon out of that company was to come in from the south to complete the circle.

Luckily I had posted another outguard down by the river to the south, so the platoon that was supposed to complete the encirclement was engaged 500-600 meters from our headquarters. This outguard proved one factor that saved us.

It is hard to recount all this in proper sequence, but as mortar rounds hit, the top of the house caught fire. I wondered how they could hit the house so accurately, but later found someone in the compound had stepped off exactly 1,000 meters, where they set up their mortar tubes. Once range data was available, gunners can do extremely well putting first-round hits on a target.

At the same time, as I came out of a deep sleep, a rocket-propelled grenade (RPG) hit the side of the building opposite where my bed had been the day before, and blew bricks all over my room. Almost simultaneously I turned my bed over and was groping around for some kind of weapon. I had had a .45 Colt on the night stand and my Thompson was at the foot of the bed on my foot locker. As I turned the bed over, my hand came across the small-caliber pistol that I carried with me at all times. I grabbed it like a drowning man at a straw. The back door to my room was blown or knocked down. I knew it was not any of my team. They would not enter my quarters that way. The first Vietcong came through the doorway firing his K-47. Luckily he was firing over my head---I was on the floor. As I shot him twice and he went down, the next Vietcong stepped into his position firing wildly through the room. I hit him twice and he also went down, and the third went down the same way. These three were lying on the floor of my room, and no more behind. I found the .45 Colt Commander that had been knocked off the table. I shot through the doorway several shots just in case and dropped the Colt. I had found the Thompson, at the end of the bed. I also found my ditty bag with 25 Thompson magazines. This bag of ammo proved another of the factors that kept us alive that night. I managed to locate a flak jacket, no helmet, no pants. I had no boots, lost somwehere under the bricks. I had only a pair of shorts, the Thompson, the bag, and flak jacket. I made my way to the bunker. I was still alive, which was not according to the Vietcong plan.

By the time I got to the bunker the rest of the team was in their places. We had occupied both the forward and back bunkers and taken the enemy under fire. We had good fields. By putting the bunkers on two diagonal corners of the house we could shoot down all four sides. But we were being attacked by a well rehearsed and organized unit. They had trained and practiced to attack these bunkers. Soon I would be forced to make the decision to leave these bunkers and defend from the front porch, where that same day we had stacked up about two hundred bags of cement. I had them stacked around the edge of the porch. We were going to use the cement on a civic action project the following week.

Before we had to leave the back bunker three or four things happened. I realized that one of the sergeants was virtually night blind. I was watching him look straight at the enemy approaching from his side and there was no shooting. I was yelling, "Why aren't you firing, why aren't you firing?" He said, "I don't see anything." I said, "Get out of the way." I stepped over and used the Thompson in that direction and five or six of the enemy went down. The rest withdrew.

I heard Sergeant Parker on the radio talking to headquarters: "We're under heavy ground attack, there must be about 300. We need some help down here. Now I have to stop talking and start shooting." He dropped the radio and picked up the M-60 machine gun.

When I looked the other way I could see Sergeant Jameson, his carbine pointed at five or six Vietcong. They were duck waddling, coming in on his left side. He shot the last one in line first, then each in succession, coming forward; the first finally stood up and looked around for the squad, then fell across the rest of them.

From nowhere a Vietcong came toward us carrying a large satchel charge. Jameson flipped the switch on his carbine to full auto and fired twenty rounds into him. The Vietcong went down.

About that time a grenade, thrown from behind us rolled into the bunker. There was nothing to do, not time to think. I moved to kick it out. Barefoot it seemed to weight about 15 pounds. As I kicked, it went off in front of me. I knew I was hit several times. Later I found I had been hit in twenty-two places.

That was when it became obvious the Vietcong were tearing this bunker down around us. That brought me to the decision to leave the back bunker. To get the team out and moving, I stepped out of the bunker to cover them.

The smoke was heavy; the team was coming out behind me, moving toward the front porch. They had to go about thirty yards. As they moved out the smoke cleared and at that moment three Vietcong appeared from the smoke in front of me all firing K-47's. I knew I was hit and going down. The tracers from their guns were tearing at my flak jacket. I remember pressing the trigger on the Thompson, which seemed to fire very slowly. Of course it was not: a Thompson fires full automatic. When the muzzle of the Thompson hit the sand, I knew I was down. But I didn't know how badly I was hurt. I had been hit in the head and left arm and right knee. I remember shaking my head, looking up and realizing I was not dead. There were three Vietcong down in front of me, fifteen feet away. The team had made it to the front bunker. I tried to follow, but fell. I stood up again, and fell. The third time I found out I could stand, and finally got to the front porch adjacent to the front bunker.

The rest of the team had also been forced to leave bunker number two.

Everywhere I looked I could see enemy around the house. The fire was bad, the district chief's house next to us was on fire, the bamboo popping and breaking up, sounding like even more rifle fire. The smoke was dense but we could see. The Vietcong were coming in on us in waves and groups. The only thing that kept them back was our automatic fire, and Sergeant Jameson throwing grenades as fast as he could pull the pins. We had several boxes of grenades that had been pulled out on the front porch by the front team before they had entered their bunker. There was not a problem with ammunition; there was not a problem with weapons; the problem was too many Vietcong.

It was a nightmare of smoke and noise. The Vietcong bullets were ricochetting from the front of the house, and cement falling on us from bullet impacts. I looked far back into the enemy through the smoke and in a flash of light could see the China Doll in the background, pointing in one direction then pointing in another and in that flash of a second I knew who was running this attack. The Vietcong had used the intelligence she had brought and practiced for a week or two in the jungles. Then she had led them back. She was doing a very good job. For a moment I could see her clearly at seventy-five yards. With a deliberate effort to slow down, I put the Thompson on my shoulder and fired twenty rounds in her direction. I did not see her again. I found out later that a company commander had been killed. I sure would liked to have known the China Doll in another time and another place.

We now were in a poor position--on the porch, the bunkers still being attacked. There is one rule when you are surrounded without possibility of relief. You must break out. If you stay you will die. We were going to have to move, die, or-worse-be captured.

The adjacent compound to the south, by now, had been overrun. We were receiving fire from it's perimeter. I remember once as I moved across to the side of the porch I could see fire coming from one Vietcong and as I fired at him I could see the sparks flying as the big heavy .45 bullets hit his rifle or exploded a hand grenade. He stopped firing.

The decision I made in the next few minutes was to try a break out. I moved twenty yards to the gate on the road in front of the house. When I got to the gate I found it had been wired closed. I do not know whether we had wired it or if our spy had wired it. But, it was not going to be possible to get the gate open.

We were not receiving fire from across the street, since that part of the encirclement had failed, the attack stopped by the river ambush. Then I saw that the district chief's gate was open. His house was burning. I knew he was in the compound. He had come to our bunker at the back earlier in the fight and said he was going to the compound to organize his troops. That was the last time I saw him alive. I got the team ready. We would attack directly into the enemy to our front. Just before we made hand-to-hand contact we would turn to the left, go out the gate in front of the district chief's house, and get to the houses across the street, thirty yards west. This would screw up their attack and they would then have to change direction or let us go.

We started to move. I was forward with the Thompson. I knew my medic was behind me and Parker was behind him. The rest of the team had not left the bunker when things started to happen. There was several Vietcong in front of me one minute, I fired the Thompson, and they were not there. I heard my medic scream and saw him go down. He had been hit hard. Parker behind him went down and started firing. I got through the gate and was hit in the foot. At the same moment I ran into the barbed wire we had put across the road to stop traffic at night. I went along the wire and crossed the street. The next thing I knew I found myself down again. I was hit, but again not seriously. I had been grazed again across the head. Somehow I got into the house on the other side. It was empty. I was able to get to a front window in time to see the rest of the team get back onto the front porch, behind the cement bags. I could still see the medic lying between the bunker and the gate. That was where he stayed for the rest of the fight. They shot at him several times. I found out later they even shot off his belt buckle. But he was down and staying there, playing dead. Parker and the rest of them had gotten back to the porch. That meant we had only one man down that could not fight. Parker had hit several Vietcong as he covered me going through the gate.

The two Marines were also still with the team. Both had been hit; both had done well. They had continuously fired at the enemy. What a visit they were having.

About this time I could see the Vietcong again advancing toward the porch. I was across the street thirty yards. They had us surrounded, but we were killing them. The poor bastards had us surrounded. Every time they would try to get to the porch I could hose them down with the Thompson from the other side of the street. The team was throwing grenades effectively. I saw my captain at one side of the porch firing and heard him yell for ammunition. Then there was fire from the compound and I saw him react, he was trying to shoot back, but was hurt. I heard him yell again, "Never mind the ammunition, I won't need it". An hour later, when the fight ended, I found he had died shortly thereafter. He had continued to fire to the last. For his action, he received the Distinguished Service Cross. He had held that side of the porch alone. He was ten days from finishing his combat tour.

The fight continued in this manner, with the Vietcong taking heavy casualties every time they had attempted to get to the porch. The house was on fire behind my team, so the Vietcong could not come through. The front wall was holding. This was the way it stayed for another hour until a Vietnamese relief column approached, led by the Vietnamese provance S-3.

I might add that during this entire three hour fight the U.S. Marine battalion three miles down the road did not come to assist us. I have never forgiven that Marine colonel, although I will say that almost surely there was an ambush somewhere on the road between the battalion and our location. The Vietcong normally would attack one unit and always ambush the most likely reinforcement route. The Vietcong never changed this method of attack. But the Marines had armor force enough to get to us. They just did not.

The S-3 had brought two trucks with forty to fifty volunteers to relieve district headquarters. I was back with the team by the time they got there. The Vietcong were withdrawing. We had a gunship over us by then and it was raising havoc with the area. I do not know if they were killing any Vietcong but they were shooting close around us.

The house was still burning. The front porch, where the captain had been killed, had held. I managed to put the captain over my shoulder and got him into the relief column truck. The rest of the team crawled onto the back of the truck and we started toward province headquarters where medical help was available. My team had taken one hundred percent casualties. The medic had been helped up by some of the relief column, he had been hit once in the pelvic area and played dead throughout the fight in the midst of the Vietcong. He had been pretty cool.

At province headquarters I got time to examine myself and found out I had been hit about twenty-five times. But my luck was holding up; I was not really hurt. It had not been my time, I was wearing my soldier's Buddha. Had it protected me? Finally I realized I was still in my shorts. My flak jacket had been shot up so much it had fallen off somewhere during the fight. Grenades in the front pockets had deflected otherwise fatal hits. I had only been scratched and burned by the Vietcong bullets, except across the head and foot. Of course, I would be picking grenade metal out of my body for years. I was a walking junk yard.

Sergeant Jameson's eardrums were damaged. He had also been nicked once or twice. Sergeant Parker was wounded in the arm. The two Marine sergeants had both been hit. The district headquarters defense had also taken 100 percent casualties.

After I got the team taken care of, and off in a helicopter to the hospital in DaNang, I got with the S-3 and we went back to Hue Nhon to survey the damage. I had acquired new fatigues and boots. I could not close the boots because of the wound on my foot but at least I had boots. I found a few more magazines for the Thompson. In Hue Nhon I found every building in the compound blown down. They must have brought in a ton of explosives. We found the district chief in the compound next to a box of grenades. He had thrown grenades as long as he could. This district chief was so hated and feared by the Vietcong that they had taken his eyes out after he was dead.

Of the thirty-two RF/PF in position that night, thirteen were dead and nineteen injured. They had stood their ground against great odds and those that were wounded and survived had crawled out into the mine field where the Vietcong would not try to find them.

The headquarters was a disaster, but when the Vietcong body count came back to us we found we had killed sixty. We also found out the next day the little village next to us had been pressed into labor and carried away ninety wounded. The Vietcong battalion was ruined. The following week one of the company commanders of the battalion defected, saying that when three hundred Vietcong could not kill seven Americans, the war was over for him.

But for us, the war was not over, and within two to three hours we had the bodies policed up and everybody alive out of the mine field and on the way to a hospital.

About the time I was going to leave for DaNang and the hospital, General Walt, corps commander from DaNang, arrived to survey this battle area. Unfortunately I suppose at the time I did not give him all the courtesies he thought he should get. He had come in by helicopter with five or six Marine staff officers to look over the area and criticize my defense. I felt this critique was extremely distasteful. He did not know what he was talking about. He kept asking something about "You were 100% alert?" I said, "General you mean to tell me after a year in this corps you don't understand what a hundred percent alert means for the regional forces. It just means they were all here that night. They weren't standing forward waiting for an attack." The general was not going to listen and said, "You can't talk to me like that, major." I suppose at that time, if I might not have been so emotionally involved I might have been more courteous. He will never know how close he came to a punch in the nose. Had his staff officers not been there to stop it, I suspect I would have wound up in Leavenworth. As it was, it meant that later on, when there was a recommendation made to give me the Congressional Medal of Honor, he down-graded the recommendation to a Silver Star. In the long run the best defense ever made in I Corps by a small unit probably cost me the army career I had expected, i.e., becoming a general myself.

The fight was over, the criticizing over, and I was ready to go to the hospital and check myself in and get some kind of assessment of how badly I was hurt. I had not lost a lot of blood, but was beginning to stiffen up across my neck and under my arms and I could not see or hear well. I did find my flak jacket and could not believe I had walked out of that. It was in pieces. A flak jacket will stop or turn almost everything except a high-velocity bullet. As I suspected, the grenades in the chest pockets turned several direct hits. We had killed sixty but, the general thought we had lost the fight. How could the general complain about our defense when his Marines had not come to our aid? But then we were Army and he was a Marine; and he was the Corps commander which made him right, I suppose. Well it was over, at least for now. The team would be replaced.

I have explained that this particular attack was rehearsed, and the Vietcong were good at what they did, there is no doubt about it. But there is one thing I should explain about a Vietcong unit. Before the attack the unit usually stops about a mile from the objective to dig enough graves for half their number. Then they go into the attack. I would like to see somebody do that with an American unit. The Vietcong were very difficult for us to understand. The motivation of the South Vietnam Government troops wasn't a fraction of this dedication. When I realized this difference I knew it would be a long war.

It takes twenty years to develop an army, and I am only going to talk about the officers. You have to train lieutenants and give them a little experience leading a platoon. Then send them back to school and train those lieutenants to become company commanders. You can not train a lieutenant in combat. When he makes a mistake he does not come back to be corrected. He dies. Training must occur before combat.

If he survives in a combat situation as a company commander you send him to a general staff school to learn the workings of a staff, at all levels. By then he is a major. He then receives a battalion and is likely promoted to lieutenant colonel. This is along about his seventeeth or eighteenth year. If he does well as a battalion commander the army will send him to War College, which will give him all the skills to become a general officer. It is not that you cannot be a general officer without these steps, but the schools give the military education required to be a commander.

We did not have the time in South Vietnam to produce such generals. To produce a good general takes twenty years. Officers and generals appointed by political action rarely serve their country and are responsible for heavy casualties. The Vietnamese army had no possibility of being trained to face the Vietcong in the time we were in the country as advisers.

There is no way we should have left Vietnam to fight alone in the '70's. It was the same as if you had expected a seven-year-old to defend his home and family. We were pulled out at least ten to thirteen years too early. A simple answer to stabilize that end of the world would have been to treat Vietnam as we did Korea and keep a couple of training divisions there, supported with U.S. air and artillery. We could have slowly stepped out of the combat role and let the Vietnamese take over, with big brother only supporting from behind. I am not a subscriber to the belief that we lost the Vietnam War. I feel that the Vietnam War was won by 1969. We were killing fourteen-year-olds and women soldiers. They were running out of manpower. If we were to withdraw it could have been done in force. The B-52s could have been used to insure an orderly withdrawal with all the time required. We could have withdrawn all U.S. supporters. It could have been done, but was not.

Somewhere along the line we fell into the belief that we must give the boss a favorable report. This is human nature, but in Vietnam it was required. This is particularly true at the province level. If you were not successful in your province you would be replaced. If you told the truth you would be replaced. The tendency of senior province advisers was to keep improving security situation on paper while they hoped the actual situation would improve. The truth was that in 1966 and 1967 the Vietcong were putting more troops into the field and we were up against units that MAC V would not recognize existed.

I have no doubt that someone will have to answer eventually for the actions of the general staff in Saigon. In the field we knew what was happening, but what was there to be done. A soldier does not call a press conference and say what he feels. You have confidence in your leaders to tell what is true and give the situation to the American public. I now feel that this might have been optimistic. I do not think Washington ever knew what a fragile army the South Vietnamese were able to put in the field. The President had been told again and again that Vietnamization was working. He was not only telling that to the public, but I am sure to those in command in Saigon. Hard to believe? Try. If the message is put out often enough that "Vietnamization is working" eventually everyone will begin to believe it. It was working, but at a normal, slow rate.

Another thing that troubled most professional soldiers was that half the province senior advisers were civilians. Most had little or no military background. Generally speaking these were successful businessmen.

A 29-year-old, very aggressive young man, stupid in the ways of military, was given a province near NaTrang. Several times he came close to getting our military advisory teams (MATS) killed.

As far back as 1967 many civilian province senior advisers that had no military background were fed into the system. A short course in Washington was suppose to "bring them up to speed". But you cannot throw a man into an area where he has battalions and regiments to advise when he was not qualified to advise a squad. This happened at all levels in Vietnam and the civilian intrusion was felt deeply by the military. I am not sure why this was done. We had enough qualified officers to take these advisory jobs. In such cases, where the province senior adviser was military he was then handed a civilian deputy senior province adviser. Since in most cases the deputy had to work with military people, they were never accepted as anything but flunkies.

I cannot blame this on any one general. I am sure there was some kind of political decision in Washington. I still feel that if the military had had control of the war we would have had little problem in solving the situation. Restrictions were placed on battle commanders, the country drawn into no-fire zones, free-fire zones, safe-haven areas, and rules of engagement established. The free-fire areas gave gunners a license to kill peasants in san pans going up and down the rivers. This sort of thing was travesty. Good body counts and reports became the name of the game.

The team at Hue Nhon had been broken up by the Vietcong attack. The idea to take the advisory effort to district headquarters was a good one. We did not make any mistakes there. It is true that the Vietcong hit us before we had time to complete our defenses. In this particular province the Vietcong never quite recovered. With a max effort they had failed to destroy the district headquarters and kill the advisers.

I was in the hospital in DaNang, but signed myself out after the third day and reported into corps headquarters to get my next assignment. I had been assigned as the Corps deputy G-3. It was a lieutenant colonel's job and probably the best I had ever been offered. I was pleased. The corps G-3 had liked the job I did defending Hue Nhon enough to put in in this operations job. But things did not go well. As the operations officer of the corps G-3, a lot of paper went over my desk every day but I was not able to keep up with it. It came to my attention one day when I called in a young captain, chewed him out for not giving me a good copy of a report of something important. He took one look at it and said, "Well, Sir what's wrong with it?"

I said, "Well, it's faded: by the time I get to the bottom of the page I can't read it."

He looked at me again, "Sir, I don't see what's wrong with it," and went out of the room saying, "I'll get you another copy, sir".

I looked at it and this time I looked at the bottom of the page first and it was clear.

What was happening? I realized that as I was reading down the page it was fading out on me. I went back to the hospital that afternoon and they came up with tests and the doctors decided I had had a concussion of some kind. I knew I was not hearing well. So I had to go to the G-3 and tell him I could not handle this job. If I made a mistake some unit might be left without support and men could get killed. If I did not read an operations order correctly, I might miss something and ruin an operation.

I asked the G-3 to release me.

He was understanding about this medical report and decided I had had enough of the combat area. I could go to Saigon, where I would be reassigned to any job I thought I could handle until such time as my physical condition improved and I was able to take another combat assignment.

Actually I knew that once I had left I Corps and been assigned some job in Saigon, or been reassigned to another area I would never see the Marine area again. I was not unhappy about that fact. Working in General Walt's Headquarters after our conflict was not really in my best interest. I could not afford another confrontation with him.

## CHAPTER 8

## SAIGON

I left for Saigon with the next C-130 aircraft. I didn't have very much baggage since the house had burned down. I had my Thompson. Also I had recovered my .45 and rebuilt it with a new barrel and springs. I had to write a personal check on the back of an envelope. My banker framed it for his office back in Indiana.

But with a few hundred dollars life seemed a little bit better. The C-130 landed and I left the airfield for a night on the town. I think I had a good time. About 2:30 the next day I found myself outside the personnel office where I was to report for reassignment. They were very kind to me. In fact I suppose the word was ahead of me about the Hue Nhon defense. So when I opened the book to look through it, to find out what jobs were available for majors, I was told I could pick out any job for a major or lieutenant colonel that didn't put me in command of a combat unit. As I went through the book and tried to keep focus on the fact that I was an infantry officer and should take some job related to the infantry I ran across several possibilities. Battalion commander of a maintenance battalion, battalion commander of a supply depot. This, that, and the other. At the bottom of one page I saw something that kind of attracted my attention. I don't know why.

The job was "reconnaissance and real estate officer" for the support command. Engineer experience was required. I did not know what my duties would be. The description required a contracting officer for real estate from the Vietnamese. I knew there were generally two ways we obtained real estate. We either leased it or obtained a "land use concurrent". The latter was permission from the Vietnam Government to use land. This was possible if it was government land. If private property, of course, we had to go the lease route. That's about all I knew.

I asked, "Well, what is this?"

The personnel officer did not know, but made a few telephone calls and said, "Well, it seems it's an engineer's position with an office somewhere in Chorlon, the Chinatown of Saigon, and we really don't know anything else. You make contacts with the local Vietnamese people."

"Well, let me look into this one," I said. "It sounds like it might be an interesting job to finish out my tour." I had about six or seven months to go in Vietnam that year. I tried to get my new office address from the headquarters at Long Ben, but only was told the office was in a small compound in the center of Chinatown. No one knew much about it. I reported to the district engineer and told him I was interested in the job and understood it was going to be vacant within a few weeks. He said, "Yes that's true." A major was going to rotate home in about a month. I had worked enough engineering jobs during my service. We talked for about two hours and I had the impression all was not going too well in the job I had chosen.

I found the office on the lower floor of an old, large, brick building in

Saigon's Chinatown. As I walked in I could hear a few typewriters and voices, obviously female. It sounded like there was a lot of nonproductive work going on. There was a lot of laughing and giggling among the ten Chinese secretaries. But maybe they were on a break?

I asked the number-one secretary where the boss was.

"Oh, Major X is always in his office, sir, would you like to talk to him?"

I said, "I'll just go on in." So I walked in and sure enough there was a major behind the desk, asleep, with his feet up. I sat down and thought, "He'll wake up in a few minutes." He did not, so I began to look around. It was a bleak little cubical.

So I stepped out for a minute to look over the area and the ten Chinese secretaries.

I say Chinese, of course I mean Vietnamese, but it was easy to see Chinese influence in almost all of their background. I walked around to the number-one secretary and asked her how many girls could speak English.

She said, "Almost all of them a little but, but they type English very well."

I said, "Well, what is in the back room back there."

She said, "Oh, well the sergeants are back there, the inspectors stay back there most of the time."

I walked back to the inspectors area. They were enjoying a poker game around an old table. Nobody bothered to get up or recognize the fact that an officer had just entered. "This would change," I thought. I turned around and went back to the front office and again sat down.

This time as I started to take my seat the major stirred, woke up, and said, "Oh, major what can I do for you? I was just taking a little siesta."

I said, "Well, major, you could brief me a bit, I may be your replacement. What do you do here?"

I wanted to say sleep all the time but I managed not to.

"Well, I keep track of all the contracts and land use concurrences and contract the Vietnamese for hotels, properties and villas that we rent for our senior officers and senior civilians. In general we take care of all the property required for support troops, supply depots, storage depots, oil storage and things like that. By-and-large we're a contracting office."

"Oh, well how do you do this?" I said. "I don't see a map or anything that shows me where these properties are located. How many contracts are we talking about?"

"Oh, in the neighborhood of six hundred."

"Six hundred contracts. I don't see a map, how do you keep track of these contracts?"

"Oh, he said, "they are all over the country. Mainly we keep track of them in this 3x5 card box." Pointing to a box about two feet long.

"Each month I hand the ones to be renewed to the secretary and she notifies the owners or their representative to come in and sign their contracts. This renews the contracts for a year and that's about all we really have to do."

I was beginning to get angry. I was also beginning to understand the

District Engineers concern for their job.

"What about the men in the back room."

"Oh", he said, "those are my inspectors. They're suppose to go out and inspect all the properties and find whether or not they are described right in the contract. But, it's really pretty dangerous for them to go to the field, so I let them stick around the office quite a bit."

Now I was angry. I also now fully understood the District Engineers concern for the way this job was being done.

Quietly I commented, "Is that right, well, well, well, it is dangerous out there. You don't think they should go out. How often have you visited each one of these contracted areas? Have you been to these six hundred areas?"

"Oh, no, I'm required to be here in town", he said.

"Well, major, where do you live? Do you live in one of the hotels?"

"I do now", he said, "but up until a few weeks ago we had a villa. I rented a villa for my team. We were just another one of the rentals and we had this villa for the past year. But, now that I'm leaving I decided I'd better turn it back into the system."

"I see", I answered, "what does your lieutenant do here?" I saw a lieutenant's sign on the next door.

"He got his job here because his father was an air force general and this is a pretty good job. He's an engineer officer and I felt he would be good to contact the senior officers we deal with and talk to them. He really can talk to senior officers. I really don't have much to do with support command. You know how it is with headquarters. The less you have to do with them the better."

"Well, major, I can understand, in your position here how that could be true." I continued, 'I'll tell you what Major, I don't need to hear any more about your job. You've got your ten months and 25 days in Vietnam, out of your twelve-month period. That means you can go out to the airport as soon as you get a relief, get on an airplane and go home. Major, I advise you to do that. This is Friday afternoon. Monday morning I'm going to be back here. By then I want your desk cleared, this office cleared. I'm going to take the job. I don't want any more briefing and I don't want you in Saigon come Monday morning. I advise you to leave before I report to headquarters at Long Ben."

He said nothing.

By Sunday afternoon Major X was on a plane heading for the States, and Monday morning I was in the office having a conference with the lieutenant and the staff of sergeants. I had not reported into headquarters yet at Long Ben because I wanted to make sure everyone understood my feelings about how this job would be done from now on. This had to be clear first, before I went to Long Ben. The chief of staff, Colonel Carson wanted to meet me, but I did not go that day. I got busy. In fact I did not report to Long Ben for weeks. I did notify the Personnel office I was on the job, and the district engineer.

One of the first things I did was to make it clear that every man was to be armed at all times with a pistol and when he went out of town he would always carry some kind of rifle (M-14 or M-16 or carbine). I would back them up with daily orders stating they were leaving Saigon. That would clear them with the M.P.'s. I did not want the team without their weapons in Saigon. They were to be soldiers again. Surprisingly, everybody took it pretty good. They knew they had had a pretty soft life for the last five or six months. With Major X leaving and somebody else coming in they were prepared for the axe. Most of them were good people. They lacked the guidance to get out and do their job.

This was to be an amazing assignment. I had heard a lot about Saigon warriors. Now I had become one. But I knew that if this job was done right, it would keep me in the field about as much as an infantry job.

I requisitioned the jeeps that would take us out of town and started to set up some personal contacts for aircraft so that I could get my people on choppers when needed, without paperwork and waiting lists. We began to operate. Soon each team member had permanent travel orders.

I felt good about this job but I did not know why. We had leases and contracts all over the Country. And limits had been set by the embassy on what the U.S. could pay. This office had just been renewing contracts. After some bookwork I found we had almost a $10 million budget. I decided to work well under the embassy limits.

I never had any problem with the embassy and I did not have any problem with my bosses, because they never came to Chinatown. The lieutenant was a fine young man, who received direction well and would execute orders explictly. He was a bit free wheeling with Senior officers and I do not know how free he was with the Chinese girls, we called secretaries, but he did his job. I depended on him for a great many things; especially to run the office when I was in the field.

The secretaries also began to do their job! They went through the files and started locating problem areas. They got the picture quickly, that they were part of this war. Attitudes changed and no one was late, no one was absent. It made a difference to them, as each began to think she had a part in what was going on.

I could not help notice that in the office upstairs there was a fine looking young lady, one of the executives in the engineers area. I had to pay attention as she would find reason to come in and out of the office. One day I stopped her and asked her what her name was, her situation, whether she was married and before I knew it we were good friends. I may not go into detail about this relationship, but most soldiers develop some kind of personal relationships during a war or between assignments. Sometimes between operations. I can only say I was pleased to find a young lady who could handle herself in any situation. She was as worried about my being an embarrassment to her as she might be to me, and things worked out pleasantly for the next five or six months.

Oftentimes she would volunteer to interpret when I had operations around the Saigon area. I would make an inspection before we made or renewed a contract. Sometimes I would walk the area to see how many acres were involved, or evaluate rooms in a hotel. It was essential to have somebody you could trust, to give answers to questions and interpret exactly. She helped determine whether we were getting that for which we were paying.

The one story I can tell about this young lady demonstrates that she had a cool mind. The problem about this one piece of property was that I could never find the exact area we were supposed to be leasing from this French company. One day I took Ann with me, twenty-five miles from Saigon, to find out what was going on. I made a wrong turn and pulled into a village. As soon as we entered I knew we were in trouble. The village was full of young men, not in uniform, but many had K-47 rifles. The Russian Kalaznikoff assault rifle was used by Vietcong local forces. Regular units were also armed with them. I had driven into a village occupied by a Vietcong Company. We were immediately surrounded and for a moment I thought my sergeant, in the back seat, was going to start shooting. It did not happen. Annie started talking and within a few minutes weapons started pointing in other directions. I could not keep up with her Vietnamese but soon the crowd parted. I could not believe it.

She said, "Drive on quickly, right on through the town. We'll figure out another way to get back to Saigon." I was driving; I finally got the jeep in gear and drove right through the crowd. Any minute I expected to be shot.

We got out of town and I stopped the vehicle and turned to Annie and asked, "What did you tell them to get us out of there?"

"I just told them" she said, "you were an Army major with the support command and you were looking for an area to put a supply depot. That they would gain nothing by killing you and the sergeant, except the command would be convinced that this was not a secure area, and if the Americans do not put a supply depot out here you Vietcong can't steal anything out of it." "You told them that?" I said.

"Yes, they must have a source of supply. They steal out of your depots all the time."

"Of course", I murmured. That afternoon I bought Annie a 24-inch TV. She had mentioned one time that she did not have one.

A soldier many times has a choice when it comes to capture. He has got an instant or two usually, and does not have to be captured, but can start shooting; he has this choice. He may choose to be killed. My team and I had made it at Hue Nhon. We were not going to be captured. The day we drove into this village that was occupied by Vietcong, I did not see any way we could have gotten the first shot off. We could have tried. We could have died. Without a doubt, this young lady had saved us from a Vietcong prison or death.

I was beginning to think the job was going too good. Maybe it was. Then a new lieutenant was assigned to my unit. This man was a young Adonis. I could not believe they had sent me a young infantry officer who looked as good as this man. It was just like sabotage. I have never seen any secretarial staff as screwed up as mine over this lieutenant. He had the entire bunch unable to do a day's work. I had a problem. Instead of a smooth-running organization I had a bunch of girls competing with each other.

In the week that followed I decided to find out how I got this infantry officer. After all, this was not an infantry assignment and no place for an infantry second lieutenant. Checking back with the personnel office I found I had been handed a conscientious objector. I do not understand how this happened. He had been to Infantry OCS at Fort Benning. He had made an outstanding record. I started a little counseling period every day at noon. In the next few days I found out he had lived in a little commune in California for thirty days before he came to Vietnam and they converted him. He had "seen the light." He had filled out his papers as an objector and it looked like there was very little I could do. But we did have counseling sessions everyday at noon. It became obvious to me that his man had no background of church-going, no theology training, and little feeling about this war, right or wrong. He should have made a good officer. I used him for small jobs and found him willing to do about anything.

After about thirty days of counseling I called him in one day. I had two papers on my desk and told him I had made up my mind. "You don't belong with us, but you have a choice." Pointing to one paper and then the other, I said, "I'll sign these papers for your court martial for cowardice before the enemy, or here is your transfer to the 25th Infantry Division. Now which do you want me to sign?"

He smiled and said, "I sure enjoyed Saigon, it was worth a try, I'll take the transfer." He went to the Infantry Division the next day. I got word several weeks later that he had distinguished himself in combat, received a purple heart and recommended for a Bronze Star. He completed his year with the division and decided on an army career.

Here was a young man with thirty days of exposure to this group in California. I wonder how they did it.

Six weeks later the job was progressing and one morning I heard the lieutenant talking to Colonel Carson, the chief of staff. I still had not been out to visit the chief of staff. I had talked to him on the phone and assured him everything was going along. I wanted to get a little better handle on the job before I met him. I assumed he did not know too much about my job since no one ever remembered anyone from headquarters coming to visit our office. So I had been able to put off this briefing for six weeks.

But that day the lieutenant was on the phone and heard him say "Oh, yes, Colonel, yes, everything's going fine here sir, it's just going fine. I just heard Major Simons turn down a $25,000 bribe a few minutes ago. It's business as usual, everything is just fine here."

I could hear the explosion on the other end of the line, the colonel yelling and screaming, "What is this business about a bribe? What do you mean 'business as usual'?" He wanted me out at Long Ben within the hour.

I picked up the telephone and talked to the colonel for a few minutes. He said, "What are you doing over there?" The lieutenant had gotten his attention. I explained this was just the normal day-to-day negotiation with the Chinese and French and the beautiful Eurasian women they sent me as negotiators. After a "god damned Simons" I was ordered immediately to headquarters.

It was 5:00 p.m. and I reminded the colonel that by the time I got there it would be after dark. I could stay the night or risk trying to travel back through closed roads. Why not come out about 10:00 a.m.? He finally agreed. I had a word for the lieutenant about how much he was supposed to say to senior officers on the phone, or more specifically what he was not supposed to say. But lieutenants are lieutenants. You accept the mistakes of your lieutenants. There is no other way.

Here I was in hot water with headquarters and I had never met anyone there. This was a fine way to report. Next morning I was up early, gassed the jeep, and got together the papers I thought I would need. I started for Long Ben to look up the colonel. I really did not have to worry about looking him up. When I arrived he had his head and shoulders half out the window looking for me. He was a big man with a big voice. I could hear him a hundred yards away. He was bellowing at me clear out on the street. I was late, I was to get in there right away, that the general wanted to see me. I had better be ready to explain.

What an ambush. I had not expected anything like this. I found later that the old gentleman was a pretty nice fellow, but somehow this idea that there might have been a bribe offered in my office got him concerned. I was going to have to explain a common occurrence when dealing with Chinese, Vietnamese, or French. It sure was not common at his headquarters.

Within a few minutes he was asking, "What the hell is your budget out there?" I told him as close as I could it was between $8 and $10 million. The blustering started all over again. He shouted, "My god, who is watching the shop?" I guess I was a little short in answering his question. A senior officer of his age and experience deserved a more courteous answer, but I had been working twelve to eighteen hours a day. I asked him what the hell he thought I was doing? "That's what you're paying me for", I said. And if he would give me enough time I would get it straightened out. Otherwise, since nobody had been out to that office in the last six to eight months, I did not see how he had a complaint. I added, "I've only been on the job five or six weeks and I've turned down at least a dozen bribes."

He was turning redder and redder when I heard the box on his desk buzz. Apparently the general's office was next door and the door to the left behind the colonel's desk was open. Colonel Carson looked over at me and said, "Just a minute," stood up and walked back to the next room. I could hear some muffled voices, but a plain clear voice stated, "Well, why don't you give him a goddamn chance and see what he gets done."

The Colonel came back out and said, "Well, I've decided that we'll let you go for another week or two, then we want a complete report. Bring your briefing materials with you and tell us exactly what's going on."

Then I asked, "How about four weeks? I'll know better what's going on by then."

"No, goddamnit, it's got to be two weeks."

I heard the buzzer--buzz, buzz, buzz. He said, "Just a minute", and he walked back again and I didn't hear what the general said this time but the colonel came back and said, "I decided four weeks will be OK." Then he said, "For Christ's sake what was this business about a bribe?"

I said, "Well, this is a simple little thing where I'd gone down and checked at the docks where we were renting an open storage area. I'd walked off the area and measured it as best I could and I found out we had been paying about $30,000 a year too much for the last four years."

He interrupted, "What, $30,000 a year?"

I said, "That's what you're paying me to do to, isn't it? Get it stopped if we are paying too much?"

He said back down at his desk and said, "Go on."

I said, "Well, I called in old Charlie."

"Charlie?"

"Yes, Charlie Chan."

The colonel flinched, "Now wait a minute Simons, don't do this to me."

I said, "Really, that's his name, Charlie Chan. I called in Charlie Chan, the Chinese representative of the French company that owns the land. I said, "Charlie, you've been screwing us $30,000 a year for about four years for that property at the water front."

He said, "I knew it, but after all the money is out of the country, back in France now. There's nothing I can do. I haven't got the money to give back to you."

I said, "Well, all right Charlie, we need the area down there, we're going to renew the lease, don't worry about that. It's just that I'm going to fine you $30,000 a year for the next four years of lease. We are going to get our money back."

That's when Charlie said, "Now, wait a minute, I pay about ten million P's a year tax or bribe and actually I could lose two million P's before I leave your office today." In effect he was offering me a $25,000 bribe. He said, "Why don't you just sign the papers and we can go along like we always have before." I know what Charlie meant, "like we always have before." Someone, sometime had been on the take.

I said, "Charlie, in the first place you haven't got brains enough to keep your mouth shut, you'd have it all over the Chinese community that I was on the take, and I would have people lined up outside my office to change their contracts. I'd get the long course in Leavenworth."

The colonel asked, "Charlie signed?"

"Of course", I said. "Colonel, I don't have the authority to fine him but can you figure out another way to get our money back?"

Colonel said, "Goddamn, you're going to get us all fired."

I said, "No, I'm not, I won't get us fired. We are going to get our money back, and every time I can do this I'm going to do it. Who's going to stop me? Are you going to stop me? Is the embassy going to stop me? Who in the hell is going to stop me?"

The colonel answered, "Well, I don't know, we'll see." Buzz, buzz, buzz, the box was buzzing again "just a minute", he said, and he walked back to the general's office again, and this time I heard something like, "Jesus Christ, isn't this what we want?", and he came back out and said, "Well, right now I guess there's no objections, but goddamnit if somebody calls your hand on this it's your ass."

I said, "Well, I'm going to do what I think is right as long as you leave me on the job." I saluted, turned around and left. But what I never told the Colonel was that three days after our conversation a grenade was thrown into my vehicle. By the slightest quirk of fate and luck it bounced off the plastic back window of the jeep broke my front windshield and fell at my feet. There was no time to do anything else but pick it up and get rid of it. To my left were school children standing on the corner so I threw it to the right under a truck where it exploded flating my rear tire.

Somehow, I couldn't get my mind off of Charlie. He died of a heart attack two weeks later.

I didn't hear anything from Long Ben for a couple of weeks and everything ran fairly smoothly.

I formed new inspection teams and we started the big task of inspecting all of the six hundred areas of interest. I found one area where I had to take an entire company of soldiers with me to gain access. We had rented some land that the Vietcong were controlling. We were still paying for it and this had been going on for six years. Needless to say, that contract was terminated.

During the next five to six months I think we reduced the contracts from six to around four hundred. Basically, the NCO's, the girls, the lieutenant, and I all felt good about being able to reduce this budget and at the same time offer the same services to our command.

## CHAPTER 9

## HIGHER OFFICIALS

There are several stories I am going to go into about this particular job. It may be a little less interesting in some aspects than the combat stories, but I think the reader should have a feel of what life was like in Saigon, how business was done. Possibly the reader will gain insight to what faced us in Vietnam.

Mrs. Vien was the wife of the chief of the joint general staff. She rented us several pieces of property. As the wife of the chief of staff she had power. I suppose that now she is in the United States. She was an exceptional woman. I have no bad things to say about her. She was rich and knew how to get her way. I had to do business with her and she was good at it. But I did not realize just exactly what power she had until I asked her to build a parking lot on land near one of our headquarters. Shacks and huts in the area were bulldozed and within two or three days the blacktop was laid. We had a parking lot. That was the use of power--of course, she was paid well for her effort.

A few weeks later she informed me she wanted a house back that we had leased from her. The house that she wanted was on the beach at Vung Tou. The U.S. was paying her $1,100 a month for this house and surrounding grounds. This was a just amount for the area and under that authorized by the embassy. I discussed her request at length. I told her we had an "area commander" in that house and it would take a little time. Mrs. Vien wanted her house back immediately

The following week I worked to get the people out of her house. I did not understand what the problem was, but decided I had to put her off a little. I told her, "I'd work on it." About a day or two later I got an invitation for lunch at her villa. I knew what this was all about; but I went to lunch. As I approached I saw several army staff cars in front of the house and a jeep with a star on it. I realized lunch was not going to be with her alone. She had invited two generals to lunch.

Now a French-Vietnamese luncheon lasts from 11:30 to about 2:00, maybe 2:30. There was plenty of time for conversation and time for four or five courses. I was enjoying myself as she was talking to the generals until she mentioned casually, "Well, major, have you made arrangements to get my house back in Vung Tou."

I said, "No, Mrs. Vien, I haven't really made the arrangements yet. Are you still sure you want your house back?"

"Oh, yes, I want my house back and I'd like to have it immediately."

I said, "Well, it will take a little time, but I'll get on it next week."

The luncheon went on with no more comment about the house. Many other things were discussed mostly social problems in Saigon. We all had a pleasant time. I left as soon as I could get away, and returned to my office.

I had been in the office about an hour when I got my first phone call. "This is General Able, Simons, what in the hell are you doing with Mrs.

Vien? You're screwing around with the chief of staff's wife. You know she can mention your name and her problem in the bedroom tonight and you'll be in General Westmoreland's office tomorrow and he will want to find out why you're not cooperating. What does it take to get you in action?"

I said, "Well, general, we've got a problem out there. I've got an area commander living there, we have a legal lease."

He said, "Well, I'm not going to say any more to you", and he hung up.

To myself, I said, "Oh, here it comes downhill again." I did not think General Westmoreland would be interested in Mrs. Vien's house, but then this was a crazy war.

I made a few phone calls to see how much this commander in Vung Tou liked the beach house. In no uncertain terms I was told it was a very fine area and his people were all happy. I told him the situation, that he might as well think about some place else, because Mrs. Vien was going to get what she wanted. There was not much he could say, I thought, I just listened, saying, "Yes, Sir."

I got another phone call within the hour, this time General Baker, who started out quietly saying, "Simons, I think your making a grave mistake by not cooperating with Mrs. Vien."

I said, "Well, general I've got some problems", and explained the same thing. I then said, "You know, it really doesn't make any difference to me whether Mrs. Vien gets this property back or not. We need it, we got it, we've got it on lease. What the hell is going on here? What's this pressure. Two calls from general officers in one day. Do you really want to discuss this? Do you want me to discuss it with my commanding general?"

"Well, that will not be necessary. We're just trying to be nice to you and let you know that you could possibly have large problems over this."

I said, "I know it and I'll give her property back when I can, but it's going to be a couple weeks."

"All right Simons, we'll be in contact."

I went over to Vung Tou to look at the house. It was an interesting trip. The trip really should be in convoy to keep from getting ambushed. When you get there it is a tropical paradise, a beach, a nice town, nice hotels, lots of entertainment girls. A resort area. I found a jeep and went out to look at the beach house. It was adequate; but not as nice as I thought it might have been. By the end of the day I found a hotel downtown that had two floors empty. This was an interesting hotel. The top floor was a sort of bar and recreation area. I did not think I'd have much of a problem getting the area commander and staff to move.

I talked to him, described the area and we went down to look over the new place. He complained a good deal about how I had succumbed to pressures in Saigon and that his troops, "in the field here" were going to suffer. I could not see much suffering but, he was a nice fellow and we eventually came to terms about when they would move. They were going to be much better off, with better security, and in Vung Tou you couldn't get more than five minutes away from the beach.

In Saigon the next day I got a telephone call from Mrs. Vien. "I understand you've been over there and made proper arrangements. I really appreciate that. Come to dinner tomorrow night."

Well, you didn't say "no" to the chief of staff's wife and I did attend a fine dinner and this time there weren't any generals around. I found her to be a very charming woman, once she got her way.

We did move the commander and staff out in a week or two and when I went over to cancel the contract with Mrs. Vien. I said, "Mrs. Vien, its none of my business really, but why do you want that house back? You are not going to live there, are you?"

"No", she said, "No, I'm going to give it to my mother and I just didn't want the house rented anymore."

Now we were paying her $1,100 a month (this was 1967) and she was going to let her mother live in it. That meant she'd have to staff it, have transportation, drivers, and guards. I wondered to myself just how much money does the Vien family make in order to let her mother live in an $1100 a month home plus all the other things that would be required. I guess I just did not understand this war as well as I thought I did.

I did get a chance to return to Hue Nhon to settle the account the army had with the widow of the captain killed in the headquarters attack on March 13, 1967. We managed to buy her a new house and set her up again. During that visit the province chief presented me with a nice Russian Kalaznikoff attack rifle. It was on a teak background with a brass plate on it that reads well. On the plate was a Vietnamese award of the Gallantry Cross and Silver Star which is one of the highest awards they give in Vietnam. I am proud of this rifle and citation. It is in my house today, displayed discreetly, of course.

The trip back to Hue Nhon was more than just business because I got to visit the old Tiger Platoon. The corporal was still in charge; he still had a grizzly beard. He spotted me at one hundred yards, came running up, and threw his arms around me like a long-lost brother. Before I left I saw to it that he was cited for his actions on the night of the attack. I found out he had brought his platoon down the road from his compound during the fight and attacked the Vietcong battalion from the rear. His action had taken some of the pressure off us. He was awarded the American Bronze Star with V.

I had been in Saigon several months when I went to Ben Hoa to inspect a hotel we were renting. Civilian employees from Long Ben were being bussed back and forth each day. It was nice, and each room very comfortable. Most rooms had a small kitchen and bath. I considered all very adequate. Certainly as good as most noncombat lieutenant colonels or colonels would have in this war. But there was one area that gave me considerable concern. Rooms 201 and 202 had been combined by knocking out a wall. A suite had been created. No paperwork or request of the owner was made, nothing. It was just ordered.

I was determined to find out what was going on, but could not get anyone to talk, so I started out with the occupant, the secretary of a two-star general. She was nice and soon I found she had been brought to Vietnam with the general. There was no doubt I was going to have a problem. Some fights are not worth losing. I contacted the owner of the building, got his permission to move the wall, and made the general's secretary's suite legal.

When I informed the general there would be some paperwork to make the situation correct he acted as if I had violated his private life, but signed everything I presented to him. He would later be charged with the indiscretion of sending hundreds of captured weapons back to the U.S. for sale. The Vietnam War brought out the best in everyone, or the worst. From my viewpoint I was taking care of the job at hand. But the incident reminded me that many things happen in a war that go unnoticed. The general was getting away with all he could. And when it was all finished he had nothing, not even a good name.

Most of the property we leased was owned by French companies or individuals living out of the country. They had representatives to deal with me. Invariably they selected a beautiful Eurasian girl who spoke good English. She was always in her early thirties. I imagine at least one or two of these representatives came in every day to talk about their leases, ask for payments, or just talk about problems.

At that time we could advance up to one year payment on a lease. The advance would go toward building or completing a building and then we would continue to lease the property for the next year or two. This way we had what we wanted and they had the advantage of having the money to pay for construction. This procedure may seem like a give away but we got what we needed. Most of these contractors gave us excellent service.

One of the ladies would often have me meet her at the Circle Sportief, probably the most exclusive club in Saigon. I am not sure that even the higher U.S. civil authorities were invited there. I never saw any of the senior staff. This lady would prefer to meet me there. From her we rented several hotels in Saigon for officers of Mac V Headquarters. We paid her $2 million a year. She admitted to me that she bought her tax receipts for about $200,000. She kept $150,000 to live on and the rest went to accounts in France or Switzerland.

This young lady was an exceptionally nice person, was beautiful, lonesome, and when given attention responded well. About a month before I left Saigon she walked into the office. I knew about her dealings and her effectiveness. I knew there was never a man in Saigon who crossed her on any transaction. She was tough. For her to drop in on me was a surprise because usually I did not see her at the office.

She said, "I have a proposition for you."

I said, "Please sit down, Mrs. Too." The title of Mrs. was a formality. She did not have a husband. Somewhere along the line, she must of dropped him or he was killed.

She opened her purse and laid two checks on my desk.

I said, "Well, what's your proposition?"

She said, "I want you to quit the army, I want you to go to California, lease a ship, and bring it back full of two year-old Chevy and Ford station wagons, with enough parts in the back of each to keep them repaired for two or three years. I'll take care of this end, taxes, entry, any problems you'd have in Saigon. You will receive this." She pushed over one check. She said, "That's half of your first year's salary. Of course you'll get expenses."

I turned the check over. It was for $70,000.

She said, "Now to tell you the truth, if you can't triple that the second half of the first year, then you'll have to leave, because you won't be making me enough money."

I said, "Well, well, that's something to think about." At that time, I didn't realize that my military career would be limited by the end of the Vietnam War. I fully intended to become a general officer. "I'll have to think about it. What's this other one?"

She said, "That's for your wife, I want you to pay her off and get a divorce."

I turned it over. That check was also for $70,000. This was quite an offer I said, "I'll give you my answer soon, but I want to think it over." I thought about it and her business dealings. I didn't know what happened to her husband. Actually, I was afraid some morning I'd leave the cap off the toothpaste tube and that afternoon she'd have me terminated. She was obviously trying to buy me, bag and baggage.

This woman was a little bit too vicious to deal with permanently on a personal basis, and as far as I was concerned certainly too vicious to live with, although she was beautiful. I have often wondered what my future would have been if I had stayed that additional two or three years in Saigon as a civilian. I might have been a millionaire today. But I may have been very dead.

These were the problems we faced while in Saigon, dealing with the people of "higher class," the monied individuals, the land owners or the beautiful Eurasian women that they hired to front for them.

My tour was rapidly coming to an end. Two weeks later I handed her checks back and told her to hold them until I could give her an answer. Shortly before I left Saigon I visited her, assured her it was nothing personal, but I did intend to make the army a career and at this time I had to go to Washington and attend to a small promotion problem. I had collected a box of medals while in Vietnam, but in Laos I had collected a lousy efficiency report for possibly the best army service I'd ever given. I had to go back to Washington to fight it, or very shortly, without promotion, I would be leaving the service.

I got my team together for a final party and told them what a fine job they had done. I selected a bright young major for my replacement. I said my goodbyes to the chief of staff and General Jones. I was presented with another Bronze Star, Purple Heart number three, Air Med number two, and the Vietnam Medal of Honor. I told the general of my promotion problem and why I would have to be in Washington. After a final goodbye to Ann I went to the airfield and caught a C-130 aircraft to Clark Air Base. I had completed my second full year of the Vietnam War--if I count the time with the Army Security Agency and the Laos tour.

Back in Washington I was able to get the poor efficiency report thrown out, the one given when I had worked for Special Forces. It had been slipped past Colonel Kerivai while he was in the hospital. Kerivai had no intention of a report like that ever getting to Washington. He put this in writing, a standby board in Washington reviewed my records, and within a few days I was not only promoted to Regular Army major, but put on the lieutenant colonel promotion list and given a year's date of rank. When I asked what did this all for me I found out that General Jones had written a letter to the chief of staff of the army, citing the action I had taken during the job in Saigon. The budget reductions involved, the dealings with the local people in Saigon who had apparently related their feelings about me to the general. For that little obscure job of administration I was promoted, not for my combat record.

The army, in its devious way instead of sending me to a quick course at this Command and General Staff School, which would have ensured my retention in service, placed me on loan to the navy at Little Creek to work with the Marine Corps. I was promoted to Lieutenant colonel and became the chief of the logistics section of the Landing Force Training Command. I instructed the Navy and Marine Corps how to land over beaches and how to support themselves once they had done so. How did I ever get into this job? No one was ever to tell me. The year was now 1968.

About twenty or thirty days after I left Vietnam the TET Offensive of 1968 started and I found out that it came right through Ann's little house, the nice young lady executive that worked upstairs from me. It was near the race track. Apparently the family she rented from had two or three sons in the Vietcong. They opened the back door, and the attack, at least in part, came from the streets which were behind the house, through the mother's house and into the race track area, which opened several routes into downtown Saigon. Of course that was not the only attack in Saigon, but this was a major one. Fortunately Annie was not at home, as I heard from her later, toward the end of the Vietnam War.

I was at Little Creek with the Marine Corps for a year and made some lasting friends. I might mention Major O.J. Elder, who was most helpful. Major Elder is a legend in the Marine Corps. An engineer, I'm sure he is retired by now. I hope he's a wealthy man. He was the most dedicated man I met in the Marine Corps and was their number-one Shore Party Officer. He was the expert on all shore-party actions. When I was assigned to the logistic section he was head of it. I was working for him. When I was promoted to lieutenant colonel, the next day he was working for me. But he was such a man who could do this and give me support. I relied on him to run the section. I taught a few classes and he gave all the technical support anyone could ever need. I learned much working with him. There are only a few army experts in over-the-beach operations. I became one of them because of Elder.

After a year at Little Creek I knew I would be going back to Vietnam. So I went to Washington and asked if I could select my assignment if I volunteered to return. They said yes that if I volunteered they would put me wherever I wanted.

I elected to work in Mac V again. I felt that if the war was to be won it would be through effective use of advisers. The American troops would eventually go home. South Vietnamese troops must be ready to stand alone.

## THE RETURN (CONT.)

Suddenly just before midnight the big jungle cat came in for a late snack. The first round fired but my homemade slug hit the cat too far back for an instant kill and to my frustration the second round failed to fire. The cat was circling and lashing wildly in all directions. He had just spotted me when I loaded the third round, pointed the old gun, and fired. Now finally at twenty feet I couldn't miss and the beast fell dead at my feet.

I returned to the village and found, to my great surprise, a bottle of Johnny Walker Red on the bunk in the hut I had been furnished. Where the hell it came from I'll never know. But it helped and I quickly fell into a deep sleep.

The next morning the cat was brought to the village. I would have loved to have the skin, but had no time to wait for it to be tanned or a way to carry it.

When the village chief found out what information I wanted, he sent twenty of his people across the border to penetrate at least twenty Kilometers into Laos asking questions about any Americans held in this area. All returned with negative information three days later.

The following day my young guide said she must return to her village. I gave a young Hmung tribesman $10 to accompany her home, almost a hundred miles. But before she left, I was introduced to another young lady, a student home from school. She wanted to practice English and together we convinced her father I'd provide for her and have her returned safely. Linn was possibly twenty, maybe twenty-one years old, it's hard to tell, and her features were more Chinese than Lao, Thai, or Hmung. Maybe she was a little too gutsy for an Asian woman, but I found her a pleasant change and the practice of English never ended. She was also taller than most Asian women and her highly arched brows over straight eyes made her a beautiful woman. Possibly she had some India ancestor that influenced her looks.

The third night she earned my everlasting gratitude and respect. But it was her English language that she had practiced so diligently, not her good looks, that turned a nasty situation for us.

We had been walking most of the day and it was dusk when we met four men. Linn told me she thought they were opium and gold smugglers. After we had talked for a few minutes I asked them a few basic questions about foreigners they might have seen during their travels in Laos. Linn was translating the answers when she added in English, "and we are really in trouble."

I asked another question for her to translate and added, "What do you mean, in trouble?" She followed with the translation and added, "They think you have money and are going to kill us both." I told her to tell them I had some pictures to show them and moved my shoulder bag in front of me. I reached in, placed my hand on the Rossi 38, and told her to step back slowly and to repeat my next words exactly. She nodded and took a short step back as she repeated my words: "I have a pistol; don't move, I will kill you, all four, before anyone of you can shoot."

I had taken them by complete surprise and the only movement in front of me was an eye or two blinking. I could tell two of them were armed. Linn had now stepped completely out of my way.

I needed a way out of this situation but they needed one more. Almost a full minute passed. "Linn, tell them they have a chance to live through the next few minutes." About a mile ahead I could see lamp or fire lights from a village.

"Tell them if they'll forget their plans I'll buy the first bottle of whiskey, if we can find a bar in that next village." The silence seemed to last forever, no one had moved, when one of the men answered her.

She looked at me and said, "Simons, they have accepted your offer."

I nodded to them and told her to tell them to lead the way and warn them I'm still holding the gun. I considered taking their guns, but decided against it.

The first building at the edge of the village was a general store that sold Mekong whiskey by the fifth. I bought two, $3 U.S. each. We sat at a back table and were brought six water glasses. I kept my right hand in the leather case. I asked Linn to pour them full and with my left hand downed mine. The four all made an effort to do the same and in thirty minutes any trouble we were in had passed. At 180 lbs. I knew I could drink more and faster than any of them. I had Linn leave first, and met her outside as soon as I could.

We faded into the background of the village and walked to the next town some five kilometers away, where we had our own celebration.

The next day we headed south to a main road and I put Linn on a bus for home. She was going to be a teacher and maybe someone of importance to her country someday. That was her dream and with her good looks and with a head as cool as hers she will become anything she wishes. I believe she wanted to continue with me, but I felt the danger of this trip now and didn't want to expose her to more. I made up my mind to find a male interpreter. Also with Linn it was too much of a temptation to get involved. I must think mission first.

I had heard of a group of American expatriots who lived in Udorn, about forty minutes by bus south of Non Khai. Non Khai was on the Mekong River, across from Vientiane, Laos. I would return there later to head down the river, but first I wanted to talk to the Americans in Udorn.

The trip to Udorn was good and the bus a pleasant change. The bus service was not up to the Bangkok-Chiang Mai trip, but then I was the only foreigner on board. The other passengers did not pay much attention to me. I slept good and was only disturbed at a check point. A Sam Hoa driver who spoke English took me to a fourth-rate hotel and after one look I decided this was not a place to stay. I then was taken to the Udorn Hotel. A room with a large ceiling fan was about $4.40. The air-conditioned room was $4 more, so I took the "Fan Room", settled in, and later after a look around town, I tried to contact one American I knew to be in the area. I had heard about my old friend, Mr. P., who had lived for years in Laos and now resides in Udorn. I managed to get a message to his house. The food in the hotel restaurant was not bad, as I found, waiting for an answer to the message I'd sent. I wondered what his real name was? I'd never known. Soon I got a message in return, he was out of town and I later confirmed this fact with the U.S. consul and some VFW members. I returned to my fan room to find it about 120 degrees. The maids turn off your fan if you leave. Hotel policy, I suppose. I read for awhile and slept until 0230 when I woke to the blast of the fan and a strange noise. I listened but heard nothing more. There had been something. I got up quickly and didn't return to the bed. My war instincts were returning and that was good. I sat in the dark room, .38 in hand, waiting for an intruder; none came.

The following morning I went to the police station to find the address of a police contact given me in Bangkok by the general. I didn't find out what I wanted, but I did establish myself with the police and was taken by police van to the American consul. I had failed to learn there was an American consul in Udorn. The consul turned out to be an interesting young man of possibly mid-thirties and for some reason I liked him immediately, even though I felt he was not an ex-military man. I frankly have little liking for the run-of-the-mill U.S. consul but after a discussion on the POW issue, which lasted well over an hour, I was convinced of his sincerity and left feeling no effort on his part was being made to cover up information on possible POWs.

The fact did arise that we don't seem to be in a good position to make a deal for prisoners because of national policy. That was quite clear. I returned to the Udorn hotel. I asked around and found out where some of the Americans in the area met daily to drink. It was a small bar owned by one of the Thai wives of their group. The afternoon was spent listening to a self-proclaimed pimp, who claimed to be the seller of over 250 women a year to nations all over the world. He offered me one of the girls just back from Greece. I'll call this man Mr. W. I guess I should have left, but in two hours he was drunk and talking about a lot of events, times and places in his life. He had been knowledgeable about the Bo Gritz mission and I soon felt he may have been, in part, the one responsible for Col. Gritz's failure. (Lt. Col. Gritz had retired from the Army, obtained CIA support and attempted a POW rescue).

As he drank, his claims got bigger and bigger. I was listening for the side comments so important when a drinker gets on a roll of bragging and mired in emotion and hate. The Bo Gritz mission came up and it seems this Mr. W. made some tentative arrangement for Col. Gritz but then was not paid to his satisfaction. At any rate it seems that because of this alleged fact, Mr. W. made the Gritz mission public and as a result presidential support or at least tacit approval had to be withdrawn. At least this premature disclosure of the Mission Lazarath makes some sense and was possibly why Bo Gritz was called off the mission. I'm not sure I believe what I heard. Little has come out of Washington about this.

I'll have to try and contact Gritz when I return. That may be a problem, but he knows me and may make his location known to me through a friend.

The VFW of Udorn centers itself in a small bar near a restaurant called the "Orange Sea Food". They all draw a U.S. pension of some kind, and most are engaged in other business. The bar had belonged to an American who recently died. His widow was in her mid-thirties or possibly forty. She was of Chinese, Vietnamese, and Thai extraction and age is sometimes hard to tell. There are some Oriental women who will be beautiful their whole lives. They were celebrating his one-hundredth day of death the following Sunday and she asked me to attend. I politely refused, but figured I might go if I was still in town.

These Americans have many problems living outside the U.S. They have no privileges normally given to military retirees, but they seem satisfied with their life in Thailand. Some were just living out their lives as best they could. Others seemed to do well and had money. The one man the consul suggested I see did not want to talk to me or so it seemed and the other Americans had little to offer me on the POW issue.

I managed to break the ice with these Americans but never drank enough to not have complete control of the situation. It's really strange the roles these men fall into, yet each has his own reason for being in Southeast Asia. Some are relatively rich since they worked in Iran and other Near East countries before retiring to Thailand. Some claim they are paid to stay out of the U.S. Others are ex-CIA operation officers of the highest quality. They live here now working, in some cases, as "advisers" for "special Thai" units.

I attended Harry's hundred-day death celebration and talked to most of the active post concerning special problems they have getting U.S. social security benefits for their wives and their children. Some of these men were wheeler-dealers while in the Air Force and had owned bars and dance halls when the G.I.'s were here, about "fifteen years ago in the good days". It's hard for us to realize that these men are in a happy situation, but consider the fact that most have had the same wife for twenty years. This small group of Americans of the VFW are one clique, the U.S. embassy people another. I wondered how many of these small groups existed.

The real problem is to get a complete conversation out of anyone before he gets drunk on Mekong whiskey and starts the "old times, I was" line meant to review his memories of the days of glory when life was dangerous and mind and body reacted as one and strength was no question.

The houses of the Americans are well kept and Thai in nature. The decoration and furniture reflects the personality of the individuals, as it does in the U.S. Their plight is simply complicated by the fact that they marry an Asian girl and chose to live outside the U.S. in the home land of their wives. The U.S. has decreed they will live as second-class citizens. Their wives will never be authorized to collect the social security an

American widow may expect. If they had had their wives in the states for five consecutive years, they might draw social security but a thirty percent tax is placed on this by the U.S. This new law was effective 1 January, 1986 and, of course the Reagan administration is blamed. I decided to try to help these people somehow. But any action on my part would have to be at a later date.

I stayed an extra day to work on an idea that had been forming.

I was still working under the assumption that POWs do exist in Laos. But frankly it's hard to find anyone here, either local or U.S., that believe it. One individual only thinks the ones who want to stay and some criminals that escaped U.S. control are alive in Laos. But unless they were killed when they landed by parachute, over two hundred POWs should still be in Laos.

I boarded a bus for NaKom Ponom, and waited. I wondered if it was ever going. Seated on the hot bus, I reviewed the past three days. I paid the driver 60 bott and he disappeared. I waited. I find it more difficult to get along now. No one speaks a good English and the new generation speak almost none. The G.I.'s left fifteen years ago in mass and only a few U.S. groups come in TDY (Temporary Duty) for training purposes. There seems to be a lot of wild country here, but the real jungle starts to the north. A lot of land has been cleared. Of course as the mountains approach the vegetation thickens.

Before leaving Udorn I had one more short session with Consul Jim and talked to one rich local lady. Both mentioned some border guard corruption and that some check points might want money. I suppose its the same game as in Latin and South America.

I had questioned over one hundred civilian and military people. The stay in Udorn only made me more aware that we don't have a quick reaction plan that's really ready to take advantage of instant information. There is no information used from long-range patrols in Laos. Of course this may not be true. I think Thai or Lao can be sent as agents to confirm any report anytime. But reports have slowed down. I felt long-range patrols, by a Special Forces team, could locate POWs. We really have a problem. It won't go away, not half enough is being done.

The fumes in the bus station were almost too much. The bus is a "local", the floors bare wood, the seats a little close together for me, but the price is right. I hoped the trip would start soon. As I remembered NKP is on the MeKong River and a lot smaller than Udorn.

I kept going over the facts I'd learned to try to make some sense of this situation.

Last night I learned we had an emergency B-52 air field south and west of Udorn. I wonder why it was so secret? It also came to me, some 20,000 Lao resistance troops are trying to start the war again. But the corruption of some leaders kept the supplies swindled to only existence level.

The Udorn visit was revealing on many issues. U.S. officials feel very little information is available and that what is available is not true. Some resident Americans feel all POWs are nonexistent and the issue should be dropped. At this point I thought, "All refugees are screened and I'm not sure a refugee camp visit would be useful." Of course, I later changed my mind. All in northeast Thailand speak a Lao-Thai dialect or straight Lao. There is a lot to learn, but those who have the answers don't give a damn or they are involved in the Lao resistance and won't talk. The problem is complex. I can't help feeling coverup. Even if they didn't have the attitude all reports are lies, there would be a problem. I feel this attitude and policy has sifted down through channels over the years not to intentionally hurt the program, but none the less leaving only a narrow portal for intelligence to pass. Again, I'm questioning seriously that if any real information on live POWs was obtained, it would be staffed until it was out of date before a recommendation could be put on the President's desk for a strike force to enter Laos. Further, would the President act?

About half the way to NKP we stopped at a small town: the market was on the main street and was a sea of activity. One beautiful girl walked by, well-dressed. I wondered if she was a Bangkok hooker home on leave. Every shop in the town was open at the front and all the merchandise displayed. The town reminded me of her or vice versa.

The bus broke down twice. Once I gave the driver a wire coat hanger to secure the drive shaft. Arriving in NKP I quickly found a nice hotel and followed directions to the Sr Nah Restaurant where I was to meet a Lao informer. We talked for three hours. I would use him on my next trip. Tomorrow I'll walk the town to look for other contacts. Back in the hotel I sent out for a comb, a bottle of whiskey, and some soda.

I wanted to get a feel for KNP. The idea I was working on was to leave my gear at NKP and return to Nong Khai. I wanted to travel the river and talk to river people along the way. Where was the information? This trip I must at least learn how to find it.

In the lobby television was coming in from somewhere. The picture was not bad, of course for $6 a night there is no air-conditioning or television in my room, but it was very nice. I hoped the food is good. There was no one in the dining room except me for breakfast. Well, it was good except for the flavor. The potatoes and beans, both tasted the same.

I wrote a letter today to Monika about the systematic discrediting of Bo Gritz and others which oppose the government policy concerning the POW issue.

Bo Gritz was described to me as a "publicity seeker, mercenary, incompetent, bungling, untrained opportunist, too old to take part actively in any action" (he's probably 45). "He can't put the war behind, he must see himself in uniform and has visions of grandeur. He is unstable and performs irrationally. He is a bad judge of character, doesn't know when to pay, etc., etc. and is always taken in by local nationals. He has taken money from Stars in Hollywood and the League of Families and is now thought of as some kind of foolish old soldier who can't let go of past glories and should never be taken seriously and is not welcome in Thailand". Frankly all of this couldn't be further from the truth. But publicly the government of Thailand cannot be supportive of him.

Mark A. Smith, retired major, (awarded the (DSC) Distinguished Service Cross, two Silver Stars, and nine bronze stars) a "basically dishonest man who passes bad checks and once pulled an M-16 on a Commander in Korea. He is mentally unstable and because he is dishonest is most probably a person who would not tell the truth. He has probably lied to Congress." Again official words meant only too discredit.

Scott Barnes (who has passed all lie-detector and truth serum tests and whose story was bought by BBC after two years of investigation) is "a flake, known soldier of fortune and therefore totally untrustworthy."

Lieutenant Colonel Howard, Congressional medal of honor winner, and me, they have not gotten to yet, but I suspect that will come.

Now I will say I've met two consuls I like despite the policy being followed, although I feel they have bought State Department policy they really believe most of what they say.

The fact exists that information is hard to come by, but available. No one wants to discuss the issue. They are too close to the problem: like a fly on a blackboard trying to read what is written there.

There are few whites in this town. I saw none in a two hour walk this morning. The hotel is nice for the price. The food is cheap, the beer still $1 a bottle, gold sells here at the world price or a little higher. I thought, "In a few days I'll go North to Nong Khai and go down the river, we'll see."

I had not been sick. But I was having a hell of a time with the heat.

I've enough to finish the book and write a report for Lugar (Senator from Indiana) and Reagan, but so far the real idea of trying to set up a recovery has not developed except in talk. The one American who doesn't want his name used is working with the Lao resistance and could get POWs out if he had any wish to do so, but he acts convinced only those who want to be there are in Laos. He was drunk when I finished with him, but he will not discuss "live Americans". He was a noted operations type in the sixties, except the company could not ever be sure he was following orders or doing it his way. In those days results counted. He also ran a program to recover flyers from Laos and North Vietnam. He talked a lot to me, but I had to sift for the truth, if there was any.

Frankly I expected to find more interest here, but there virtually is none concerning our POWs.

Many times I felt that alone this may well be a foolish trip, but I knew this was not my last trip to Southeast Asia. The Americans have left--the Japanese are everywhere as tourists. The Europeans are in protected areas. No one, except me, was working along the border areas of the POW issue.

My ideas to date, just to keep them well in mind:

Increase the effort from Washington down (the POW effort needs more men in the field, language qualified).

The President should understand that character assassination of Americans by the State Department will not be accepted.

The procedure to process intelligence reports is much too long and slow. I doubt if a real "live report yesterday" would or could be reacted to.

Establish a real "standby strike team" to have six-hour reaction time.

The fact Bo Gritz is called a bungler is amazing to me, a highly trained special forces professional. He was able to get the money from Hollywood stars, get a presidential "nod", probably had CIA help to get his equipment into Thailand through customs, and then when his plan was made public, by persons unknown, the government stepped back. This is not a credit to Reagan or his administration, and the fact that a recon patrol had located two or three live Americans in a camp in Laos is sworn to by Scott Barnes. This is not good. Now a campaign of discredit has been fairly successful and Gritz is in seclusion in California or Nevada, with allegations widespread that his team had made threats against the President. If so, why isn't he in jail? Probably because it's not true, and could never be proven. I was becoming overconcerned this smear campaign was perpetrated by people in the State Department. This is not what I came here for and it's not what I want to hear. I tried to keep an open mind. I was looking for facts. They were somewhere.

Tuesday afternoon I went to the police station to see a Captain Leket, referred to me by Bangkok Police Captain Cham. The discussion went on for two hours. I learned a lot about how refugees are handled. But I had to answer more questions than I asked. He wanted to know about the chances of the U.S. changing policy, again like in Vietnam, and leaving Thailand to the Communists and also, what were the objectives of the Vietnam War. But, in general we got along fine and later Captain Leket took me to the NKP Hotel to meet a Mr. Jay. who turned out to be Jay T. Privette, a "civilian" worker at refugee camps for ten years. He wasn't in but I arranged to meet him later. I didn't know what kind of reception I'd get. The 5:30 call failed and I was told to call again at 6:00 or 7. I'd decided to eat before I would go personally to see Mr. Privette. Perhaps the personal approach would do it.

As I looked over the rusted tin roofs of the village or town of NKP, I wondered if a thought of our POW across the river ever entered the conversation of the local people. My hostess at the Serb Hotel had told me, "We talked of it fifteen years ago, even twelve years back when the Americans were still here." She is about thirty-five now and speaks good enough English to have known a GI or two. Married and with three children, she had trouble understanding me at first but got better as she remembered her English. I got a few leads to some border crossers.

In my room I picked up Radio Vietnam in Hanoi, in English. Communist-slanted, the Voice of Vietnam told about Nicaragua, Honduras, Cuba, of anti-Reagan troops in movement against eighteen U.S.-held bases in the Mediterranean, the Libyan provocation, U.S. chased out of Libya. U.S. Contra Policy will lead to another Vietnam. U.S. forces' spring-board against Nicaragua from El Salvador and Honduras; pour more oil for world peace problems. International Communism is invisible, and will win over U.S. Kampuchea, bridge repaired. Solidarity commission all agree about national import. Trade union open forum, working class of people, higher production is the goal, 60,000 of the party of Vietnam to meet this year. Vientaine was site for meeting of the trade unions of Vietnam, Laos and Cambodia. U.S. strikes are in progress to improve working conditions. Protests in the Philippines. (The line of Communist crap never quits.) All U.S. strikes are to improve living conditions of workers and bring them up to **subsistence level.** This is the only news some of Southeast Asia people have.

I went to the NKP hotel to wait for Jay T. Privette. I found this man of thirty-five to be extremely dedicated. He went into detail about his work in several refugee camps for the past ten years. He speaks Lao, Cambodian, Thai and some Vietnamese. He helped me to find out how the system worked. He was doing his job and was very interested to see all POW information was forwarded.

Early the next morning I left for Nong Khai. The bus left within thirty minutes of schedule and then proceeded along the MeKong River north to a point where Laos was on three sides. It's a poor country when the rice paddies are dry. Summer was here but the rice will grow again after the coming rains. I sat in the back of the bus where there is some leg room. The baggage area was full of boxes, chickens and produce. I suppose the local Lao thought I was crazy.

As the old bus crawled north along a dirt road, the Mekong River was often in view. Watching northeast I had plenty of time to look over the mountain range in Laos. They started twenty kilometers northeast of the river and faded into a blue haze. This is a strange part of the world. The mountain range, worn down by time, was paralleled by not-so-large mountains to the south, indicating the river in this part of the Mekong was fifty times as large and hundreds of feet deep in ages of unwritten history before man was known in this world. Whether it was my imagination or not, I could feel the presence of our kinsmen somewhere in the dark jungled mountain area to my north. I know they are there and the feeling became overwhelming. I now understand the tremendous pull this forbidden Laos has to some Americans seeking to aid the escape of our comrades. I had learned in the past two weeks all is not well in the intelligence collection effort. This information came from the Thai captain of police and what I could put together from Jay and the U.S. consul.

The time may be approaching soon that some Lao refugee swims the river and arrives at an immigration check point on the Thai side of the river with current POW information.

Through my investigation of the current situation we will not be ready to react to the knowledge he may have. The escapee is not really concerned about the possibility he has basic information we want. His interest is in his next meal and how he'll be treated. Will he be sent back and if so what fate lies ahead? The swimmer's shirt will dry on his back in the Thai jail holding area. He is interrogated until he is classified and a dossier is built. All this happens before he sees his first American interrogator at the refugee camp. This very thorough Thai action may take up to thirty days and at no time, according to the police captain, is the refugee asked about Americans. This then precludes the United States from having immediate information on which to act, if in fact there is a plan to make a rescue.

Before I started my river trip I decided to return to Udorn to discuss this fact with Jim Bruno. He was courteous as always, but acted as if I were trying to pick on U.S. embassy policy. His attitude changed a little as we pursued the subject and he did concur that there could be a five or ten-day delay in normal procedure. I encouraged him to take a second look at the system, maybe it was having a slight malfunction, but I knew for sure the thirty-day delay was there and built in and it was not going away without some real action. The action would be required in all provinces and Jim only handled the NE-17. I thought, "Well, in Chiang Mai I'd speak to the consul there and in Bangkok I'd have a crack at the people who direct the refugee program."

Back at the Udorn VFW, I learned that Richard Childress had asked for a local membership. Childress was Reagan's personal representative and adviser for the POW issue and I had heard before he might be slated to work in the northeast area. I'm not sure if he was to be located in Udorn or just visit often, but that was a bit of intelligence I had not expected. Later in the day I also learned more about Gary's job as vice consul and how his job was closely connected to that of Mr. P. There had been hints dropped, but now I began to put together the pieces. As an intelligence officer I knew I was picking up classified information or maybe I was just able to conclude facts based on my experience. I should ask for a briefing and act accordingly. I mentioned this fact to the consul. I felt it would be to our best national interest for me to know what not to discuss or write about, but all U.S. officials wanted to hang tough. Without a briefing I was free to write what I please. I have no knowlege of any classified data, officially. But, much classified material was obvious to me. Who are we kidding? But I won't make a point of going into detail on things I feel are supposed to be of a classified nature. It would be against my training and belief.

Once again I had traveled all day by bus along the Mekong River. The mountain on the other side was dark and ominous. It was the forbidden world where I was not permitted or wanted. But that was where the secret lay to the issue foremost in minds of several hundred American families. Somewhere just beyond the range of my binoculars were prison camps with guards who had grown old with our POWs. I could feel their presence even at this distance, but how would I be able to affect their future? To let my mind wonder was dangerous. I knew a lot about the terrain of Laos from the 1960s when I was here. I knew it was possible to move great distances and virtually see no one. Reality was also very present. Anyone looking for Americans would have to have explicit information and it would have to be current. Besides, an American could be spotted a long way off, unless he dressed as a farmer or fisherman. I know any in depth look at Laos was foolish for now. I would stick to what I could do on the Thai side of the river. I got back to my plan, and details started to form. I must go down this river until it entered Vietnam and talk to fishermen and traders who cross every day.

I arrived at Nong Khai and made arrangements with a fisherman to use his boat for a few days. I needed a Thai/Lao interpreter. The fisherman's son was about eighteen and had been to school. He was happy to find he would be able to practice his English for a few days. All three of us left carefully at night, so as not to arouse notice, and moved northeast on the river almost all night. I found that trying to paddle the dugout was useless after a few hours and that I was slowing down the trip. I shall call the fisherman and his son L and M.

Traffic on the river at night is different than during the day, and both L and M had no trouble stopping boats as they made their way from one shore to the other. These were traders, and smugglers who paid no attention to the river as a border, but L and M did not want to become too involved with these night travelers, so our contacts were quick: we would pass behind a fisherman using nets, with some lines out, and questions and answers were short and to the point.

Toward morning we pulled to the Thai side, and found a sandy spot behind some trees and went to sleep. They had seen to it that my clothes were as poor as theirs, and the old Chinese-style hat covered my head and face. At any distance I was just another fisherman. That day the river was dotted with boats, and we stopped frequently to talk. I asked about Americans or any tall foreigners seen on the Laos side. Occasionally I'd get an answer that some foreigners were in a village just over the first mountain range, or was it the second mountain-no one could really tell. It was obvious that American prisoners were kept out of sight of river people--back beyond the blue haze of the mountains. There is jungle all the way to the top of these aged and eroded mountains and triple-canopy foliage will let an aircraft fall through and burn without leaving a smudge on the top. Maybe locals will find parts of it someday and make things they need from the scrap metal. This is a remote land and will not easily give up its secrets or its dead.

We stopped for lunch with a family that had rice and fish (what a surprise), but during that visit I got my first real story that might lead to an American POW. A cousin or close relative had talked about seeing about twenty Americans working thirty to forty klm from the river. My attention quickened as this information came, but I tried to remain calm and passively interested. When was this report made? Was it unusual in that area? The answer came in a roundabout way, but as I gathered five or six tall white men had been seen working in a sawmill project about 30 days before and the others in fields. I asked questions for over an hour. Were they guarded? Were they working in chains? All was to no avail. They just did not know. It would take an effort to get the information, far beyond my capability or that of the U.S. personnel I had seen in Thailand. A spy would have to be sent. Well, I could forget about getting anyone to move on this. But I had learned POW information is still available and that fact was of great interest to me.

One of my objectives was to find if current information was available. The answer is simply, yes, if it's gone after. This information was not from a refugee.

There are other ways to get information out of Laos. I wondered if we sent agents. I had no way of finding out, but somehow I felt that real operational covert agents were far and few between. We found in Vietnam that if an American did not accompany local forces, patrols or agents, many times they went over the first hill and sat down for two days. This was safe, and the enemy avoided. It was always hard for me to debrief an agent and get a straight story, even when I was working in the Intelligence business in Europe. It is difficult to know if the agent really goes to an objective.

That night we went ashore and found a friendly family. I gave them 100 bott for our food and a floor with a mat for each of us to sleep upon. We could not have been treated better if I had been President. Later I found that 100 bott was about equal to a month's wages for that family. The house was built off the ground, with thatched roof, and was very clean and neat. The bamboo floor had space between the strips, and any dirt brought in fell to the ground.

We were off before daylight and met several fishermen as they started the day. They all seemed happy with their life: they displayed only a mild interest in me or my questions. None had seen any white men in Laos. But one spoke of a large black man who spoke good Lao and Vietnamese. This was a new report, as far as I know. My expectations again rose, but again the location was vague, the time unsure. But it was firsthand, and again this fisherman had never before been asked about big foreigners in Laos.

Here was another important point to report. Those who cross the river were not being sought out, and potential sources had no reason nor incentive to seek us out. Also, someone in our system is always trying to discredit anyone who makes such a report, so why should any person come forward? There is no reward system. However difficult to administer, a reward system should exist.

The day was hot, the river now moved a little swifter, time passed without much action. I watched the same Lao mountains approach that I had seen going north a few days before on the bus. That night we found no place to land at dark, and proceeded for a few more hours. We had a ball of rice each, provided by the friendly family. We ate it with water and a bottle of Mekong whiskey I'd brought. The night was hot and again I was able to let my mind drift.

# CHAPTER 10

## II CORPS, 1969-70

When I left Indiana for the next tour to Vietnam my wife Jeanne said good-bye. She had enough of the Army, the moves, and the separations. I cannot blame her. She wanted to raise our daughter in a small, quiet Midwestern town, and let her go to one high school all four years. The Vietnam War had extracted another casualty. We had lived together only about two years, from 1960 to 1969. Enough was enough. The divorce would be final if I returned from Vietnam this time. If not, she and my daughter would have the benefit of being survivors of an active-duty officer. Either way I lost my family. But I was a soldier, Vietnam was the assignment, and when I found that it was no use to pursue a reconciliation, I reported to Travis Air Force Base in California, thirty days early, for this combat tour.

The air force officer at the terminal was surprised anyone would report early, but nonetheless put me on a flight to Saigon via Clark Air Force Base. The stop over in Hawaii was worth remembering, but short.

I went to Waikiki Beach for an evening "on the town", and at the Bare Foot Bar met Bob Mitchum by accident - a real accident. We were both at the bar and I was having my first drink when this big man turned and took a step back. My drink went over my shoulder and on the floor. Mitchum ordered a new drink and introduced me to his friends. They were interesting people. I had a pleasant night and left for Saigon the next afternoon. I would not see him for months, but we were to meet again during a fire-fight in II Corps. The next time I was to be the host, he was the guest.

For some reason the processing in Saigon and Ben Hoa was much quicker than I remembered, and I was transported to the II Corp area by a C-130. We landed at Canranh Bay (now a Soviet naval base) and I transferred to a helicopter for a quick fifty-mile flight to NaTrang. I had never traveled along this coastline, and its beauty amazed me. The South China Sea was a deep blue, and washed against endless white sand beaches, behind them the bright green Mangro and then the medium-size hills and deep-green jungle. Beyond the hills the land flattened into rice paddies. To the seaside numerous fisherman were netting the day's catch. The tide is considerable, and it was in as we made our way north.

The airfield was at the south edge of NaTrang. I was met by a staff car and taken to a seaside hotel. It seemed that life might be rather pleasant in NaTrang. It had been a French vacation resort in years past and houses were modern, compared to other towns in Vietnam.

NaTrang would be only where I kept my gear and slept when I could. But of course, on my arrival I didn't know that.

The hotel had a restaurant and five or six floors. Each room opened on a small balcony, and the ocean was just across the street.

I might have known it was too good, but I found a room I liked in the back, where civilian Red Cross workers lived, and settled in for the afternoon. I was hungry, but settled for a fifth of cognac. Later that evening I found most of the officers were headed for the club about six blocks away. I found the club to have a pleasant bar and dining room. Each night there would be a different movie, and the compound was fairly well guarded. NaTrang was an armed compound if I had ever seen one. The II Corps commander had his headquarters there, Special Forces had a "C" team headquarters there, commanded by a lieutenant colonel, and many signal and support organizations, also the Vietnamese had logistics support stationed there. There was also a Vietnamese NCO academy and district headquarters. Intelligence agencies had people everywhere. Air America had a part of the airfield, and in general life seemed similar or better than Saigon.

Next morning I reported to the G-1 office for asssignment. When my record was looked over and after an interview I was assigned to the office of territorial forces as the senior regional forces adviser for II Corps.

The office was a few blocks from the hotel, and quite nice by any standard for Southeast Asia. The director of territorial forces was Colonel Penny, my boss. My assigned duties were rather broad.

I was responsible for II Corps staff - supervision of ninety-six Military Adviser teams (MATS). Penny made clear that my duties would go beyond just briefing. I must insure that they had maximum security in their remote field positions. I was to issue extra weapons, insure communications, a fire-support plan, and an escape and evasion plan. The colonel made the additional assignments.

1. I would visit each district and province commander to ensure maximum security of Americans and advise on compound defense;

2. I would brief the II Corps commander (a three-star general) on request, after any successful action on the part of the Vietcong or our Territorial Forces;

3. I would investigate each and every action when over six regional forces troops were killed and write a personal briefing for the general;

4. I would be prepared to relieve any province senior advisor if he needed a replacement;

5. I would make further recommendation for any action I felt necessary to improve U.S. adviser's security in II Corps and use any and all means to effect these measures.

I had a small staff to make our reports, and one major to assist me. There was also a captain to cover the office when I was in the field.

During my first few days I found it impossible to keep up with the requirement to investigate the defensive problems of adviser teams. We were not doing well, the Vietcong could attack at will, and almost always inflicted heavy casualties.

I asked Colonel Penny to let me speak directly to the corps commander about a helicopter for Territorial Forces. He felt I had no chance, but gave me permission to talk to the general.

The general listened to my argument and request for a helicopter, so I could be on site as soon as I learned there was an attack somewhere in II Corps. Also, I would need it to make a monthly visit to all districts and provinces and inspect the MATS as often as possible. To my great satisfaction the general agreed, and later found this "dedicated helicopter" so valuable that he assigned his deputy (a brigadier general) to visit all the II Corps adviser compounds. It upgraded our adviser effort, and I got the kind of cooperation that would not have been easy without General Brown's support. Colonel Penny was pleased with this step forward, and as he finished his tour the Territorial Forces office had developed into an action unit. Penny had given me his confidence, and he was not sorry.

Colonel Penny was replaced by Colonel Wheeler and I was given even more latitude. The truth is I probably had more adviser experience in province and district, and really more exposure in this war, than almost any other officer in II Corps and this experience was now paying off.

Each military adviser team assigned to II Corps came through my briefing, which I gave each week for a full day. I covered all I could, concerning team and personal security. These men would be in the small towns and villages throughout II Corps. The teams, commanded by lieutenants, were always in jeopardy, and almost always too far from help to be reinforced if attacked. Support had to be planned by artillery or air, and a good escape and evasion plan devised.

The dedicated helicopter kept me flying 196 days that year.

NaTrang was a resort area, and an armed camp, but without the real protection of U.S. Forces you might expect. Although I was not there much, the town was off limits to all U.S. soldiers. This fact caused many problems. I would never have thought a town as large as NaTrang should be off limits...at least not off limits all the time. There should have been a 10:00 curfew to get people off the streets, but our toops quickly found that they could go into town whenever they wanted. There was not enough military police to keep them out. There were whorehouses, opium dens, and bars everywhere. Of course they were not open to the street but in the backroom areas of little restaurants or tailor shops. Prostitutes were always available, the beer was easy to get and pretty good, and of course someone local was always around to sell the soldiers marijuana or whatever else they wanted. Soldiers took their chances, knowing that maybe one out of a hundred would get caught.

As long as they stayed out of the compound the entire night, they were pretty safe. If they got to work the next morning no one said anything because no one knew about their all night adventure.

Some of the girls lived within a few meters of the compound. The back gate of the compound was supposed to be locked, with a guard but it was common knowledge that if you came in before 10:00 the gate guards did not pay much attention. The little houses immediately behind the compound were always busy. The majority of troops lived near the airfield. The young ladies were allowed to gather at the gates at night and troops could take them to the movies. The movies began at 7:00 and lasted till 10:00 or 11:00, and the girls were supposed to be out by 12:00. Most of the time I think they were. After all, if you cannot do what you want in six hours, it really is not worth it.

This was the way things were running in 1969 and 1970. It was a quiet town. There was not much trouble. The troops were well taken care of, either by girlfriends visiting them or by going to town. Officers went to the club at night to eat, and then they would sit around the bar and have a few drinks and then go back to their hotel rooms. That was about the size of it. If you were fortunate enough to meet one of the Red Cross girls, and there were several in town, or one of the CIA secretaries or analysts, or one of the nurses, life could be pleasant but local women were tabu and could lead to big trouble. All the senior officers from captain up, had to do was make one mistake. The generals were exceedingly straight and most of the staff towed the line. There were beach parties and swimming anytime you could get away. Almost everyone spent the lunch hour on the beach. We would often play football.

NaTrang was a relaxed area where rarely was there an incident. Sometimes the outskirts of the airfield got mortared, but as far as having a war around NaTrang in 1969 and 1970 it did not happen.

As advisers for the RFPF and the Vietnamese my office personnel were allowed a great deal of latitude in doing what we wanted to do, or going where we wanted to go in NaTrang. No one took advantage of his position, and we never got challenged on the privileges we had when working with the Vietnamese. Staying out after hours, and carrying concealed weapons was doing the sort of thing we had to do to stay alive and at the same time be the kind of people that could get a relationship going with the senior Vietnamese officials.

In 1969 and 1970 we were beginning to win the fight in Vietnam. I could drive a jeep anywhere in II Corps almost anytime, as long as I did it in daytime. At night the Regional Forces Popular Forces (RFPF) would block the roads with barbed wire to try to stop the Vietcong from moving, but in the daytime I can honestly say that except for once or twice I never got shot at on the road. Once in a while I would get caught in one of the Special Forces bases or one of our team areas, when it would come under attack. But in general it was obvious that the South Vietnamese were beginning to win the war. Why it did not work out in 1971-1973 I will never know, because all we really had to do was put pressure on during those years instead of talking about withdrawing and it would have been the Vietcong who would have withdrawn.

There are several things that happened in the first months I was there that helped shape events. I was briefing all the MAT teams* and this made me known to everyone in the Corps. I had arrived just at the time the MAT teams were rotating. So within three or four months I had briefed almost every team in II Corps. I had visited all the province headquarters within the first few weeks. I made myself known to the senior province advisers, their

* This was the way our Military Adviser Teams were referred to - so MATS were all called MAT Teams. As today SWATTS are called SWAT Teams.

deputies, and their teams, and always traveled with minimum equipment. I carried an M-14 rifle or an AR-15, along with side arms, so when I arrived in an area they did not see a desk soldier from NaTrang. They saw a field soldier ready to go to the most remote areas and stay until the problem was cleared up. This set well with most of the teams in the provinces and the districts, because they did not have a good impression of staff officers. In this manner, I found I was accepted. I was taking action or insisting on action aimed to save their lives. I am happy to say that during the year I was there, I am sure, I was able to influence the situation. Not too many soldiers in Vietnam could say that.

The colonel, my boss, and I had a great many social activities to attend among the higher rank Vietnamese. We were expected to be armed most of the time, but you could not go to these affairs with arms showing so I had to obtain concealed weapons permits and also permits to drive Vietnamese officials or their wives in our vehicles.

These small details helped keep us secure and insured we would have little trouble with the local U.S. military police.

While in NaTrang I can remember one time, however, that I was required to undertake an odd mission. We had received information that there was going to be a Vietcong attack of a particular compound. I was asked to get into the area and make sure of the defenses. Many in II Corp felt defense of a compound was my specialty. We were also supposed to have a general officer with us. The general was to be there to improve the morale of the unit and show complete U.S. support. We lined up air support and artillery. It was to be a classic defense, if the Vietcong attacked.

During the Second World War there was a story about "The Imitation General". I do not want you to think I am comparing what happened the next few days with that story, but as a matter of fact the general involved became ill and could not go. When I arrived in this area everyone was expecting a general. Usually I had my collars turned under for personal security. This had become a habit and this day was no different. As I got off the aircraft I received the generals welcome given by the Vietnamese commander. When we got into the advisers area I explained that I was not a general and that he was ill. Everyone was dismayed. They felt it would be hard to explain to the local Vietnamese commander. For the next three days I was the general, the attack came on schedule, the defense was extremely successful, none of the local forces doubted my rank, and I was given a nice farewell. We had destroyed the enemy attack. I do not know how the story ever got back to headquarters but there was a quiet remark from the corps commander about a week later that he "didn't realize there was an extra general in the area". With that comment the whole thing was dropped. The remark was made only to me personally and I'm sure he just wanted me to know I didn't get away with imitating a general, even for three days.

The helicopters that I flew in were extremely well piloted, usually by warrant officers. As far as I remember they never refused a mission, or refused to take me into a hot area. These were not gunships: they were what we called "slicks". With no door guns. The safety of the aircraft depended on the skill of the pilot. Once we had been flying a couple miles out over the ocean, to avoid enemy fire as we approached a certain area. Many times it was a lot safer than flying over the jungle, but that day we flew over some junks we thought were fishing boats. All of a sudden we got a hail of bullets and the helicopter was hit several times. The ship filled with smoke. It was only a matter of time until we were going down. The pilot headed toward the beach. As we came in I knew we were going to get wet, but at the last moment the pilot pulled pitch to flare out and we came in hard on the beach about 20 feet above the highwater mark. As the bird settled into the sand, the engine came to a screeching halt. We had just had another close one. But the day was not over. We were not in the greatest of positions. We were in Charlie's territory, so we got out of the aircraft to form some kind of defense. We had picked up a few riders that day so we had seven or eight on board. All of us had arms. As senior officer on the ground I ordered a perimeter around the helicopter, but not too close. We moved away from it a little, because I felt it would be the primary point of attack. We could better protect the helicopter with good fields of fire if the Vietcong had seen us go down. We were there for fifteen or twenty minutes when the pilot went back to the aircraft to use the radio. He hoped to contact a U.S. aircraft in the air who might be able to cover us until a relief column could be sent. We would also need another aircraft to come in to pick us up. At that point it would be decided whether or not to destroy the damaged helicopter or to try to bring in a crew and make a change of engine.

Just at this time we saw troops at a distance. The enemy was coming for us, and soon we realized there must have been three or four hundred of them. Things looked bad. This was either going to be a long hard day or a very short one.

But at the very last moment, before we were ready to open fire, one of the enemy stood up, shouted something that sounded like English, and walked toward us. My luck was still with us. This was a local Vietnamese battalion-size patrol. Apparently they saw us go down and were only a mile or two away.

Not only did we have enough troops to protect the aircraft until we could get in a repair crew, but this battalion had radio contact with their headquarters and within thirty minutes we were on our way out in another helicopter. The maintenance crew was on their way with a new engine and the means to change it. Next morning the helicopter was flown back to NaTrang.

We lost several thousand helicopters in Vietnam to enemy ground fire. That one we saved.

It seems as if I was forever trying to get to the airfield, and always too early to get a ride easily. I needed transportation. There was a jeep allocated to my office, but it never had been issued, and the paperwork would take months. I knew I could get one with pressure from the general, but I decided to solve my own problem. I started to look around for a jeep.

About two weeks later I found an old beat-up junker at CamRonh Bay advisor headquarters. It had been shot up and written off, then parked in back. I found they did not want to answer questions about it. Would it run? Well, sort of. I got it started, and with no spare or tools and the tailpipe dragging on the drive shaft, drove it fifty miles to NaTrang. I kept it out of sight until I made sure it could not be identified, then drove it to the motor pool.

I left it with an amused sergeant and asked him to do what he could. I also left five cases of beer and two bottles of Scotch in the seatless vehicle. Actually I had used three cases to sit on, to get it to the motor pool.

Some people know how to accept a challenge. The sergeant was one of them. Next day I got a call to pick up my jeep.

When I got to the motor pool I could not find it until the sergeant pointed it out. Unbelievable! Body repaired, dents out, and painted. It had a new top, tailpipe, muffler, bearings, seats, tires, oil changed. A new windshield with wipers, and a radio mount and antenna installed. It looked like the general's jeep, maybe a little too good. The next day I put Vietnamese markings on it, so the military police would leave me alone in off-limits areas or carrying Vietnamese in towns of II Corps. I found a sergeant at the gas pump who would fill me up anytime, and obtained three gas cans, an extra spare tire and tools.

I would be able to visit areas close to NaTrang. Actually when weather prohibited flying, or the helicopter was down, I would drive all over II Corps from NaTrang to Delate to Kontum. Of course, the general did not go on these trips and I wore no rank showing and an old Vietcong-style hat. Usually one of my sergeants rode shotgun. I also put in a military long range radio and scrounged up a trailer. The advisers rarely wore helmets, and it was the one thing no one ever tried to regulate. The old Vietcong hat kept me out of a lot of trouble.

When I was in NaTrang one Sunday I took a few hours to work out on the beach. It may be hard to believe, but the staff in NaTrang worked from 7:00 a.m. until 7:00 p.m., seven days a week. Twelve hours a day was normal, and some put in more. I actually had more time to myself because I was always at some province or district headquarters and could set my own schedule.

But this one Sunday I met one of the CIA analysts.

She was trying to sunbathe when I accidentally rained sand all over her as I ran by. After a few well chosen words of apology I was asked to dinner. Miss Jones was on a two-year assignment and had a house with guards at the gate twenty-four hours. In general she lived well for a woman in Vietnam. I can say that my one link to the real world during my II Corps experience was the frequent visits to her house. We became close friends and kept contact for several years after the war.

It might be interesting to discuss some of the single women who supported the war as CIA analysts, secretaries, nurses, doctors and medical technicians, but I won't.

These women were exposed to all of this war and some did not survive. Those that did should have the same respect offered to our young soldiers who returned. Those that did not return were soldiers in every sense of the word. They were caught up in a man's world and a war no one wanted. Some stayed for two or three years. Each have their own stories, little loves and big loves. Terror and war have effected many. If they went to Vietnam for adventure they got it. If they went to serve their countries they did. If they went for the higher than normal pay they were to return home better off than their counterparts. But the nurses and doctors and each and everyone of the American women in Vietnam were thought well of by our troops and did their job despite the bombs and dangers of the time and place. Most felt it was the most useful time of their lives...just ask a few.

One thing that bothered me as an adviser was that South Vietnamese families of Regional Forces lived almost within the compound. The closeness of families to this war was hard for me to accept. During every attack some family members were killed. This war had been on going for twenty years. Where else would a soldier's family live? Some villages came right to the edge of compound areas and I was forever in trouble trying to get the huts away from the compound fence.

Maybe this simple problem bothered me more than it should have, but I kept wondering how it would be in the U.S. if we were fighting in our hometowns and counties. Just imagine if you could not put your children to bed without fear of a Vietcong attack aimed to kill everyone in the area. Maybe that's a reason to fight communism as far away from the U.S. as possible.

I was able to spend a lot of time with the teams in the field. I tried to be useful to the small teams located far from U.S. support.

Once I had taken a few days to visit a team in the mountains. There had been some action, and the team was training local groups to ambush. Of course, I was urged to participate. The night was hot, and time dragged by hour after hour. I was sitting on a recently-cut tree stump behind a tropical plant that obscured my position. The moon came up and some of the jungle sounds seemed to quiet down. Then it happened. I felt as though I was being watched. I shrugged off the feeling, but as I looked up at the moon, which had just moved behind a large dead tree to my left, the feeling became real. The shape of a jungle cat was clear, only about fifteen feet above me. He had also been on ambush. As our eyes met he jumped for me. I started to raise the double barrel shotgun and everything went black as the cat's shape covered the moon in his leap. I only moved the muzzle a few inches. The shotgun had fired as I just pointed and pulled both triggers. The gun went one way, the leopard and I the other. He had hit me headlong. I was down, the animal on top of me, and the ambush ruined. As I realized I was not hurt I rolled from under the beast. I was covered with warm blood and when members of the team got to me I was picked up and carried off. I protested I was not hurt, but I was back in the temporary camp in a few minutes. When it was sorted out the next morning, they recovered my shotgun and the headless cat. Was it the golden buddha which had been given me years ago in Laos that was still protecting my life?

The administrative captain, that I thought a great deal of, elected to meet his wife in Hawaii for R&R. I felt this was a good idea and approved his request. To my surprise he did not return on the appointed day. I had a captain AWOL, a situation not common in any war. There was little I could do except wait to see if he would return with a reasonable excuse. It did not happen soon enough. I had a dilemna. Should he be court-martialed? What should I do with him? He had been good at his job.

When he finally showed up I had replaced him. I gave him an assignment to DucTo. This was as close to Siberia as I could send him. It was the farthest outpost away from civilization that we had in II Corps. He had four or five months (if he lived that long) to consider his AWOL adventure. I hope it was worth it to him and his wife.

I never had another AWOL.

Many South Vietnamese casualties could be credited directly to the old French-style bunkers. Most of them had small shooting ports. There was no way to see out at night. The enemy could virtually walk up to these bunkers and drop in a grenade, killing or injuring everyone inside.

I was finally in a position in II Corps to do something about these bunkers. First my boss and then the general had to be convinced. Everyone in II Corps had to be convinced. By 1969 most U.S. forces were doing well in a mobile concept and the Vietcong were losing ground, but the local forces had a long way to go and already there were rumors of withdrawal of U.S. forces. We knew American politics would dictate an eventual withdrawal.

I had only this one year to influence the Vietnam War. I really felt it would be my last tour.

Colonel Wheeler used what experience I had to everyone's advantage, and urged me to change the defensive posture of all adviser compounds and influence the Vietnamese where ever I could. The idea was to open these old bunker windows and be able to defend during an attack, but it was not easy and took most of the year to convince advisers and local commanders. I had 92,000 local forces to deal with, and a lot of combat commanders whose war had lasted twenty years. But the Vietcong lost when they attacked our newly fortified village and compounds. My reputation in II Corps seemed to grow beyond my expectations. Finally I did not have a problem getting people to listen.

I was presented the Bronze Star during this tour, for improvement of the defensive posture of II Corps South Vietnam Regional Forces, and later a Legion of Merit for the year's work, which is one medal I am proud of. It represented a year of work, not just a few moments in action.

## CHAPTER 11

## A VILLAGE IN TERROR

## AND OTHER EVENTS

Most of us arrived too late in Vietnam, about thirty years late. The country people supported the Vietcong, and a lot of Americans ask why. The answer is not difficult. Communists can easily appeal to the poor and landless. They give them "rising expectations", hope for a better life, or they use terror tactics unfamiliar to Americans.

The village of Kam is fifty miles from Province headquarters. Only a few volunteer home guard or regional forces were in the area. Early one morning, before any of the village was up, a Vietcong squad walked through Kam and intentionally fired their automatic weapons into every house, about four feet off the floor. The intention was not to kill villagers. They sleep on the floor or on low bamboo racks. But for the rest of that night the villagers all slept under the beds or slipped off into the jungle. And when it got daylight they returned to find their chief cut in four or five pieces, around the town center. They found the only on-duty policeman hung, upside down, with his belly cut open and his entrails hanging over his face.

Where did they sleep that night? Who took the chief's place or the place of the village policeman? Nothing happened that night or the following week. Then when a new chief was appointed there were a few more days of quiet, and the same thing happened. Now who took the official's place?

Next day the Vietcong sent a platoon to take care of the village. These attacks would not happen again. Of course, the village would be expected to support that unit, make uniforms, give grain and supplies. A few of the village young men would be taken into a Vietcong unit. The village would be Vietcong for a long time. It was hard for an American adviser to come into that village and tell the people "we are the good guys. Your protectors and your sons are the bad guys."

Another way power can be taken is by use of an infra-structure set up over the years.

A few young men from the village will be taken to a central training area, maybe Hanoi. They will return fully indoctrinated, to support the communist political movement.

The village of Duc Hoa was a farm village, but all villagers worked the land of a landlord who owned the area. The young men returned well-trained. Some called a meeting of the townspeople. No one was in the field, so the landowner went into the village to find out what was going on. When he came into the village the people were incited to seize him and bury him alive up to his head. They were told to punish him with bad words and criticism.

The townspeople did not know what the young trainees had hitched a water buffalo to a plow and when the time was right one would drive over the helpless landlord and sheer off his head.

At this point the whole town had been involved. Would they cooperate with government forces when they inquired about the landlord? The Vietcong hold on the town was permanent.

We heard a lot about the black market in Saigon, NaTrang and DaNang, but little was known of its depth.

While in NaTrang I was given a tour of the black market area by the district chief. I was amazed that one could buy anything, D-8 engine head or a tube of toothpaste. I was quite surprised to find many types of weapons also for sale, and the price was right. An M-16 would bring one-hundred dollars, an M-1 about sixty, a carbine fifty and hand grenades were five dollars each, a good pistol one-hundred and fifty. A Thompson .45 submachine gun might bring one-hundred and thirty. I was never able to find how these weapons found their way to the black market. Either U.S. or Vietnam officials were able to steal and sell these guns. Maybe the Vietnamese economy depended on the black market. I often wondered why no one attempted to stop it.

Money traders were on both sides. The army used script, but there were so many greenbacks around the system really did not work.

One hundred dollar bills brought one and one-half to two times the regular exchange rate. Gold traded well, and money dealers made a lot of money to buy the gold.

Dollars were the lifeline for the Vietnamese, to assure he would be able to get money out of Vietnam when the U.S. left. Many Vietnamese knew we would leave and felt the Vietcong would overrun the South Vietnam army, and they were right.

## THE GUEST

While I was taking the province senior commander's place in Pleque province, I seemed always to be in the wrong area. This time the Vietcong planned an action exactly where I was visiting.

This particular afternoon we had contact with a Vietcong unit and were not doing at all well. There had been some men wounded, and a "dust off" (medical helicopter) landed to pick them up.

To my surprise a civilian jumped off the helicopter and ran toward my position. He had a helmet and when he hit the ground it rolled against me. It was Bob Mitchum. He did a doubletake and said something about the fact I could buy the next drink. At that moment I didn't know if I would ever get another drink.

But then some gunships I had called for arrived, and the fight turned better. The Vietcong withdrew, and this time I was Bob's host. A great guy. We all liked him.

A few weeks later while senior adviser at Kontum I was asked to look into the defenses of an artillery position. The Commander of the battery was new and the II Corps commander was concerned. I spoke to the captain and his lieutenants about using patrols, and tried to get him to use regional-force troops. The battery did not have men for patrols, but the U.S. commander wanted to use his own troops. He really did not trust the regional forces, but his troops were not infantry-trained. Usually a battery is within infantry perimeter protection or at least the infantry furnishes patrols. It was not going to be easy to get the men to patrol aggressively or patrol at night. Maybe night ambushes would be the place to start.

I talked to the troops, but it was evident many did not want to go with their lieutenant. He was young, I knew the only thing that would get the patrols out was for me to take them. A lieutenant colonel on patrol again, this was the life of a MAC V adviser. I could not get out of it.

Within a week I was able to get them to work with the Vietnamese. As far as I know, the Vietcong never made an attack on the U.S. battery. The patrols kept them from getting set and slipping into a position from which to attack. I was being paid to advise the Vietnamese or supervise adviser security. So I decided I had better get back to that.

I dropped in to see that battery four months later and I doubt if their commanding general was treated better. It almost embarrassed me. I was proud of them.

## HOLDING OFF DANANG

Once on a liaison visit to I Corps I was picked up at NaTrang airfield by an Air America plane that never turned off its two engines. We headed for a meeting I had scheduled in two hours. "We'd make it easy", I thought. I should have known that two hours for a thirty-minute trip was not good planning.

The pilot was older than most in Vietnam, a civilian, and probably had worked for Air America since its creation. As we left the ground he was pulling the flaps and had no more than leveled off when he looked over to me and said, "Take over, heading 345 degrees, keep it at 3,000 feet", and without more proceeded to check out several pieces of equipment including gas gauges. After ten minutes I noted some concern on his face. As I tried to hold the heading and altitude I asked, "What's the matter?"

Without emotion he said, "We may run out of gas, the damn gauges have screwed me. Something is wrong, but we are as close to DaNang as going back to NaTrang. This plane needs a long runway for real safety under these conditions."

I was glad to hand the controls back to him, but then I had nothing to keep my mind off our situation. To add to the poor feeling I was having, we were at least ten miles off the coast and had just entered a cloud bank. He was flying on instruments. I found myself hoping he did not die of a heart attack as he called DaNang for landing instructions and was told to enter a holding pattern. We were still five miles out, at least, and I could not see through the clouds.

Each time he would call he got louder and finally with an alliteration of four-letter words, some of which I did not recognize, he threw the microphone down with the words, "Well, you have held me out here until I'm out of fuel. Notify air sea rescue and clear the runway if we happen to make it. Out."

He cut the pitch on the props and we started down. At 1,000 feet we broke out of the clouds and the shore line appeared in the distance. My guess of five miles had been optimistic.

Bert Cramer's jaw was set and he was swearing under his breath. Again he said, "Take it," and he got up to check what I thought was a life raft. Now I worried. I felt a little better when he took his seat again. Then one engine changed sound. Bert made some change in controls. The shore line seemed to remain in the distance and it seemed the plane had quit moving. My imagination was playing tricks. Bert pulled out a cigar and without changing his expression bit off a piece and started to chew. Now I began to see; he was not afraid, he was angry, mad as hell. I felt a little better, but not much. We were still over the water, at three hundred feet, and the motion of the aircraft was considerably less than comfortable.

Minutes stretched out, and then we were on the ground touching down at the runway's very end. A few hundred feet down the runway one engine stopped and as we pulled up to the control tower the other quit.

I took my first full breath in many minutes, but Bert was already out of the aircraft. He ran to the control tower and started up. Before the bodies started coming out of the tower, I heard a familiar voice and an old NCO friend of mine was calling my name. He motioned me to his jeep.

"Sir, the whole damn headquarters is waiting for you. You may catch some hell about this." I thought, "Won't that be a shame-maybe not the high point of my day, but not the worst."

I hoped to see Bert at the Club that night if he was not in jail for murder of an air controller.

## BRIEFINGS FOR THE GENERAL STAFF

It was impossible to go a day or two without one of the Regional Forces Popular Forces units getting hit hard. I had to brief it the next day, describing what happened and who was responsible. I can remember once trying to explain how the Vietnamese felt about an ambush.

The morning I had to brief about ambushes (we had two or three that week) I got up early and watched the general leave his house and timed him from his house to work. It was the same route he had taken every morning for three or four months. When we got into the briefing I put a vivid description in front of the group about the vulnerability of the general on the way to work that day. "The general knew he could be ambushed this morning on the way to work but he still went down the same route the same road and he made it. Someday he may not make it. At that time what are we going to do? Are we going to criticize the general for not going a different route every day? He only has two ways to go when he leaves his house. Right or left. He is going down the same street because he only has one gate in the front.

"So the problem of ambush is just the fact that everyone, everyone of you, all of us, everyday, must accept. I don't think it is a big disaster when the local Vietnamese go the same route on patrol once a week and get ambushed. It's just going to happen."

The story went over pretty good with the general, but some of his staff did not think much of it and there was more security taken for the general after that. It really was not the object of my story, but that is the way it worked out.

As I have related, when Colonel Penny left us, Colonel Neil Wheeler replaced him as chief of the office of Territorial Forces. I want to tell you about him. Colonel Wheeler was a big man with explicit ways of talking. He was a man of compassion, and reason and it did not take him but about two or three weeks to demonstrate that he was a man of courage, action and bravery. The office of Territorial Forces indeed had a new leader.

Colonel Penny had his own quiet leadership. He was a sophisticated senior officer, I always thought destined to be a general.

Wheeler was a bit more forward, a bit more outspoken, and I think sometimes the word "fear" was not in his vocabulary. I remember one incident during a trip I arranged. We were near Dalat when we got word that the big game hunter, Captain X, was in a little trouble. Captain X was not an ordinary captain of the Vietnamese Forces. He knew his area and really did not take into consideration province boundaries. We never knew in which province to find him. I carried him on my books and supported him as "a special friend of the government". He had about 160 troops. All these men had worked for him before the war when he had been a big game hunter near Dalat. The war ruined his business. He took his employees and formed a company and started to raise havoc with supply lines of the North Vietnamese as they came across the border from Laos. He would move anywhere, anytime, to interrupt supply lines.

This day he was in the Dalat area and in trouble high on a mountainside; he needed a resupply of food and ammunition. He also needed to evacuate a couple of wounded.

As soon as we heard this unit was in trouble Wheeler made his helicopter available for the mission. I checked with the pilot to make sure we had plenty of fuel, we loaded the supplies, and headed for the mountain. Before we left Wheeler looked around the headquarters compound and picked up an old M-14 he liked and loaded his jacket pockets with ammunition and magazines. We also picked up several cases of "C" rations. We did not know where this unit was but we had them in radio contact and Captain X said that by the time we got there they would have a helicopter pad cleared. I felt we could find him on that mountain. There would be only one cleared area.

We flew about thirty minutes. Wheeler had his M-14 and I had a M-60 machine gun. We were going into a hot landing zone. The pilot spotted the landing zone they had cut with machetes and explosives. The ammunition and C rations were enough to keep them going for another few days before he could again attack Vietcong supply lines and resupply himself. When we landed we were met by a man in his late thirty's or early forties. He carried a submachine gun of some kind and an old German Lugar pistol under his left shoulder. He spoke very little English, but he knew we had come to help him, and while we were there he handed the colonel a captured K-47 and thanked him for coming in under this dangerous situation. We had picked up fire one time coming in, but did not get hit.

Altogether we were on the ground only about five or six minutes. We put his wounded men on the aircraft. The fight was raging around us. Apparently the Vietcong were making an attempt to get to the landing zone and the helicopter. His people were holding well and we only got a few rounds coming in our direction as we lifted off. We took no hits and in thirty minutes were back in Dalat.

Colonel Wheeler, only two weeks in country on his first tour to Vietnam, had done extremely well. So much so that for this act he received an Army Commendation Medal with a V for Valor. He had started his tour right. With his feet in the fire, so to speak, and he had started to make his reputation. He would soon be known all over I Corps as a man of action.

I continued to go from one camp to another visiting our MATs, who were in the most remote location possible. They had a morale problem and I think you can see why. The feeling of being alone and always open to Vietcong assassination was hard to accept. Often when I arrived, spirits went up a bit. After all, if a lieutenant colonel, or a general were visiting, maybe it was not so dangerous.

This tour in Vietnam seemed to go by rapidly, and I had little time of my own. The combat adventures were not as common as on my previous tours, but in the end I felt I had done a lot toward making it safer for our advisers to do their job of training South Vietnamese Regional Forces.

The one thing we lacked in Vietnam was the reporter or photographer who had a feeling for the unit or the soldier in front of their cameras. There were no Ernie Pyles in Vietnam. Why? Because the newsmen had helicopter access everywhere and most Commanders gave them a free rein. It does not work. It is too easy to drop in on a unit, write a story, take pictures, and leave, oftentimes praising the Vietcong attack or defense.

I had the same situation every day of my tour in II Corps. I dropped in by helicopter, went on one or two missions, and left. It was easy to criticize and leave. I found I had a stay in the area or come back often to get a picture of how a province or district was functioning. It is necessary for a newsman to be with one unit over a period of time to see how an operation is developed. If it fails he can feel a part of the failure, and the U.S. public might get a truer picture. War is made of people. Sometimes we fail. Sometimes we look like heroes. It takes time to see both sides.

## A WORD ON DISSENTERS

The disenters in the States were a terrible morale factor with our troops. One prominent actress went to Hanoi and gave aid and comfort to the enemy while we had prisoners of war held there. She hurt us a great deal. The troops will never forgive her. I'm surprised she's lived as long as she has since there are many Vietnam Vet's I know that hate her so much.

The dissenters who hurt us a great deal are the successful young people of today. Most now are willing to support the Army and our government because without it they couldn't be making the "big money". They may have had every right to dissent, but to actively support the enemy was a great tragedy. I don't know if any of them realize just how much damage they caused.

On the other hand those who followed their true belief during the Vietnam era had the right--after all that's what this country is all about. There were legal ways to be declared a conscientious objector. But many used the right of dissent to evade duty to their country and a risk of their personal safety. Some felt they were above such service. Whether or not a man agrees with the political leaders of the country his obligation to serve when called is real. If he cannot morally serve in a combat unit then he should serve in a non-combat status. To object on "legal grounds" is not good enough. Who can set himself above the law of the land? If Politicians make mistakes the system will replace them, but for the good of the nation an individual cannot go his own way. The United States was built in "United" revolution a civil war was fought to keep the country united even when some states did not agree with the Federal Government. Then what is the right of the individual to put himself beyond the law. Our revolutionary leaders were risking everything.

Those who opposed the revolution went to Canada, to stay, Loyal to the crown.

That's the way it all started. Those who didn't support the revolution were not permitted to benefit from the results. Financial gains were enjoyed by those same men who risk their lives, land and fortune. Why should that idea of democracy change?

Only about five million Vietnam dissenters existed--they were vocal, but did not represent the majority of the U.S. **Democracy must be controlled by the majority, not a vocal demonstrating minority**....Many of the Politicians listened too closely to these dissenters and were led to believe the American public in general felt the war was wrong. The truth is, most felt that if we were to fight it should be a fight to win. But the loud dissenters got the attention and in many ways mislead the politicians. Will it ever happen again?

Certainly there should be a list compiled of the deserters and the Veterans organizations should make sure none ever hold public office in this country. Those who failed to meet the call to duty and took no legal action to declare their conscientious objections should have no chance to become public leaders of the future. Why should those who reported for duty forget and forgive those who did not take equal risk?

## OTHER THOUGHTS

In general the time I worked in II Corps was well spent. The troops in II Corps did their job as well as they could, under the restrictions imposed by the U.S. Government. I would very happily return to NaTrang for vacation. I highly recommend that area to anyone who is motivated to visit Vietnam. If the present regime was ever deposed to become more friendly to the U.S. this is one of the most interesting and in some ways beautiful places in the world.

Unfortunately the withdrawal phase of our Vietnam War began long before it should have, and the Vietcong began to think they were winning the war. The withdrawal in the early 70's was a grave mistake. We had either been there seven years too long or we were leaving seven years too soon. It was a great mistake to leave when we did and let the good people of Vietnam go down the drain with promises of support that we never gave. We got them started winning and then we turned our backs and left them to a fate at the hands of the Vietcong. The morale of the Vietnamese went with us and they in effect stopped resisting. Yet there are some units today still in the hills. I suspect the Captain who was a big game hunter, is still fighting. They're now the rebels. the Vietcong are in control of the legal government. The loss of this area and the killing of over a million Cambodians is directly the fault of the U.S. untimely withdrawal. I feel most of the soldiers did their job in Vietnam. By soldiers, I mean all our service men, all levels and grades and they should be proud of their Vietnam service.

# CHAPTER 12

## HONG KONG

It was late in my tour, and I must have been showing signs of fatigue, because my boss told me to take a week off. He had arranged for me to be dropped off in Hong Kong by an Air America plane on its way to Taiwan for repair. I would have four days, and be picked up on return.

It sounded great to me, but the catch was that I had forty-five minutes to be at the airfield. We were in a slow month and I really had done about as much in II Corps as I could. Without changing clothes I picked up money on the way to the airfield.

The boss also had a long list of things for me to buy for other senior officers. He had known I was going before he gave me the week off. Altogether I must have had $4,000 in cash.

I did not know much about Hong Kong, but the list would give me something to do. Hell, who doesn't like to spend money.

I only had a small bag. I was wearing worn fatigues and had no idea that to arrive in uniform was against the rules in Hong Kong. As I walked across the airfield a jeep came out to meet me and there were two British-looking police, about 6'6 each. They made it clear I was to come with them, that the commandant wanted to see me. I had no idea what was going on, but this was not a time to argue. Across the airfield I was presented to a red-faced commandant. To my dismay this man of apparent Scottish heritage was extremely angry. He was pacing up and down and finally sat down behind his desk and said, "Well, maybe you're here to invade us. You realize, of course, that uniforms like that are not allowed in Hong Kong."

This was not early in the war, but I did not know anybody who had ever been to Hong Kong. I explained that I did not realize this was the case.

I was asked to sit down, while his officers waited outside. I was led into a discussion of the Vietnam war far beyond that which I enjoyed. I was being asked questions that should have been asked of the President. The commandant wanted to know about the rights and wrongs and moral issues of the U.S. envolvements in Vietnam. I did what I could to answer him, within the perimeters of my own judgment, from the viewpoint of a professional officer. I'm sure that my answers in his opinion were inadequate and finally he just shook his head and said, "Now I want you to accompany these police to the car that's waiting out in front and as you go through the terminal building don't cause any problems." He asked me how long I expected to be here, and I told him four days. He said, "Well, we will see to it you get back on your airplane. You just accompany these policemen where they take you. Very quietly now get him out of here."

I went through the airport with these two men, one on each side, trying to act as casual as I could. We got into the back of the car, one was on each side, and the driver took us into the main part of town. Actually we were in Kowloon. Hong Kong Island itself is off the coast. The airfield is on the mainland. We stopped at a couple of stoplights, then pulled over to the side of the curb and I looked out the window. It didn't look to me like a jail. One of the police got out and asked me to follow him.

As I got out I said, "What is this?" He answered, "This is a tailor shop. Go get your clothes changed. We will wait."

I thought, "Well, I guess this is where I pick up civilian clothes. They sure were particular how I dressed in jail." I went into the tailor shop and an Indian tailor greeted me quickly. I noticed he had some new clothes laid out. I asked him, "What is going on?"

He said, "The commandant has told us to take care of you. Of course, these are just for tonight. You will have a suit by tomorrow. We will measure you now and have it delivered to your quarters in the morning."

My quarters? Suit? I began to think it sounds less and less like I'm going to jail. I decided to go along and play this game very carefully, because I didn't know what was going to happen next. Of course, I had plenty of money.

Next he walked around me a couple of times with his tailor's tape and after taking a couple of measurements asked me, "What type and color of material do you want?"

I said, "Well, I've always wanted a white, tropical suit. This is just as good a time as any to buy one, what type of material do you have?"

After looking over several bolts of material I selected one.

He said, "That's pretty good for a suit, yes that will make a fine suit."

I said, "Well, what about the quarters, where am I suppose to stay?"

He said, "The commandant has taken care of that. I think it's time to change clothes." So I went in the dressing room and changed. Everything fit except the socks, I handed them back out and he gave me another pair. I came out dressed in civilian clothes. The uniform was wrapped up and put in a bag.

I said, "Now tell me about those quarters you've been speaking of."

He said, "Yes, we've been told to take care of your quarters."

I said, "Oh, you have."

"Oh, yes, the commandant said to take good care of you and make sure you didn't get into any trouble while you were here in Hong Kong. So we have taken care to get exactly what you need in the way of not only clothes, but an escort, a guide who will take you throughout Hong Kong without a problem," he said.

"Is that right." I answered. "You have a guide for me." Thinking, "What in the hell am I in for?"

"Oh, yes, she is observing from the balcony above." The balcony went all the way around the shop, as was the case in many of the old Hong Kong shops. The workers would work in the balcony while the shop was downstairs.

As I looked up I saw this vision of Chinese beauty. She made Susie Wong look like a Sunday School teacher. She had on a long Chinese split dress.

I mumbled, "That is my guide?"

He said, "Oh, yes, we were told to get only the finest guide and she has just nodded her head in approval that she will take the assignment."

I said, "I see, she has her choice to take the assignment or not."

He said, "Oh, yes."

I thought, "Well, I don't think at this time I should argue with the commandant's judgement."

I asked, "What are the arrangements." The young lady sat down in a very plush chair. He said, "It's very simple. While you are here you'll need a guide and she will furnish your quarters, and at the same time you will need a car which she will furnish. I assume during your stay in Hong Kong you are going to be buying for other people and yourself and because she knows Hong Kong very well, you must understand, that she can make better buys than you can. You give her your list and she will take you to these places and you will do much better than if you went by yourself. She will make five or ten percent on each sale she makes from the man who is selling you these items. Your fee for her guide services, the car, and your quarters is $35 a day."

I said, "Now let me see, let me go over this one more time. I get a car, guide, she is going to be my buyer, my escort for $35 a day." To think, I went to a mirror to look at myself in my civilian clothes and it wasn't too bad. I really did not like the shirt very much, but what the hell. I was going to have a new suit next day. So I picked up a couple of white shirts and a tie. I looked up and noticed my guide was gone, but a car had pulled up out in front and I noticed the police car was gone. The young lady was seated in the back seat of the car that had just pulled up. I said goodbye to the tailor and asked him when my suit was coming and he said, "Oh, yes, we know where to deliver the suit and about seven o'clock in the morning should be about right."

I said, "You mean your people are going to make this suit tonight. Without a fitting you're going to bring it to me."

He said, "It will fit, don't worry about that, you're going to be extremely pleased with this suit."

I thought, "All right, maybe I should order another one tomorrow." And I did.

The young lady was waiting for me in the back of the car. As I got in I was introduced to her by the tailor and I was whisked off immediately. A few blocks and a few turns and I did not know exactly where I was, but it did not matter, my attention was undivided upon my guide. This was one of the most beautiful women I had ever met. She was obviously not all Chinese, she had some European background, and was a good deal taller than most Chinese women. If one could have produced a Chinese Barbie Doll, that is what she would have been.

We stopped at a little stairway between two buildings and I noticed there were some words exchanged in Chinese between the driver and the young lady. She had been introduced to me as Susan. I assumed this was her adopted American name, and was right. She told me later her Chinese name. Susan had apparently acted as a guide for other Americans. She told me I was the first soldier for whom she had ever acted as a guide.

We went up the stairway to the second floor and entered a very nice apartment. It was a good deal larger than I expected. The floors had thick carpets and there was a TV. Also a bar, and an older Chinese lady busying herself around the room. I saw two or three rooms down a hallway, a nice dining room and living area. There were several pictures on the wall of Susan and some of her friends. She had it well decorated. At this time I was beginning to wonder exactly what I was getting into. The pictures on the wall were taken with movie actors and celebrities from around the world. But, after all, the commandant had arranged this so I thought there was nothing for me to do but go ahead with the situation. I was not unhappy. What was Susan? Just a high-class hooker. I really did not care. I was going to have a trip to remember.

The bar was open and I was asked what I wanted to drink, Scotch or whatever. Susan and I sat down to become acquainted. She was explicit in a few of her comments. She said, "You have just come out of the Laotian or Vietnam jungle. As you can understand, here in Hong Kong we have a few problems with this."

I said, "Well, what are your thoughts."

She said, "Well, I don't know very much about that area, I don't know very much about what you have been doing. Before we get too well acquainted, understand this is nothing personal, but I'm going to ask you to have a physical examination."

I could hardly believe my ears but that's what she said. I said, "What are you talking about?" She said, "Well, there are all kinds of jungle diseases and so on and I just don't care to be exposed to them. My sister is a Chinese doctor, and will make the examination if you agree. If not, it's all right, but our relationship will be somewhat curtailed, but I will carry through with my duties as your guide and buyer."

She was talking good sense and any objections lessened as I began to understand what she was talking about. I said, "I have no objections, but when is this going to happen?" She said, "My sister is in the apartment now and I will call her if it's all right with you and she will give you an examination in the back room."

I said, "All right." She brought her sister out and introduced her as Con Mi. Con Mi was a very beautiful woman also, not as exquisite as Susan, nor did she try to be. She was more or less what you would expect as a Chinese doctor. However, though, she did show a few of the Eurasian or European virtues. Tall, slim, and nice looking. Con Mi took me to the back room and proceeded with a thorough examination. In fact it was one of the most thorough examinations I have ever had. When I told her this, she seemed very pleased. At the end she went out to talk to her sister while I got dressed. Apparently I had passed. Con Mi immediately disappeared and Susan seemed pleased that everything was all right.

We got acquainted the next two to three hours. I suppose by then it was seven or eight o'clock in the evening and I do not need to describe the whole action. Needless to say, this young lady was as good as she looked.

About 8:00 she explained that she had to go to work. We had some Chinese soup and a small piece of steak. I did not have any idea what she was talking about when she said she had to go to work. As delicately as she could she explained to me, as she got out of the large queen-size bed, that her fee for guide services and what she could make on the commissions being a buyer for people, was not adequate to send her younger brother, who was still in Red China, to medical school. She had to maintain a night job. This job was as a dancer at one of the cabarets. I was curious. What kind of dancer? She explained that she did a fire dance and I would have a chance to see it if I wanted, the next night or two. This young lady was quite an athlete, but I had no idea just how far she had developed this exotic dance.

She explained that she would be gone from about 9:00 to 12:00. During this time she had to put on two different shows, one at 9:00 and one at 11:00. Each lasted for thirty minutes, so she would return about midnight. She had arranged for my entertainment during this time she was going to be gone. I thought I had about enough entertainment this night, but she insisted as she took me down the hallway and knocked on a door at the far end. I did not know there was anyone else in the apartment other than her sister and the old lady. The door opened and I was introduced to Ni Ton, a girl of about nineteen, very Chinese. Her broader face and slanting eyes gave her a special beauty. She was well groomed and dressed.

At this point, not knowing what to say, I said, "Susan, what is this exactly?"

She said, "Well, Ni will take care of you this evening while I'm gone. I hope you will like her. I'm sure she will be satisfactory and please you."

More than surprised I said, "All right, that's fine, I'll sit down and Ni and I will get acquainted." So Ni and I tried to communicate for awhile in her room. She was young but very nice. As we heard the door close, and knew Susan was going to her work, we went to the living room and she prepared a drink or two. All this time I realized that as we were talking to each other, I was speaking English and she was speaking Chinese, but it did not seem to make much difference. I think she knew what her job was. She proceeded under the assumption I knew. It did not take her long to explain it with international language. I can only say that from the four days I thought I was going to spend in jail this entertaining situation was a pleasant reprieve. The entertainment that Susan had provided was outstanding. For awhile I wondered whether I cared if Susan came back. But that was the way it was and I was not going to argue. About 11:30, Ni insisted that I go back to Susan's room and be there when she returned. She was not going to displease the boss. I returned to await her return. Happily, I might say that Susan was exhausted from her rigorous dance and did not insist on any attention.

The following morning, after a nice breakfast and an early morning shot of cognac, which I never miss if I can help it, we went downstairs. Her driver was waiting and she whisked me off on a nice drive around the town to see the sites. Also I think she wanted to get to know me a little better. She asked if I wanted to see the Tigerbalm Garden? Would I really be interested? Did I want to go to bars? Was I interested in fine restaurants in general getting acquainted with Hong Kong? We stopped for some tea and she wanted to see the list I had brought, which was extensive.

She took one look at my list and said, "Oh, my goodness, we've only got a couple of days for this."

I said, "Well, do you want to get started right away?"

She said, "We better, or we certainly won't get this list finished and still have time for you to see as much of Hong Kong as you would like."

I said, "Well, lets go and get started." For the rest of the day we went from one shop to another. I really did not have any doubt that when the arguments ended I had bought everything as cheaply as possible. Later when I compared the prices to the army/navy commissary prices I found that sometimes she had purchased items thirty percent cheaper.

We had a very pleasant day. She made no secret of the fact that in these places she was well-known and that she would receive a commission. She kept a little book of what every store owner owed her. Later she would go back and receive her pay. They let her keep the book and paid her what she claimed.

By the end of the first day we had accomplished quite a bit. The following day we were to see Hong Kong Island.

That evening I said, "Why don't you invite the doctor and Ni and we can go to your club. I want to see you dance, I'll buy dinner, and we will all have a nice time this evening."

I really did not expect to have a good time. I would be entertaining her sister and employee. I found out that Susan worked at an exclusive-looking place. Not just a cabaret, as I suspected, but a ballroom, with large pillars going all the way to the ceiling. Tables and chairs were outside the large dance floor.

I noticed I was the only guest with three beautiful women. But there were several Chinese in attendance who had wives number-one and two with them. This is something that deserves a little bit of comment. It is often the case in Chinese society that wife number-one and wife number-two will appear together in public. It is not exactly legal but it is done. Wife number-two is accepted by wife number-one as the helper, not only to take care of her husband but her home. Of course wife number-one continues to be the boss.

To get back to the pleasant evening ahead of me I found that by letting the girls order I had many surprises. They ordered Chinese soup, large fried mushrooms, prawns, good steak, baked potato and several bottles of Chinese wine. I cannot think of one thing about that dinner that I disliked. I took my turn dancing with each of the ladies, until it was time for Susan to go to work.

I watched this fire dance, with fascination. She used two batons that sprayed lighter fluid, different colors. From time to time she would appear to be a human torch. This dance lasted almost 40 minutes. I did not see how she could do it. I am sure that she was working just as hard as if she was running ten kilometers. The dance included acrobatics and movements that were extemely impressive. I am sure she could have made a living anywhere in the world. I wondered how she kept her long black hair from burning.

The evening ended about 12:00 and we all went back to the apartment. Susan was fatigued. She asked me if it was all right, again, if Ni took over her duties. I did not have any problem with that.

The next day was probably one of the more interesting days I remember. We had lunch at a Chinese restaurant on the water, and watched the san pans and junks move about the bay.

Quickly, to my surprise, my buying list was complete. I do not know how much of the $4,000 remained, but it was considerably more than I would have had without my guide. I bought a one-carat diamond at about a third of the U.S. price. It carried the standard guarantee that ninety percent of the money would be returned if anyone in the world would sell an equal diamond cheaper. I carried that diamond in my pocket in a little sack for five months before bringing it to the United States. I did not know what else to do with it. I figured that if someone wanted it badly enough he would have to get me before he could get the diamond. In that case, what difference would it make.

This was a nice day and Susan's job as a guide was done with the greatest of sophistication. I never had the feeling that I was being escorted by a call girl. She sold her services. I never felt she was doing anything except living the way she wished. I do hope readers understand that in different areas of the world the social structure is such that Susan had a fairly honorable job.

There was an excellent dinner prepared for us when we returned to the apartment that evening. Sister Doc, as I had been calling her, was in attendance, as was Ni. This evening I got a little help with translations so I could understand what Ni was saying. We laughed about getting along without English on one side and without Chinese on the other. It was an interesting evening. Susan excused herself at about the same time as usual, and as she left the bedroom she told me to enjoy myself and have a few drinks. I do not know whether this evening was arranged by the girls, but I suspect it was. That evening Ni was not feeling her best, and also asked to be excused. This was fine with me. I had been doing quite well.

I was not to get away that easily.

About the time Ni disappeared, Sister Doc showed up. Within a few minutes it was obvious that Sister Doc was interested in entertainment that evening. The doctor was not what you would call a beauty but she did have qualities that neither of the other girls had. Her education had taken her a lot farther in English, and her studies had made her a great deal more worldly. I remember that she insisted I say nothing to Susan. I do not think I had to say anything. Susan knew what her sister was up to. But of course I agreed, as a gentleman should, and Sister Doc proceeded to show me her room.

The doctor was not a sophisticated lover, by any means, a little wilder than I imagined, but then again the doctor was not a professional entertainer. I had the feeling that only occasionally she took advantage of her sister's customers.

Like Ni, she insisted that I be in her sister's room when she returned. That night Susan came in with a little different attitude and I do not think we got to sleep until about four.

Next day we went to the beach. They had a nice beach, and behind it a pool. I think this is what the girls enjoyed, not going to the beach so much as to the pool. It was sort of the wind-down of a three or four-day stay. Everyone was having fun, there were waiters everywhere bringing drinks, and it was a continental atmosphere. There were quite a few British diplomats or executives in the crowd. Most everyone was discreet enough not to say hello to Susan, but they knew her. At least I had the feeling that quite a few knew her. Discretion in that part of the world is a respect given to everyone.

All of the items I had ordered had been delivered to the airfield. I was skeptical that everything would arrive on time for the plane. I arrived early to pay my respects to the commandant and thank him for the four days in Hong Kong. Susan had arranged to come to the airport to see me off. In fact Susan brought Ni and her sister. All of the girls were treating me as if I was the only person in the world. Of course they were good people and since they saved me so much money I was able to give them a generous tip. I left the doctor in charge of the tip. Apparently they had all been pleased with that arrangement. I could talk to the doctor in many ways, a lot easier than Ni or Susan. The driver arrived with all the packages, and Susan was there, very businesslike, checking off the list, ensuring I got each item. We had about an hour before the plane would take off. She had arranged this so that if there had been a mistake she could go back to the store an be sure we got what we had paid for.

This is an extremely efficient operation and I had the feeling that it was something they did every week.

With all three girls of my apartment to see me off, you can imagine what the crew of the air craft had to say after seeing this fanfare walking me to the airplane. And I must admit it wasn't my worst day of the Vietnam War.

## AFTER VIETNAM

I left Vietnam in 1969, for the Defense Language Institute to study Spanish, and then was sent to command the Third Civil Affairs Group in Panama. In this job I felt in some ways my experiences in Vietnam might work to the advantage of the people of Latin America. I became a friend to General Somoza and the Somoza family, when I was commander of the earthquake disaster relief effort to Nicaragua which devastated Managua beginning Christmas eve of 1972. I suppose commanding the disaster relief was the high point of my military career. Readers Digest published an article on the actions of my unit and I received a meritorious service medal and a personal commendation from President Nixon. There was talk about a promotion, but action stopped at rumor stage. "Close but no cigar", only a medal and commendation. General Somoza referred to me as the Salvador of Managua, sometimes to my embarrassment.

I retired in 1974 after the Vietnam and Panama assignments, as lieutenant colonel unqualified to be promoted to full colonel because of the years spent in Vietnam, which had taken me past the age for Command and General Staff School at Ft. Leavenworth.

For ten years there after I sought to rebuild an old yacht, living in the Caribbean and exploring the jungle areas of Panama and Latin America. Many times I helped in the search for lost foreigners or Americans, at the request of one embassy or another. This life in the Caribbean was to end as my concern grew that the U.S. Government was not getting our POWs home from Southeast Asia. I worked on the POW problem in my mind and eventually returned to the United States to conduct my own investigation.

I had really taken up a new profession as a private investigator and been licensed in Indiana by the Superintendent of State Police. My Indiana cases were mostly uninteresting and routine. Mainly I only took "out of state" or international cases, and most of them were searching for lost Americans in Latin America. It was a carryover from the days in Panama where I assisted the American consuls. These reflections brought me up to date.

## THE RETURN (Cont.)

Shortly afterward, the boat owner and his son suddenly became quiet and I then saw the reason. There was some kind of boat with a spotlight playing on the water about 1½ miles ahead. We headed for cover on the Thai side of the river, and pulled in close to a high bank. Some brush was quickly pulled over the boat. The Lao patrol boat was close now and there was talking. I could not understand a word but the old fisherman and his son were whispering something. The boat passed close to the Thai side but soon was out of sight.

The old fisherman and his son stayed quiet another fifteen or twenty minutes and then told me the Lao River Force was looking for someone in the river they thought may be a refugee or the body of one. The boat had come close enough that we could hear them talking and see the K-47 rifles and what looked to me like American .30 caliber. I was not really sure in the dark and only when their light was reflecting back on their boat could see anything of the men on board.

The patrol boat went north upriver and we quickly got underway south. Nothing was said and we all paddled, the old man steering. Then they stopped suddenly and I listened to catch what slight noise caught their attention. I heard nothing, and then it came; ahead of us was a log, and the wind and current was pushing water against it, or so I thought. As we got closer we could see that there were also two people in the water. One on each side of the log. One was a girl with long black hair that reflected the moonlight, the other a young man. These were the ones the patrol boat had been looking for. The shore of the Thai side was 200 yards away. My worst fears then came to life; the lights were coming back. Our boat was not large enough for two more so we pulled the girl on board. I slipped over the side and with the young Lao pushing hard and both the old fisherman and his son paddling we began to make good time. The girl had pulled a waterlogged pack in the boat with her. I guessed it contained their only possessions. It was no contest, and we made the Lao side before the patrol boat was able to cover half the distance. It seemed to be one of our old commando boats. They had not seen us and we pulled into a small river and tied the boat to a tree. Then we made our way inland and stopped to rest. The fisherman stated flatly the next morning that he had had enough of this trip and not bargained for that kind of trouble. I paid him and his son, gave the young couple 100 bott, and we all went our separate ways.

I did, however, have a chance to question them about white men in Laos. They had seen none, but told me that the uncle of the girl had come across the mountains from the Vietnam border last year and told of seeing a prison camp with ten or twenty foreigners.

Next day I found another boat and proceeded. I obtained an interpreter by speaking to a priest. He was fair, and also believed there was something to the POW issue. We proceeded south for ten more days. Most reports were like those already described. But the point I wish to make is, simply, that there is a lot of information not being sought after, and we will most likely miss the next current report as we have missed many before.

By then I had had enough of the river, and had learned how easy it was for a refugee to cross. But the young couple we assisted would probably not have made it without our help.

I had at least eight separate reports of big white and black foreigners behind the mountains, and I got a feel for just how many locals cross and recross the Mekong River on a daily basis. I learned later that patrol boats are not a common sight on some parts of the river.

I caught a bus to NKP, to discuss the situation further with a refugee official, then back to Udorn and on to Chiang Mai for the three-day water festival. You remain wet for the entire three days, but it must be the happiest time of the year for the Thai. In Chiang Mai, I made a non-profitable visit to another American Consul. How do we get those types to represent the U.S.? I sure hope he does better with the locals than he did with me. He had checked with Bangkok and been notified that I was to be given no help-no assistance, no information. He is the kind that makes the whole POW issue look like a coverup. "Everything is classified so of course I can't discuss it with a mere American civilian citizen", was his attitude. Well, by then I didn't need help. There was no use trying to pass him information. He stated that he really did not want anything I had learned, because he would "have to spend time checking it out and it wouldn't be good any way if I'd got a hold of it."

By now I felt in many ways that the fact-finding mission had accomplished something. It had taken the two months I gave myself. I hoped not to have the delay in returning that I had experienced on the way over. But, then space available travel is all luck. I made a note that I must get a Japanese visa in Bangkok, to go through Okinawa if necessary.

What I had discovered here was much as I had suspected, except more complicated. I found the trip more difficult in respect to language. A lot fewer Thai now speak good or even passable English. Also, the economy of Thailand is changing.

I was talking to one hotel owner's wife, a pretty Thai lady of twenty-one or twenty-two, and she said she had an eight-and-one-half year old daughter and a boy of four. I thought that there was one rich Thai hotel owner who bought himself a "baby doll". She had to be no more than tweleve when married. She did OK, and now helps him by managing the hotel. I asked her about the restaurant and she said it was very expensive and largely used by rich Thai and visiting tourists. Live music and twenty to thirty girls for entertainment these days meant money. Quite a change from the days I could afford the best in Southeast Asia on captain's pay. Frankly the Thai food is OK but I had lost my desire for the "Asian Brown", as we used to refer to Thai girls. As in most areas of Southeast Asia there is the working class of girls and somewhere in the social structure is the bar girl or "hostess", as they like to be called now. Some must make good money, most are able to purchase a small Honda. A Honda 100, new, costs $600 cash, or about $1,000 in payments for one year.

In summary of the POW issue, based on information I collect: 1) there is a built in delay, which I feel can be corrected; 2) a rescue reaction plan is needed; 3) authority to react should be delegated below presidential level if possible; 4) the Lao resistance movement should be encouraged to help the POW operation and direct attention to patroled prison areas; 5) full U.S. air support should be available for the mission; 6) the entire evolution of intelligence must be shortened to an Entebe reaction schedule, not a Son Tey operation; 7) all effort should be coordinated at one center, commanded by a general officer authorized to act on justifiable cause, with the sole purpose of a POW recovery, not just an office to process and eliminate intelligence. As it is now, the Embassy will give the POW issue little attention.

Having decided to spend the Water Festival in Chaing Mai, I knew there would be nothing else I could do for three or four days. In Chiang Mai, I would feel better, being in a larger town where I was not the only "Flong". I had been the only white man in many of the border towns. The bus was crowded, but a lot better than the local buses I had been taking. I had not lost any gear. I had given some things away and retired an old bag and bought another. Although I worked my excess clothing down, I still felt overloaded for the heat. I had just forgotten how to travel in Southeast Asia - a few shirts, two pairs of pants, shorts and that was all, maybe an extra pair of shoes, together with toilet articles, camera, good knife, compass, and binoculars (depending on the task). The best possible way is to carry nothing except a stack of money, and buy local.

The local radio was setting the scene for celebration, as Chinese-Thai music goes on and on. Once in a while I heard an American country-western translated into Thai or Lao. Of course I could only catch a word or two. I was watching the ceiling fan as I wrote and as many times before it took me back to Vietnam days, but this visit was different. Americans here were different, and I was a real foreigner, from a different age, maybe a different era. Besides, on this trip I was the outsider officially. Everything I needed to know seemed to fall into a classified area. It was no wonder the American public had no confidence that "everything is being done that is possible".

As I reflected over the past month, I could not lose my feeling of near success-as I made my way down the MeKong River, speaking to someone in each boat about Americans on the far side of the river. I had kept well to the Thailand side, but was tempted to look for a small river on the far side to make my way inland. But that would have been foolish. At a distance, with my Ho Chi Minh-type Chinese hat and black pants and white shirt I caused no notice, but a close inspection of any kind would have ended such a guise. Besides, where would I start? The POW solution must come from information that would lead to release or rescue.

How many were left? How many had survived 6,000 days and nights of captivity in poor accomodation, with poor food, maybe without medical or dental care? Germans who survived Siberia proved it could be done for up to twenty years.

I had been changing my perspective: the idea of the next trip was firm, but it was the how that I was wondering about. The language problem was greater. It seemed that my best bet was to press for better intelligence and the shortening of processing.

The basic premise, "It's just a matter of time and money", is sound. On my return I would urge that a standing offer for information leading to recovery of each POW, and $1,000,000 on delivery C.O.D.

I feel strongly, after talking to two resistance leaders, that the possibility of using the resistance is not being exploited. We are working with the resistance, but locked into State Department and CIA security. I should have been briefed. If I can dig this deep, so can any other good detective or reporter.

My job for now was over. I now had to get back to the U.S. The system had too many built-in delays. My return to Bangkok was uneventful, except that I baby-sat one of Germany's twenty-one-year-old little rich girls. She was too self-centered to be interesting, but was company during the twelve-hour bus ride. At least she spoke excellent English-a change from even the Americans I had been dealing with.

Back at the Malaysia Hotel I made the initial preparation to return to the U.S., or at least the Philippines. Friday would be a big day-the Japanese Consul, U.S. Embassy, JCRC? I went to JUSMAGTHAI to mail a letter informing Monika and Mark I was leaving Thailand.

Getting a Japanese visa meant standing in line with at least sixty people for two hours, then being ordered back the following morning to find I had been granted a transit visa good for five years, but only fifteen days at a time. It would do, and only cost $8 taxi fare for the two trips.

I briefed Lieutenant Colonel Mathers of JCRC for about two hours, then had lunch with him and his wife. She is the Vietnamese woman who had been accused of being an intellectual communist and possibly a spy for North Vietnam.

Paul Mather is a modest man who will probably never be promoted to full colonel, in his opinion, because of these allegations. He has been at JCRC a long time and I feel has been overrun by a lot of attention and pressure from above. He recognized each problem I brought up. It was hard to read his reaction. He did state that he felt all my comments should go forward to Washington just as I explained them. This was somewhat of a surprise. I left the embassy, suddenly, because of a warning of a small demonstration on the street outside. I was escorted quickly to the front gate, my ID card returned, and I was on my way to JUSMAG to sign up for a flight on Friday, if something happened to my Tuesday flight with Air France. I wanted to get back to the Philippines and to Clark AFB. My job was done for the present. At least I had established myself as an import-export dealer who might want to go into Laos for business next year. I was hopeful that my experience with customs would be better than before.

As my Thailand investigation closed I kept wondering why I had to come 12,000 miles to point out a basic intelligence problem.

Much to my surprise the trip out of Thailand was easy, and customs sent an agent with me all the way to baggage check-in. I really got more attention than necessary. The Air France plane left on time. It was a very pleasant flight to Manila. I passed customs with no problems and boarded a bus to the Manila bus station, missed the Angles bus, and got on one to Sanfrando. There I caught a jeepney to Clark AFB, without much cost, about $2 total-with two buses, 1 jeepney-and then $1.70 from gate to Steve's house. I do not believe the people on base should pay four or five times the off-base taxi rate. Some contract was renewed, with no thought of local wages and cost, and the U.S. airman and his family are still paying.

I had a pleasant two days, but then I got word that OSI, the Air Force "Office of Special Investigations", wanted me detained at the airport. I was supposed to be carrying classified papers. I was not going to make it easy for some Air Force policeman to spoil my return to the U.S. with a lot of questions and delays. I left Clark the next morning by bus for Manila. I did not understand this effort to detain me, and search my baggage for "items of interest". Was it just harassment? I knew I would have to wait a week for a flight space available and this order to detain me just made me angrier than hell. Besides the word detain had an indefinate ring.

I relaxed that afternoon in Manila around the hotel pool. I wondered how far the DIA would go. Why would they think my report important, unless I was right in all my conclusions? Somehow they had gotten the word--maybe through Mather of JCRC. I did not know. If I could get out of the Philippines I had it made, but there was the airport ahead of me. Security measures were toughened. I did feel the guns would be an issue if they were found. But what I didn't know was that the new President, Mrs. Aquino, had put a death order out on anyone carrying weapons. If I felt it was that big of an issue I would of given them to Steve or thrown them away. They were in a box, sealed by Thai customs, but would the American OSI be sharp enough to have the Philippines police stop me, and if so then what? I would run out of money with a long delay. They might get me put away in a Philippine jail. I wondered about what kind of people we must have working in DIA or Air Force OSI. I had done nothing illegal, but that does not always mean some charge could not be put together.

I had done the best I could, and must return to the real world and take care of other business. I drafted a report to President Reagan.

The return from Manila to El Retiro (my estate on the Tippecanoe River) was via Korea, then a direct flight to O'Hare in Chicago. The flight was a refugee flight of Southeast Asians and Philipino immigrants. Of the 542 passengers I was the only U.S. citizen.

All went well, except that U.S. Customs must have been alerted to give me a real inspection. I could hardly believe it, but the 541 refugees and immigrants passed customs with only casual inspection. One and a half hours after they had all passed, I was still being detained by a "lady" of customs. She did understand the law that I was only required to declare my guns, not answer personal questions about their use, but questions persisted until I asked to see her supervisor. Only then, after his arrival and some threats from me to take legal action about the whole situation, was I allowed to repack and pass. I had missed two buses south to Indiana, and it was approaching 2200 hours when I found another.

I am glad there was really nothing in my old bag she could pick on. She tried to confiscate a cobra skin I had bought for a friend, only to find it was not on the endangered species list. I really did not expect this petty trouble. I was going to give our government a lot of hell over the POW issue. But who was behind this harassment?

I had done what I could, without official sanction or authority. For me the Vietnam War was over. The thought felt good for about one minute, and then I knew that as long as the POWs are there, the war will never end for me. Somehow there must be a way to get them out.

I wrote a report to President Reagan which I've enclosed in the following pages. I sent copies to about 75 Senators and Congressman and I also sent the whole miserable POW story to my old commander, General Westmoreland so that he might be able to discuss in detail the POW issue.

## REPORT TO REAGAN

The following report was sent to President Reagan by Lt. Col. Simons, Ret. USA.

REFERENCE: My letters of March 1986 and previous communications.

**1 MAY 1986**

Mr. President: To my great dismay and regret, I must inform you up front---there will be no POWs recovered from Laos as long as the present system of intelligence collection is being used.

The POW problem has simply lasted too long and our intelligence methods have decayed. Intelligence lags or delays of a basic nature go unrecognized and uncorrected.

I no longer suspect a "cover-up" but instead an assembly of stupid mistakes and misguided policies that have evolved over the years since the Vietnam War and casts great doubt on our intelligence capability to collect information in Southeast Asia. This fact finding trip brought to light some of our real problems.

After several weeks of extensive field investigation, I'm more than ever convinced live American prisoners exist in Laos. Information is available.

I base this conclusion on numerous discussions with the Thai Police at various levels, Lao Resistance leaders, boat people along the MeKong River, smugglers, U.S. expatriates living in the area, Thai officer of General Rank, U.S. Consuls, and countless Thai and Lao civilians. To my surprise the following facts and information were not difficult to uncover. However, I did spend several weeks traveling along the Lao/Thai border to insure my findings were correct.

All U.S. officials in Thailand were courteous to me. However, I received no official help or briefings. The investigation was conducted from the ground up and although I was not required to debrief, I chose to discuss my conclusions and recommendations with Lt. Col. Paul Mather of the Joint Casualty Resolution Center (JCRC) in Bangkok, before I left Thailand. I hoped to move him to actions which might improve the POW situation. However, I doubt he has the authority to take real action to correct the problems. The problems go beyond JCRC charter and in some cases concern U.S. Policy or at least State Department Policy.

It first must be understood that 98% of all information, concerning the possibility of POW's, comes from refugees. However, there is a built in delay in the initial intelligence collection from the refugees. A refugee makes his way to the Thai side of the MeKong River, usually by small boat. He immediately tries to become known to the Thai immigration or turns himself into the police. That's the safest course for him. The Thai Police question him and builds his file for an average of about 30 days before he is turned over to the refugee camp where eventually he will be questioned by an American official. This period of delay can be up to 60 days. At the refugee camp the State Department contracted JVA (Joint Volunteer Action) people who are very dedicated, but are not intelligence trained interrogators. They ask "trip wire" questions about any Americans seen in

Laos and forward the information faithfully to JCRC through the U.S. Consul. They understand the importance of getting the information forward, but what they get will already be out-dated. Thirty day old information precludes any reasonable rescue mission as a practical operation.

When I confronted one U.S. Consul with this fact he became very defensive and denied the truth of my allegation or the accuracy of my information and stated some American field representative will see the refugee within the first ten to fifteen days. His statement, though possibly well meaning, did not check out as I double checked this situation with various police in different areas. After confirming my findings as in fact true, I reported this to Lt. Col. Mather (JCRC) in Bangkok, who made no effort to deny this delay was possible.

We agreed that a new attempt to coordinate with the Thai Police at all levels must be made but since the U.S. no longer has Police Advisors it would be difficult to get the Thai Police's full cooperation from top to bottom. The only way we'll ever get current "yesterday" type information is to have the police ask the critical question during the refugees first interrogation.

Although I'm convinced live Americans are being held in Laos, currently, the Hard Proof will never be produced in time for a rescue mission to be feasible.

But, the problem of current information then has other ramifications. Information passed to JCRC in Bangkok, is passed on the Hawaii office of JCRC and not evaluated "on the spot". It's then turned over some how to Defense Intelligence Agency (DIA) and the real evaluation starts. A report is criticized, cross checked and massaged to death until any hope of an "Entebee" type rescue is lost forever---if in fact one ever existed. I'm sure all involved in this situation will deny, side step and bluster around about me "not having all the facts", but now you know the truth--disgraceful and tragic as it is.

## ANOTHER POINT THAT NEEDS A CLOSER LOOK

Although we have a Special Forces Unit in Okinawa capable of organizing a rescue if furnished current information and given the contingency mission, I failed to find the link between the Special Forces Unit and any one principal person in Thailand for such a mission. In fact I could find no one who had the sole mission or concern of a POW recovery. Certainly if this issue is one of the Presidents ten top priorities there should be one officer with an appropriate staff, mission oriented to press full time for a POW recovery.

The above lag in intelligence would not exist with such an American Unit or Command and if a lag did exist there would be someone to fire. As it is now all concerned "on the ground" have other jobs which take the majority of their time--and there is no one with the capability to evaluate immediate information and request Presidential approval for a rescue--if it was possible to ever get a "yesterday" type report--which as of 21 April, 1986 there was no possibility. There is a lot of information available from smugglers and border crossers who are not now being asked questions by anyone on a regular basis. You see: **all is not being done that could be done.**

All concerned have principal work which takes the majority of their time and the POW issue is of interest, but in most cases not even a secondary interest.

The U.S. Ambassador in Thailand can hardly be held accountable "after all the problem is really in Laos, Vietnam or Cambodia".

The head of mission in Laos can hardly run a covert operation the lady probably is not trained for that mission and "our fragile relationship with Lao would not survive much stress".

The Army Defense Attache, in Bangkok, told me it was not his concern, although he was always interested, but not to expect him to come up country if I had a real hot prospect.

The U.S. Consuls, in the field offices, have a vast multitude of problems to handle. The POW issue is of great interest but little time can be devoted to it.

The contracted JVA personnel, hired to ask questions, are all dedicated people, but their job is to process refugees. They are not intelligence trained for interrogation. They faithfully pass along information if it surfaces, but admittedly 30 days late.

The other refugee officials have a large number of people to process and thats their main concern.

The U.S. Military Advisors JUSMAGTHAI have a passive interest, "It's not really our business".

Lt. Col. Mather, JCRC, is devoted to both the POW reports and the MIA, but does not have a section to evaluate intelligence. And in addition of not having an intelligence staff, he says he is not an intelligence officer.

The point is there is no one responsible for a coordination center, which is required to make a rescue mission feasable and make direct request for Presidential approval if and when the opportunity exists. The recovery of our dead is important to the families of the MIA. The recovery of our POWs is of great importance to this Nation.

## ANOTHER INCREDULOUS FACT EXISTS

There is no on going offer to officers or civil authorities of Vietnam, Laos or Cambodia on an individual basis, to induce them on their own to defect and bring a live American POW with them. In return they would receive "C.O.D.", U.S. asylum, a substantial reward and relocation somewhere in the world. No such offer is now made officially, yet we bought our first Russian M.I.G. from North Korea with such an offer---and I remember several years ago we obtained a Soviet aircraft and tank with such an offer. The President is justified to reconsider the "no reward policy". This type of a reward is not a ransom and would not be offered to adventurers or mercenaries. The official U.S. "Blood Chit" was issued to our fliers and Special Units in Vietnam. This was a piece of silk material overprinted with the U.S. flag and made it clear in several languages that anyone who would get one of our men out safely would be rewarded. The reward system eventually will get a taker and show U.S. determination to recover our POW's. In reality I don't feel this Policy reflects our Presidents feelings. It does reflect some "Career Diplomats" approach. "The solution might cause some problems, therefore it's not diplomatically recommended".

The reward system will work and the POW issue will be clear before the world and be a fact instead of conjecture, supposition and assumption. If it works it's justified and if not the POW's are none the worse off.*

## FURTHER FACTS BEARING ON THE SITUATION

I talked to some leaders of the Lao Resistance (no names). They are being told by some "U.S. types" that only U.S. criminals who escaped U.S. confinement in Vietnam or deserters from the U.S. services married to Vietnamese or Lao women are in Laos. I find a problem with this...the figures just don't match up...But, the fact remains the Lao Resistance may be a useful tool in the POW issue if we used extreme care. In my opinion U.S. money is being channeled for their use and the POW issue should benefit if possible.

There seems to be another poor official policy that is counter productive to the POW issue. This is perpetrated by the State Department once again and its effect on the active servicemen, veterans and the public in general, is bound to also appear as some kind of cover up attempt.

The policy is to discredit in any way possible those who take action or speak out on the POW issue such as: Lt. Col. Ret. Bo Gritz, Maj. Ret. Mark Smith, M/Sgt. Ret. McIntire, Soldier of Fortune Scott Barns, witness before Congress against DIA who has seen, photographed and recorded at long distance American POW's in Laos.

All of the above are now being described as: unstable, not reliable, liars, not to be trusted, dishonest, self serving, adventurers, publicity seekers, mercenaries, and it goes on and on.

Lt. Col. Howard, Congressional Medal winner, so far is not subjected to the same type of character assassination, but I expect it. (I hate to think how I'll be labeled.)

This sorry and miserable State Department effort does not go well with the 28,000,000 U.S. Veterans now representing (with families) 36% of U.S. voters.

Best leave the national heroes alone; Distinguished Service Cross, Silver Star and Medal of Honor winners. It is true they don't always fit a common mold, but to degrade, demean and discredit them is a political mistake.

* In 1988 2.4 million was being offered by the American Def. Institute. Hopefully as a direct result of this report.

## ANOTHER POINT

Over classification of much POW/MIA material also increases the chance for the public to yell cover up. The truth is any good intelligence officer of any country can put together extensive information during such an investigation as I've just made. The usefulness of any security classification (except names and places) is highly questionable. Also, a cloak of security keeps the public from being informed of all this administration is doing.

## ANOTHER UNBELIEVABLE SITUATION WHICH HAS EVOLVED

It seems that on the POW issue, if an informer wants to be paid for his service or information or risks, he is automatically dishonest and untrustworthy and not be believed or dealt with.

The services of an informer or spy do not come free. We have paid spies and informers for over 200 years. Why stop now? What makes this POW intelligence effort that much different? This approach also makes the public wonder about the sincerity of the DIA. The real question is, if the DIA's approach has not worked in the past ten years, why should it work the next ten years, and that will conclude our POW effort because "Then there will be none, our POWs will have died in captivity."

When I previously wrote to President Reagan I stated "I didn't feel all was being done that could be done". After that I made the required trip to Southeast Asia and conducted an extensive investigation to insure I'd done all I could do. I truly hope this report will help to obtain more official action and correct some of these problems which preclude POW recoveries.

**Editors Note:**

The recommendation section of this report is not published at this time to preclude compromise of possible future action on the part of Government Action Agencies or civilian groups. However, a POW/MIA Presidential or Congressional Commission was strongly suggested, and the report ends with a comment on this proposed Commission.

## CIVIL COMMISSION A POSSIBLE SOLUTION

The Civil Commission, to be headed by Ross Perot, Dallas Industrialist, now endorsed by over 150 Congressmen, will let the current POW effort transcend the Presidency and preclude a slow down in the effort when President Reagan leaves office. This recommendation must receive more serious consideration. **(By 1988 neither a congressional nor a presidential commission materialized.)**

## RESULTS

A result of this report and other pressure brought on this administration by POW Activists all over the U.S., by 1 March 1987, the Government had taken the following action:

1. The Defense Intelligence Agency increased from 18 to 41 the analysts working on the POW issue.

2. The Staff of the Joint Casualty Resolution Center, JCRC, had been increased from 14 to 22 (12 in Bangkok according to Col. Hill, Office of the Secretary of Defense.)

3. Although a Presidential Commission was not formed by 1 March 1987 the President has given Ross Perot sanction to take certain actions to recover the POW in Southeast Asia. (Not confirmed.)

4. The issue of Intelligence delays is being looked into by the National Security Council.

These results seem to justify the actions of the writer, but the problems have not ended and will not end until the POW are recovered.

Certainly the governmental increase in the staff working on this issue attests that many in the Government now believe we have POW in Southeast Asia.

The pressure on Washington must continue until the statement "all is being done that can be done" is a true fact.

Almost two years after the report the POWs were still not recovered and every effort of the Reagan administration seems to have failed.

However, the reward I recommended was established by over twenty congressmen, senators and prominent POW/MIA activist through the American Defense Institute. The reward in 1988 stands at 2.4 million in gold for any indigenous Lao, Vietnamese or Cambodian who will defect with two of our men.

The Joint Casualty Resolution Center in Bangkok was upgraded with personnel and the Central Intelligence Laboratory in Hawaii revamped. The Defense Intelligence agencies again increased personnel in their analysis section and a renewed effort was made by the white house to speed up normalization of relations with Vietnam. In 1987, General Vessey was sent as an envoy to Vietnam and another envoy was sent to Laos.

All these actions, which I feel I had some part in influencing, have failed to produce even one of our POWs by early 1988.

The sleeping tiger of this country, the American people, has yet to take anything beyond a passive interest in this forgotten battalion of American men and women.

I hope my next return will be with a plan, adequate financing, correct updated intelligence information, logistic support as required and the good wishes and sponsorship of my government.

But regardless of this dream, there will be another return.

During these two years General Vessey had become the Presidential envoy, but he had by-in-large been ineffective as far as the POWs are concerned.

Laos was still the best bet for locating our POWs, possibly over 200 of them but negotiations were not being aggressively pursued.

The League of families, Gen. Vessey and U.S.Government had only been able to get Vietnam to send a few bodies of U.S. servicemen back. Some of these failed to pass forensic examination and many are still thought to be -indigenous. In the last group only 30 of 70 bodies were identified by October 1988.

By the end of November 1988, in general the POW issue was faultering and the 40 eyewitnesses whose testimony couldn't be shaken by the DIA (Defense Intelligence Agency) were being ignored and some of these discredited.

The POW issue seemed to be getting worse. The following Associated Press article appeared throughout the country in October 1988.

**U.S. POW-MIA section head says no Americans are still being held**

LOUSIVILLE, Ky. (AP) - There is no credible evidence that Americans are still being held against their will from the Vietnam War despite persistent reports to the contrary, according to the head of the Defense Department's POW-MIA effort.

Army Col. Joseph A. Schlatter, chief of the special office for prisoners-of-war and missing in action for the Defense Intelligence Agency, said there has been some progress in the work to recover the remains of American servicemen from Southeast Asia.

Schlatter acknowledged there have been thousands of reports received by his office about Americans still being held against their will in Vietnam or elsewhere in Southeast Asia.

"I have to tell you, speaking both professionally and personally, I don't see the evidence of it," Schlatter said Monday during an address to the 70th annual American Legion convention.

A delegation is scheduled to leave Friday for Vietnam to discuss technical aspects of a search for the 2,393 Americans who are unaccounted for from the 14-year involvement by the United States in the Southeast Asian war, Schlatter said.

Schlatter said the delegation hopes to resolve questions with the Vietnamese government about the makeup of a possible search team, locations to search and other technical issues.

A final resolution to the nagging problems of prisoners of war and missing in action is up to the Vietnamese, Schlatter said.

"The answer is not in my files. The answer is in Hanoi," Schlatter said.

There are remains being held in the Hanoi area right now. "The only question is where and how many," Schlatter said.

One possible explanation for the reports of Americans being seen would be a deserter who voluntarily stayed in Vietnam. Such was the case with former Marine Robert Garwood, who deserted, but returned to the United States and was court-martialed.

There are 22 people listed in his office records as deserters.

"If one more Bobby Garwood popped up we wouldn't be surprised," Schlatter said.

Garwood has said he saw other Americans in Vietnam, but he has been inconsistent in his story, Schlatter said. The results of a complete investigation of the information provided by Garwood should be released to Congress in the next three months.

Schlatter's comments notwithstanding, many in this country believe there are prisoners of the Vietnam War still being held.

(Article continues with questionable references to the POW issue.)

## The Following Passage Seems To Apply

War is a violent and terrible time but not the worst thing that can happen to a country or a man.

The decayed moral and patriotic feelings of those who think nothing is worth a war are worse.

When personal and financial safety are the only things a man can think of and when he takes no responsibility for his freedom or being free, he is a despicable person, a cringing creature who has no chance in this world....unless he is defended by better men or women than himself.

He will never know what a man has never lived until he has almost died in the defense or service of his homeland.

A feeling the "Protected" will never have as he safely stands behind his betters and counts his political or financial gains.

But, something worse than that man is a political group that will not recover and bury the MIA dead or bring home the POW from a war that was never declared.

(My expansion of a thought expressed by John Stuart Mill written in the Eighteen Hundreds.)

It's true "YOU DON'T CRY FOR HEROES" but as a nation we must cry out about this national disgrace. We must not let the POW stay in enemy hands, forever. They will all die soon.

But obviously we can not depend on the U.S. Government and present initiates to free them.

It's time to make a real plan. This time it won't be just an investigation along the Lao border.

**F.D.S.**

**NOT THE END**

Enclosed:
POW List
Lessons that should have been learned in Vietnam.

## MIA'S & POW'S
## CATEGORIES OF DEGREES OF INFORMATION
## ENEMY KNOWLEDGE OF MIA's & POW's

| CATEGORY | DEGREE OF KNOWLEDGE |
|---|---|
| 1 | Confirmed |
| 2 | Suspect |
| 3 | Doubtful |
| 4 | Unknown |
| 5 | Unrelated |
| CVL. | Civilian |

### CATEGORY 1-CONFIRMED KNOWLEDGE

This category includes 166 individuals who were:

A. Identified by the enemy by name.

B. Identified by reliable sources, received from releasee/escapees, or

C. Reported by highly reliable intelligence sources

D. Identified through analysis of all-source intelligence.

### CATEGORY 2-SUSPECT KNOWLEDGE

This category includes 1122 individuals who were:

A. Involved in the same incidents as individuals reported in category 1.

B. Lost in areas or under such conditions that they may reasonably be expected to be known by the enemy.

C. Connected with an incident which was discussed but not identified by name in the enemy news media; or

D. Probably identified through analysis of all-source intelligence.

### CATEGORY 3-DOUBTFUL KNOWLEDGE

This category includes 342 individuals whose loss incident is such that is is doubtful that the enemy would have knowledge of the specific individuals (e.g., aircrews lost over water or remote areas).

### CATEGORY 4-UNKNOWN KNOWLEDGE

This category includes 429 individuals.

A. Whose time and place of incident are unknown (e.g. aircrews members downed at unknown locations or ground personnel that were separated from their units at an unknown time or place), and,

## CATEGORY 5-CATEGORY UNRELATED TO DEGREE OF ENEMY KNOWLEDGE

This category includes 434 individuals whose remains have been determined to be non-recoverable as outlined in Department of the Army Technical Manual 10-286, January 1964, Section 39.

Data provided by the Defense Intelligence Agency
January 20, 1982

This list is the best available in early 1988. About 150 bodies have been returned by Vietnam and only time will tell which of the list may be crossed off.

The category number is given for each individual after his name:

Abrams, Lewis H., 2
Acalotto, Robert J., 2
Ackeley, James H., CVL.
Acosta, Rosario Humberto, 2
Adachi, Thomas Y., 2
Adam, John O., 4
Adams, John R., 2
Adams, Lee A., 2
Adams, Oley N., 5
Adams, Samuel, 1
Adams, Steven H., 4
Adkins, Charles L., 4
Adrian, Joseph D., 4
Aduentio Rudolpho
Ahlmeyer, Heinz Jr., 2
Alberton, Bobby J., 2
Albright, John S., 2
Aldern, Donald P., 2
Aldrich, Lawerence L., 3
Alford, Terry L., 4
Alford, Gerald O., 2
Algaard, Harold L., 2
Allard, Michael J., 2
Allard, Richard M., 4
Allee, Richard K., 3
Allen, Henry L., 4
Allen, Merlin R., 3
Allen, Thomas R., 2
Allen, Wayne C., 4
Alley, Gerald W., 2
Alley, James H., 2
Allgood, Frankie E., 5
Allison, David J., 2
Alloway, Clyde D., 3
Alm, Richard A., 5
Almendariz, Samuel, 3
Altizer, Albert H., 3
Altus, Robert W., 3
Alwan, Harold J., 5
Amesbury, Harry A., 2
Ammon, Glendon, 2
Amos, Thomas H., 2
Amspacher, William H., 2
Anderson, Denis L., 3
Anderson, Gregory L., 3
Anderson, Robert D., 2
Anderson, Thomas E., 5
Anderson, Warren L., 4
Andre, Howard V., 2
Andrews, Stuart M., 3
Andrews, William R., 2
Angell, Marshall J., 3
Angstadt, Ralph H., 3
Anselmo, William F., 4
Anspach, Robert A., 2
Antunano, Gregory A., 2
Apodaca, Victor J., 2
Appelhans, Richard O., 2
Appleby, Ivan D., 2
Ard, Randolph J., 2
Armistead, Steven R., 2
Armond, Robert L., 2
Armstrong, Frank A., 2
Armstrong, John W., 2
Arnold, William T., 2
Ashall, Alian F., 2
Ashby, Clayborn W., 3
Ashby, Donald R., 5
Ashlock, Carlos, 2
Asire, Donald, 2
Asmussen, Glenn E., 5
Aston, Jay S., 2
Austin, Carl B., 3
Austin, Charles D., 2
Austin, Ellis E., 2
Austin, Joseph H., 2
Auxier, Jerry E., 3
Averly, Allen J., 2
Avery, Robert D., 2
Avolese, Paul A., 5
Avore, Malcolm A., 5
Ayers, Darrell E., 2
Ayers, Richard L., 4
Ayers, Gerald F., 2
Ayers, James H., 2
Babcock, Ronald L., 2
Babola, Robert L., 2
Bacik, Vladimir, 2
Backus, Kenneth F., 2
Bader, Arthur E., 4
Badley, James L., 2
Badolati, Frank N., 3
Bailey, Danial
Bailey, John E., 2
Bailey, John H., 5
Bailon, Ruben C., CVL
Baker, Arthur D., 3
Balamott, Michael, 2
Balcom, Ralrh C., 1
Baldridge, John R., 3
Bancroft, William W., 2
Bankowski, Allons A., 1
Bannon, Paul W., 4
Barber, Robert F., 5
Barber, Thomas N., 5
Barden, Howard L., 2
Bare, William O., 2
Barker, Jack L., 2
Barnes, Charles R., 4
Barnett, Charles E., 2
Barnett, Robert R., 3
Barr, John F., 2
Barras, Gregory I., 3
Bartocci, John E., 5
Bates, Paul J., 4
Batt, Michael L., 4
Bauder, James R., 4
Bauman, Richard L., 1
Baxter, Bruce R., 2
Beach, Arthur J., 5
Beals, Charles E., 2
Bebus, Charles J., 2
Becerra, Rudy M., 3
Beck, Edward E., 3
Beck, Terry L., 5
Becker, James C., 3
Beckwith, Harry M., 4
Bednarek, Jonnathen B., 4
Beecher, Quentin R., 5
Beene, James A., 3
Begley, Burriss N., 3
Behnfeldt, Roger E., 2
Belcher, Glenn A., 2
Belcher, Robert A., 2
Belknap, Harry J., 5
Bell, Holly G., 3
Bell, Marvin E., 2
Bell, Richard W., 5
Benedett, Daniel A., 3
Bennefeld, Steven H., 2
Bennett, Harold G., 1
Bennett, Robert E., 3
Bennett, Thomas W., 2
Bennett, William G., 2
Benson, Lee D., 5
Benton, Gregory R., 3
Benton, James A., 5
Berdahl, David D., 3
Beresik, Eugene P., 3
Berg, Bruce A., 2
Berg, George P., 2
Bergevin, Chalres L., 4
Berry, John A., 2
Berube, Kenneth A., 2
Bessor, Bruce C., 4
Beutel, Robert D., 3
Beyer, Thomas J., 3
Bezold, Steven N., 2
Bibbs, Wayne, 2
Biber, Gerald M., 1
Bidwell, Barry A., 5
Bifolchi, Charles L., 2

**Biggs, Earl R., 1**
**Billipp, Norman K., 4**
**Bingham, Klaus, 2**
**Birchim, James D., 3**
**Bird, Leonard A., 2**
**Biscailuz, Robert L., 2**
**Bischoff, John M., 1**
**Bishop, Edward J., 2**
**Bisz, Ralph C., 1**
**Bittenbender, David F., 5**
**Bivens, Herndon A., 1**
**Bixel, Michael S., 5**
**Black, Paul Y., 2**
**Blackburn, Harry L., 1**
**Blackman, Thomas J., 5**
**Blackwood, Gordon B., 2**
**Blair, Charles L., 4**
**Blackenship, Charles H., 5**
**Blanton, Clarence F.**
**Blassie, Michael J., 4**
**Blessing, Lynn, 3**
**Blevins, Lural L., 3**
**Blewett, Alan L., CVL**
**Blogett, Douglas R., 4**
**Blood, henry F., CVL**
**Bloodworth, Donald B., 1**
**Bloom, Darl R., 5**
**Bloom, Richard M., 5**
**Bobe, Raymond E., 4**
**Bodahl, Jon K., 2**
**Bodden, Timothy R., 2**
**Bodenschatz, John E., 2**
**Boffman, Alan B., 2**
**Bogard, Lonnie R., 4**
**Boggs, Paschal G., 5**
**Bogiages, Christos C., 2**
**Bohlig, James R., 5**
**Bohlscheid, Curtis C., 2**
**Bois, Claire R., 5**
**Boles, Warren W., 5**
**Bollonger, Arthur R., 1**
**Bolte, Wayne L., 2**
**Boltze, Bruce L., 2**
**Bond, Ronald D., 4**
**Bond, Ronald L., 4**
**Bookout, Charles F., 2**
**Booth, Gary R., 5**
**Booth, James E., 3**
**Booth, Delmar G., 4**
**Booth, Lawrence R., 4**
**Borah, Daniel, 1**
**Borden, Murry L., 2**
**Borja, Domingo R., 2**
**Boronski, John A., 3**
**Bors, Joseph C., 4**
**Borton, Robert C., 2**
**Bosilevac, Michael, 2**
**Bossio, Galileo F., 2**
**Bossman, Peter R., 3**
**Boston, Leo S., 2**
**Bott, Russell P., 2**
**Bouchard, Michael L., 2**
**Bower, Irvin L., 2**
**Bower, Joseph, 3**
**Bowers, Richard L., 1**
**Bowles, Dwight P., 2**
**Bowman, Frank, 5**
**Bowman, Michael L., 5**
**Boyanowski, John G., 5**
**Boyd, Walter, 3**
**Boyer, Alan L., 4**
**Boyle, William, 2**
**Bradshaw, Robert S., 5**
**Bram, Richard C., 4**
**Branch, James A., 1**
**Brand, Joseph W., 2**
**Brandenbury, Dale, 1**
**Brandt, Keith A., 2**
**Brashear, William J., 2**
**Brasher, Jimmy M., 2**
**Brassfield, Andrew T., 2**
**Brauner, Henry P., 2**
**Brazik, Richard, 2**
**Breeding, Michael H., 5**
**Breiner, Stephen E., 5**
**Bremmer, Dwight A., 5**
**Brennan, Herbert O., 2**
**Brenning, Richard D., 5**
**Brett, Robert A., 4**
**Breuer, Donald C., 2**
**Brice, Eric P., 5**
**Bridges, Jerry G., 4**
**Bridges, Phillip W., 4**
**Briggs, Ernest F., 4**
**Briggs, Ronald D., 4**
**Brigham, Albert, 5**
**Brinckmann, Robert E., 2**
**Broms, Edward J., 2**
**Brooks, John H., 2**
**Brooks, William L., 2**
**Brower, Ralph W., 2**
**Brown, Donald A., 3**
**Brown, Earl C., 2**
**Brown, Edward D., 2**
**Brown, Frank M., 5**
**Brown, George R., 4**
**Brown, Harry W., 4**
**Brown, James A., 4**
**Brown, James W., 5**
**Brown, Joseph O., 2**
**Brown, Robert M., 4**
**Brown, Thomas E., 3**
**Brown, Wayne G., 2**
**Brown, Wilbur R., 4**
**Brown, William T., 2**
**Brownlee, Charles R., 1**
**Brownlee, Robert W., 1**
**Bruch, Donald W., 1**
**Brucher, John M., 2**
**Brunson, Jack W., 3**
**Bucher, Bernard L., 2**
**Buck, Arthur C., 3**
**Buckley, Louis, 2**
**Buckley, Victor, 2**
**Buell, Kenneth R., 4**
**Bullard, William H., 5**
**Buerk, William C., 4**
**Bullock, Larry A., 4**
**Bundy, Norman L., 5**
**Bunker, Park G., 2**
**Burd, Douglas G., 2**
**Burgess, John L., 3**
**Burkart, Charles W., 3**
**Burke, Michael J., 3**
**Burnes, Robert W., 3**
**Burnett, Donald F., 5**
**Burnett, Sheldon J., 2**
**Burnham, Donald D., 4**
**Burnham, Mason T., 2**
**Burns, Frederick J., 1**
**Burns, John R., 2**
**Burns, Michael P., 2**
**Burns, Donald D., 3**
**Busch, Jon T., 2**
**Busch, Elbert W., 1**
**Bush, John R., 2**
**Bush, Robert E., 3**
**Bush, Robert I., 3**
**Bushnell, Brian L., 5**
**Butler, Dewey R., 3**
**Butler, James E., 1**
**Butt, Richard L., 1**
**Byars, Earnest R., 2**
**Bynum, Neils, 2**
**Byrd, Hugh M., 4**
**Byrne, Joseph H., 2**
**Cadwell, Anthony B., 3**
**Caffarelli, Charles J., 3**
**Cairns, Robert A., 5**
**Caldwell, Floyd D., 5**
**Calfee, James H.**
**Calhoun, Johnny C., 2**
**Call, John H., 2**
**Callahan, David F., 5**
**Callahan, Richard J., 2**
**Callies, Tommy L., 2**
**Calloway, Porter E., 2**
**Cameron, Virgil K., 2**
**Campbell, Clyde W., 2**
**Campbell, William E., 2**
**Caniford, James K., 2**
**Canton, Suzan, CVL**
**Canup, Franklin H., 4**
**Cappelli, Charles E., 2**
**Caras, Franklin A., 2**
**Carlock, Ralph L., 2**
**Carlson, John W., 2**
**Carlson, Paul V., 5**
**Carlton, James E., 2**
**Carpenter, Howard B., 3**
**Carpenter, Nicholas M., 2**
**Carpenter, Ramey L., 2**
**Carr, Daniel L., 3**
**Carr, Donald G., 4**
**Carroll, John L., 1**
**Carroll, Patrick H., 2**
**Carroll, Roger, 1**
**Carter, Dennis R., 2**
**Carter, George W., 3**
**Carter, Gerald L., 5**
**Carter, James D., 4**
**Carter, James L., 4**
**Carter, William T., 5**
**Cartwright, Billie J., 4**
**Cartwright, Patrick G., 5**
**Carver, Harry F., 3**
**Case, Thomas F., 2**
**Casey, Donald F., 3**
**Castillo, Richard, 2**
**Cassell, Robin B., 5**
**Castro, Reinaldo A., 5**
**Causey, John B., 5**
**Cavalli, Anthony F.**
**Cavender, James R., 4**
**Cayce, John D., 5**
**Cecil, Alan B.**
**Cestare, Joseph A., 5**
**Chambers, Jerry L., 4**
**Champion, James A., 2**
**Chan, Peter, 5**
**Chandler, Anthony G., 5**
**Chaney, Arthur F., 2**
**Chapa, Armando, 5**
**Chapman, Peter H., 2**
**Chapman, Rodney M., 5**
**Charvet, Paul C., 4**
**Chavez, Gary A., 3**
**Chavira, Stephen**
**Cheney, Joseph C.**

Cherry, Allen S., 2
Chestnutt, Joseph L., 1
Chipman, Ralph J., 2
Chivia, Stephen, 2
Chomel, Charles D., 2
Chomyk, William, 2
Chorlins, Richard D., 2
Christensen, Allen D., 4
Christensen, John M., 3
Christensen, William, 5
Christian, David M., 2
Christiano, Joseph, 4
Christiansen, Eugene F., 4
Christie, Dennis R., 2
Christophersen, Keith A., 4
Chubb, John J., 2
Chung, Yen Binh, CVL
Cichon, Walter A., 2
Clack, Cecil J., 4
Clafin, Richard A., 2
Clapper, Gean P., 4
Clark, James W., CVL
Clark, Jerry P., 2
Clark, John C., 2
Clark, Lawrence, 2
Clark, Phillip S., 2
Clark, Richard C., 2
Clark, Robert A., 2
Clark, Stanley S., 3
Clark, Stephen W., 2
Clark, Thomas E., 2
Clarke, Fred L., 2
Clarke, George W., 1
Claxton, Chalres P., 4
Clay, Eugene L., 4
Clay, William C., 5
Cleary, Peter M., 4
Clem, Thomas D., 3
Cleve, Reginald D., 2
Cline, Curtis R., 3
Clinton, Dean E., 5
Clydesdale, Charles F., 5
Coady, Robert F., 2
Coakley, William F., 3
Coalston, Echol W., 3
Coates, Donaly L., 5
Cobbs, Ralph B., 4
Cocheo, Richard N., CVL
Cochran, Isom C., 4
Cochrane, Deverlon C., 4
Cody, Howard R., 2
Coen, Harry B., 2
Cogdell, William K., 2
Cohron, James D., 2
Cole, Legrande, 2
Cole, Richard M., 2
Coleman, Jimmy L., 3
Collamore, Allan P., 2
Collaio, Raphael L., 2
Collette, Curtis D., 4
Collins, Arnold, 5
Collins, Guy Fletcher, 2
Collins, Richard F., 4
Collins, Theothis, 5
Collins, Willard M., 2
Colombo, Gary L., 5
Coltman, William C., 4
Colwell, William K., 4
Comer, Howard B., 4
Compa, Joseph J., 1
Compton, Franck R., 5
Conaway, Lawrence, 2
Condit, Douglas, 2
Condit, William H., 3
Condrey, George T., 2
Confer, Michael S., 5
Conger, John E., 2
Conklin, Bernard, 2
Corley, Eugene O., 2
Conlon, John F., 3
Conner, Edwin R., 5
Conner, Lorenza, 2
Connor, Charles R., 4
Consolvo, John W., 2
Conway, James B., 3
Cook, Dennis P., 5
Cook, Donald G., 1
Cook, Dwight W., 1
Cook, Glenn R., 4
Cook, Joseph F., 5
Cook, Kelly F., 2
Cook, William R., 4
Cook, Wilmer P., 2
Cooke, Calvin C., 2
Cooley, David L., 4
Cooley, Orville D., 5
Coons, Cherster L., 3
Coons, Henry A., 5
Cooper, William E., 2
Cooper, Daniel D., 5
Cooper, Richard W., 2
Comparct, Joseph B., 2
Copenhover, Gregory S., 3
Copley, William M., 2
Corbitt, Gilland W., 2
Cordova, Robert, 5
Cordova, Sam G., 1
Corefield, Stan L., 5
Corle, John T., 5
Cornelius, Johnnie C., 2
Cornelius, Samuel B., 3
Cornwell, Leroy J., 2
Corna, Joel, 4
Cota, Ernest Keno, 5
Cotten, Larry W., 2
Cozart, Ronert G., 1
Craddock, Randall J., 2
Crain, Carroll O., 5
Cramer, Donald M., 3
Crandall, Gregory S., 2
Craven, Andrew J., 2
Creamer, James E., 2
Crear, Willis C., 2
Creed, Barton S., 2
Cressman, Peter R., 1
Crew, James A., 2
Crews, John H., 2
Cristman, Frederick L., 2
Crockett, William J., 2
Crody, Kenneth L., 3
Crone, Donald E., 2
Crook, Elliott, 3
Cropper, Curtis H., 5
Crosby, Bruce, A., 3
Crosby, Frederick P., 3
Crosby, Herbert C., 4
Crosby, Richard A., 4
Cross, Ariel L., 4
Cross, James E., 3
Crossman, Gregory J., 2
Crosson, Gerald J., 2
Crow, Raymond J., 3
Crowley, John E., 3
Croxdale, Jack L., 4
Crumm, William J., 5
Cruz, Zarlos R., 2
Cruz, Raphaell, 4
Cudlike, Charles J., 3
Cunningham, Carey A., 2
Cunningham, Kenneth, 4
Curlee, Robert L., 1
Curran, Patrick R., 4
Curry, Keith R., 5
Cushman, Clifton E., 2
Cuthbert, Bradley G., 2
Cuthbert, Stephen H., 2
Cutrer, Fred C., 2
Czerwiec, Raymond G., 2
Czerwonka, Paul S., 5
Daffron, Thomas C., 2
Dahill, Douglas E., 2
Dailey, Douglas V., 2
Dale, Charles A., 1
Dallas, Richard H., 5
Dalton, Randall D., 2
Danielson, Benjamin F., 2
Danielson, Mark G., 2
Darcy, Edward J., 4
Dardeau, Oscar M., 2
Darr, Charles E., 2
Davidson, David A., 2
Davies, Joseph E., 2
Davis, Brent E., 2
Davis, Charlie B., 2
Davis, Daniel R., 4
Davis, Donald V., 3
Davis, Edgar F., 2
Davis, Francis J., 5
Davis, Gene E., 4
Davis, James W.
Davis, Richard G., 2
Davis, Robert C., 2
Dawes, John J., 5
Dawson, Daniel G., 2
Dawson, Frank A., 3
Dawson, James V., 4
Day, Dennis I., 5
Dayao, Rolando C., 5
Dayton, James L., 2
Dean, Donald C., 5
Dean, Chalres, CVL
Dean, Michael F., 2
Deane, William L., 1
Deblasio, Raymond V., 5
Debruin, Eugene H., CVL
Decaire, Jack L., 4
Deere, Donald T., 3
Degnan, Jerry L., CVL
DeHerrera, Benjamin D., 4
Deichelmann, Samuel M., 4
Deilsch, Chalres E., 4
Deleidi, Richard A., 5
Delong, Joe L., 3
Demmon, David S., 1
Dempsey, Jack I., 4
Demsey, Walter E., 2
Dennany, James E., 2
Dennis, William R., 4
Dennison, James R., 5
Denton, Manuel R., 3
Derby, Paul D., 5
Derrickson, Thomas G., 2
Desoto, Ernest L., 3
Deuso, Carroll J., 5
Deuter, Richard C., 2
Dewberry, Jerry D., 2
Dewisperlaere, Rexford J., 2
Dexter, Bennie L., 1
Dexter, Ronald J., 2

Dibble, Morris F., 2
Dickson, Edward A., 2
Dilger, Herbert H., 5
Dillender, William H., 5
Dillon, David A., 4
Dinan, David T., 2
Dingwall, John F., 4
Dion, Laurent N., 5
Dix, Craig, 1
Dixon, David L., 1
Dodge, Edward R., 4
Dolan, Edward V., CVL
Dolan, Thomas A., 4
Donahue, Morgan J., 2
Donato, Paul N., 3
Donnelly, Verne G., 4
Donovan, Leroy M., 2
Donovan, Michael L., 4
Dooley, James E., 5
Dority, Richard C., 5
Dotson, Jefferson S., 4
Doughtie, Carl L., 3
Douglas, Thomas E., 2
Dove, Jack P., 2
Downing, Donald R., 2
Draeger, Walter F., 2
Drake, Carl W., 3
Dreher, Richard E., 2
Driver, Clarence N., 2
Driver, Dallas A., 4
Dubbeld, Orie J., 2
Ducat, Phillip A., 5
Duckett, Thomas A., 2
Dudley, Charles G., 2
Duensing, James A., 5
Duffy, Charles J., CVL
Duffy, John E., 3
Dugan, John F., 2
Dugan, Thomas W., 2
Duggan, William Y., 2
Duke, Charles R., CVL
Duncan, James E., 2
Duncan, Robert R., 2
Dunlap, William C., 4
Dunlop, Thomas E., 2
Dunn, Joseph P., 3
DiTommaso, Robert J., 2
Dunn, Michael E., 4
Dunn, Richard E., 2
Dusing, Charles G., 1
Duvall, Dean A., 4
Dyczkowski, Robert R., 4
Dye, Melvin C., 4
Dyer, Blenn Colby, 5
Dyer, Irby, 2
Eads, Dennis K., 4
Earle, John S., 5
Earll, David J., 2
Earnest, Charles M., 5
East, James B., 4
Eaton, Curtis A., 2
Eaton, Norman D., 2
Eby, Robert G., CVL
Echanis, Joseph Y., 3
Echevarria, Raymond L., 2
Eckley, Wayne A., 4
Ecklund, Arthur G., 4
Edgar, Robert J., 4
Edmondson, William R., 2
Edmunds, Robert C., 2
Edwards, Harry J., 3
Edwards, Harry S., 2
Egan, James T., 2
Egan, William P., 3
Egger, John C., 2
Ehrlich, Dennis M., 5
Eidsmoe, Norman E., 4
Eilers, Dennis L., 4
Eisenberger, George J., 2
Eisenbraun, William F., 1
Elkins, Frank C., 4
Ellen, Wade L., 3
Ellerd, Carl J., 5
Elliot, Robert M., 2
Elliott, Andrew J., 2
Elliott, Jerry W., 2
Ellis, Billy J., 2
Ellis, Randall S., 2
Ellis, William, 2
Ellison, John C., 4
Elzinga, Richard G., 3
Emrich, Roger G., 2
Enger, Robert J., 2
Englander, Lawrence J., 2
Entrican, Danny D., 1
Erickson, David W., 2
Eriskine, Jack D., CVL
Erwin, Donald E., 5
Escobedo, Julian, 5
Espenshield, John L., 4
Estocin, Michael J., 2
Evancho, Richard, 5
Evans, Billy K., 2
Evans, Cleveland, 2
Evans, William A., 2
Eveland, Mickey E., 5
Evert, Lawrence G., 2
Fallon, Patrick M., 2
Fanning, Hugh M., 2
Fanning, Joseph P., 2
Farlow, Craig L., 3
Farris, William F., 5
Featherston, Fielding W., 2
Fegan, Ronald J., 5
Feldhaus, John A., 2
Fellenz, Charles R., 2
Fellows, Allen E.
Feneley, Francis J., 3
Ferguson, Douglas D., 2
Ferguson, Walter, 1
Fickler, Edward J., 4
Fieszel, Clifford W., 2
Finger, Sanford I., 5
Finley, Dickie W., 4
Finn, William R., 3
Finney, Charles E., 2
Fischer, John R., 3
Fishcher, Richard W., 2
Fisher, Donald E., 4
Fisher, Donald G., 2
Fitts, Richard A., 4
Fitzgerald, Joseph E., 2
Fitzgerald, Paul L., 2
Fivelson, Barry F., 3
Flanagan, Sherman E., 3
Flanigan, John N., 2
Fleming, Horace H., 2
Flynn, Sean L., CVL
Fobair, Roscoe H., 2
Foley, Brendan P., 4
Foley, John J., 2
Forame, Peter C., 2
Ford, Ecward, 4
Forman, William S., 5
Forrester, Ronald W., 2
Fors, Gary H., 2
Fortner, Frederick J., 2
Foster, Marvin L., 4
Foster, Robert E., 2
Foster, Paul L., 2
Foulks, Ralph E., 4
Fowler, Donald R., 4
Fowler, James A., 2
Fowler, James J., 5
Fowler, Roy G., 5
Frakes, Dwight G., 5
Francisco, San D., 2
Franks, Ian J., 4
Fransen, Albert M., 5
Frawley, William D., 5
Frazier, Paul R., 5
Frederick, David A., 2
Frederick, Peter J., 4
Frederick, William V., 2
Freng, Stanley J., 4
Frenyea, Edmund H., 5
Frink, John W., 1
Fritsch, Thomas W., 5
Frosio, Robert C., 5
Fryar, Bruce C., 2
Fryer, Charles W., 5
Fullam, Wayne E., 2
Fuller, James R., 2
Fuller, William D., 2
Fullerton, Frank E., 4
Gage, Robert H., 2
Galbraith, Russell D., 2
Gallagher, Donald L., 5
Gallagher, John T., 4
Gallant, Henry J., 3
Galvin, Ronald E., 5
Gan, Leonard J., 5
Ganley, Richard O., 2
Ganoe, Berman, 3
Garbett, Jimmy R., 4
Garcia, Andres, 3
Garcia, Ricardo M., 2
Gardner, Glenn V., 5
Gardner, John G., 2
Garner, John H., 3
Garrett, Maurice E., 4
Garside, Frederick T., 1
Gassman, Fred A., 2
Gates, Albert H., 5
Gates, James W., 1
Gatewood, Charles H., 4
Gatwood, Robin F., 2
Gaughan, Roger C., 5
Gauley, James P., 3
Gause, Bernard, 3
Gauthier, Dennis L., 2
Gee, Paul S., 5
Gehrig, James M., 5
Geist, Stephen J., 4
George, James E., 2
Gerber, Daniel A., CVL
Gerstel, Donald A., 2
Gervais, Donald P., 2
Getchell, Paul E., 2
Giammerino, Vincent F., 2
Giannangeli, Anthony R., 2
Gierak, George G., 2
Gilbert, Paul F., 2
Gilchrist, Robert M., 3
Gillen, Thomas E., 2
Ginn, David L., 5
Gish, Henry G.
Gist, Tommy E., 2
Glandon, Gary A., 2

Glanville, John T., 2
Glasson, William A., 5
Glover, Calvin C., 4
Glover, Douglas J., 4
Godfrey, Johnny H., 2
Godwin, Solomon H., 1
Goeden, Gene W., 5
Goeglein, John W., 3
Goetsch, Thomas A., 5
Golf, Kenneth B., 4
Gold, Edward F., 4
Gollahon, Gene R., 3
Golz, John B., 3
Gomez, Robert A., 2
Gonzalez, David, 4
Gonzalez, Jesus A., 4
Gonzalez, Jose J., 2
Goodman, Russell C., 2
Goodwin, Charles B., 2
Gopp, Thomas A., 2
Gore, Paul E., 5
Gorsuch, William D., 5
Gorton, Thomas F., 5
Gould, Frank A., 2
Gourley, Laurent L., 4
Govan, Robert A., 2
Grace, James W., 2
Graf, John G., 1
Graff, Albert S., 3
Graffe, Paul L., 4
Graham, Dennis L., 2
Graham, Gilbert J., 5
Grainger, Joseph W., 1
Graniela, Jose A., 3
Grantham, Robert E., 2
Grauert, Hans E., 5
Graustein, Robert, 2
Graves, Richard C., 5
Gravitte, Connie M., 5
Gray, Harold E., 2
Grayson, William R., 5
Graziosi, Francis G., 4
Green, Donald G., 5
Green, Frank C., 2
Green, George C., 2
Green, Gerald, 5
Green, James A., 2
Green, Larry E., 5
Green, Norman M., 2
Green, Robert B., 2
Green, Thomas F., 5
Greenleaf, Joseph G., 3
Greenly, Jon A., 2
Greenwood, Robert R., 2
Greer, Robert L., 2
Gregory, Paul A., 5
Gregory, Robert R., 1
Greiling, David S., 2
Grella, Donald C., 4
Grenzebach, Earl W., 2
Grewell, Larry I., 2
Griffey, Terrance H., 2
Griffin, Rodney L., 2
Griffith, John G., 5
Griffith, Robert S., 4
Grissett, Edwin R., 1
Grosse, Christopher A., 2
Groth, Made L., 4
Grubb, Peter A., 4
Grzyb, Robert H., CVL
Guajardo, Hilarid H., 5
Guerra, Raul A., 3
Guillermin, Louis F., 2
Guillet, Andre R., 2
Guillory, Edward J., 2
Guillory, Hubia J., 2
Gumbert, Robert W., 4
Gunn, Alan W., 4
Haas, Leon F., 5
Hackett, Harley B., 2
Hackett, James E., 3
Hagan, John R., 4
Hagan, Craig L., 1
Haight, Stephen H., 5
Hail, William W., 4
Hale, John D., 2
Hall, Donald J., 2
Hall, Frederick M., 3
Hall, Gary Lee, 2
Hall, Harley H., 1
Hall, James W., 2
Hall, Walter L., 1
Hall, Walter R., 2
Hall, Willis R.
Halleberg, Roger C., 2
Halpin, David P., 5
Halpin, Richard C., 2
Hamilton, Dennis C., 4
Hamilton, Eugene D., 2
Hamilton, John S., 2
Hamilton, Roger D., 2
Hamm, James E., 2
Hammond, Dennis W., 1
Handrahan, Eugene A., 2
Hangen, Welles, 1
Hanley, Larry J., 3
Hanley, Terence H., 5
Hanna, Kenneth, 1
Hanratty, Thomas M., 2
Hansen, Lester A., 2
Hanson, Robert T., 1
Hanson, Stephen P., 2
Hanson, Thomas P., 2
Harber, Stephen J., 2
Hardie, Charles D., 5
Hargrove, Joseph N., 2
Hargrove, Olin, 2
Harley, Lee D., 2
Harned, Gary A., 3
Harper, Ralph L., 5
Harper, Richard K., 2
Harris, Bobby G., 1
Harris, Gregory J., 2
Harris, Harold L., 4
Harris, Jeffery L., 2
Harris, Paul W., 5
Harris, Reuben B., 3
Harris, Stephen W., 2
Harrison, Donald L., 2
Harrison, Larry G., 2
Harrison, Robert H., 2
Harrold, Patrick K., 2
Hart, Joseph L., 3
Hart, Thomas T., 2
Hartness, Gregg, 2
Hartney, James C., 2
Hartzheim, John F., 3
Harvey, Jack R., 4
Harwood, James A., 2
Harworth, Elory, 2
Hasenback, Paul A., 2
Hassenger, Arden K., 4
Hastings, Steven M., 3
Hatley, Joel C., 3
Hattori, Maskai, 4
Hauer, Leslie J., 2
Hauer, Robert D., 4
Haviland, Roy E., 5
Havranek, Michael W., 2
Hawkins, Edgar L., 2
Hawthorne, Richard W., 4
Hayden, Glenn M., 3
Heep, William A., 5
Heideman, Thomas E., 2
Heiskell, Lucius L., 2
Heitman, Steven W., 2
Helber, Lawrence N., 4
Held, John W., 2
Hellback, Harold J., 2
Helmich, Gerald R., 2
Helwig, Roger D., 2
Hemmel, Clarence J., 5
Hempel, Barry L., 4
Hendrix, Jerry W., 4
Henn, John R., 3
Henninger, Howard W., 4
Henry, David A., 5
Hensley, Ronnie L., 2
Hensley, Thomas T., 2
Hentz, Richard J., 3
Hepler, Frank M., 3
Hernandez, Frank S., 2
Herold, Richard W., 3
Herreid, Robert D., 2
Herrera, Frederick, D., 2
Herrick, Charles, CVL
Herrick, James W., 2
Herrin, Henry H., 5
Herrold, Ned R., 5
Hertz, Gustav, CVL
Hesford, Peter D., 2
Hess, Frederick W., 2
Hess, Gene W., 2
Hessom, Robert C., 3
Hestle, Roosevelt L., 2
Hetrick, Raymond H., 2
Hewitt, Samuel E., 4
Heyne, Raymond T., 5
Hickman, Vincent J., 2
Hicks, Prentice W., 2
Hicks, Terrin D., 2
Hiemer, Jerry A., 2
Hillbrich, Barry W., 4
Hill, Arthur S., 3
Hill, Billy D., 2
Hill, Charles D., 5
Hill, Gordon C., 4
Hill, John R., 5
Hill, Joseph A., 2
Hill, Rayford D., 5
Hill, Richard D., 3
Hill, Robert L., 4
Hills, John R., 2
Hilton, Robert L., 3
Hines, Vaughn M., 5
Hise, James H., 5
Hodges, David L., 3
Hodgson, Cecil J., 2
Hoelfs, John H., 4
Hoff, Michael G., 2
Hoff, Samie D., 2
Hoffman, Terry A., 5
Hogan, Jerry F., 2
Holdeman, Robert E., 2
Holden, Elmer L., 3
Holguin, Luis G., 4
Holland, Lawrence T., 1
Holland, Melvin A.
Holley, Tilden S., 2

Hollinger, Gregg N., 5
Hollingsworth, Hal T., 5
Holm, Arnold E., 3
Holman, Gerald A., 5
Holmes, David H., 2
Holmes, Frederick, 3
Holmes, Lester E., 2
Holt, James W., 1
Holt, Robert A., 2
Holton, Robert E., 2
Holtzman, Ronald L., 5
Hom, Charles D., 5
Homuth, Richard W., 5
Hopper, Earl P., 2
Hopps, Gary D., 3
Horchar, Andrew A., 5
Horne, Stanley H., 2
Horsky, Robert M., 2
Hosken, John C., 3
Hoskins, Charles L., 2
Hoskins, Donald R., 2
Hoskinson, Robert E., 2
House, John A., 4
Housh, Anthony F., 4
Howard, Lewis J., 2
Howard, Luther H., 4
Howell, Carter A., 2
Howes, George A., 4
Hrdlicka, David L., 1
Huard, James L., 4
Hubbs, Donald R., 5
Huberth, Eric, 2
Hubler, George L., 5
Huddleston, Lynn R., 4
Hudgens, Edward M., 2
Huggins, Bobby G., 3
Huie, Litchfield P., 5
Hull, James L., 4
Hume, Kenneth E., 5
Hummel, John F., 1
Humphrey, Galen F., 5
Honeycutt, Charles J., 2
Hunsicker, James E., 3
Hunt, James D., 3
Hunt, Leon A., 2
Hunt, Robert W., 1
Hunt, William B., 3
Hunter, James D., 4
Hunter, Russell P., 2
Huntley, John N., 2
Hurst, John C., 2
Huss, Roy A., 5
Huston, Charles G., 4
Hyde, Jimmy D., 5
Hyde, Michael L., 2
Hynds, Wallace G., 3
Iandoli, Donald, 4
Ibanez, Di R., 2
Innes, Roger B., 3
Ireland, Robert N., 2
Irsch, Wayne C., 2
Irwin, Robert H., 2
Ivan, Andrew, 2
Jablonski, Michael J., 4
Jackson, Carl E., 4
Jackson, James T., 2
Jackson, James W., 4
Jackson, Paul V., 2
Jackson, William B., 2
Jacobs, Edward J., 5
Jacobsen, Timotny J.
Jacques, James J., 3
Jakovac, John A., 2
Jamerson, Larry C., 2
James, Samuel L., 3
Janqusek, Ronald J., 5
Jarvis, Jeremy M., 3
Jefferson, James M., 2
Jefferson, Perry H., 4
Jefferson, Derrell B., 4
Jeffs, Clive G., 2
Jenkins, Paul L., 3
Jenne, Robert E., 2
Jensen, George W., 2
Jerome, Stanley M., 5
Jewell, Eugene M., 2
Jimenez, Juan M., 2
Johns, Paul F., 2
Johns, Vernon Z., 2
Johnson, August D., 3
Johnson, Allen L., 2
Johnson, Bruce G., 1
Johnson, Dale A., 3
Johnson, Edward H., 2
Johnson, Frankie B., 2
Johnson, Gary L., 2
Johnson, Guy D., 2
Johnson, James R., 4
Johnson, Randolph L.
Johnson, Richard H., 2
Johnson, Robert D., 5
Johnson, Stanley G., 5
Johnson, William D., 2
Johnston, Steven B., 2
Johnstone, James M., 3
Jones, Bobby M., 4
Jones, George E., 5
Jones, Grayland, 4
Jones, James E., 2
Jones, James G., 5
Jones, John R., 3
Jones, Johnny M., 3
Jones, Louis F., 2
Jones, Orvin C., 2
Jones, Thomas P., 5
Jordan, Larry M., 5
Jourdenais, George H.
Judd, Michael B., 2
Jurecko, Daniel E, 2
Kahler, Harold, 2
Kahl, Tanos, CVL
Kane, Bruce E., 5
Kane, Richard R., 4
Kardell, David A, 2
Karger, Barry E., 2
Karns, Joseph J., 2
Karst, Carl F., 4
Kasch, Frederick M., 3
Kaster, Leonard L., 2
Kearns, Joseph T., 4
Keefe, Douglas O., 4
Keiper, John C., 3
Keller, Jack E., 2
Keller, Wendell R., 2
Kelley, Daniel M., 2
Kemmerer, Donald R., 3
Kemp, Clayton C., 5
Kemp, Freddie, 4
Kennedy, James E., 2
Kennedy, John W., 4
Kenney, Harry J., 5
Kent, Robert D., 2
Kerns, Arthur W.
Kerr, Ernest C., 5
Kerr, Everett O., 2
Kerr, John C., 2
Ketchie, Scott D., 2
Ketterer, James A., 2
Kibbey, Richard A., 2
Kiefel, Ernest P., 2
Kieffer, William L., 2
Kier, Larry G., 2
Kilcullen, Thomas M., 4
Killen, John D., 4
Kilpatrick, Larry R., 3
Kimsey, William A., 4
King, Charles D., 2
King, Donald L., 4
King, Gerald E., 5
King, Michael E., 3
King, Paul C., 2
King, Ronald R., 4
Kinkade, William L., 2
Kinsman, Gerald F., 2
Kipina, Marshall, F., 4
Kirby, Bobby A., 2
Kirk, Herbert A.
Kirksey, Robert L., 3
Klemm, Donald M., 2
Klenda, Dean A., 2
Klimo, James R., 4
Kline, Robert E., 4
Klingner, Michael L., 2
Klinke, Donald H., 2
Klugg, Joseph R., 5
Klute, Karl E., 2
Kmelyk, Jonathan P., 2
Knabb, Kenneth K., 2
Knapp, Fredric W., 3
Knapp, Herman L., 2
Knebel, Thomas E., 4
Knight, Billy, 1
Knight, Henry C., 4
Knight, Larry C., 5
Knight, Larry D., 4
Knight, Roy A., 2
Knochel, Charles A., 5
Knuckey, Thomas W., 2
Knutsen, Donald P., 2
Knutson, Richard A., 1
Koenig, Edwin L., 5
Kohler, David L., 5
Kollmann, Blenn E., 5
Kommendant, Aado, 2
Konyu, William M., 2
Kodt, James W., 2
Koonce, Terry T., 4
Koons, Dale F., 1
Kosko, Walter, 2
Koslosky, Howard M., 5
Kott, Stephen J., 2
Kraner, David S., 5
Krausman, Edward, 2
Kravitz, James S., 3
Krech, Melvin T., 5
Krogman, Alva R., 2
Krommenhoek, Jefrey M., 4
Kroske, Harold W., 2
Krupa, Frederick, 4
Krusi, Peter H., 5
Kryszak, Theodore E., 2
Kubley, Roy R., 2
Kuhlman, Robert J., 4
Kuhlmann, Charles F., 2
Kulland, Byron K., 1
Kusick, Joseph G., 2
Kustigan, Michael T.
Kuykendall, Willie C., 4
Labohn, Gary R., 4

Lacey, Gary R., 4
Lacey, Richard J., 4
Ladewig, Melvin E., 2
Lafayette, John W., 1
Lagrand, William J., 2
Lahaye, James D., 5
Laker, Carl J., 2
Lambton, Bennie R., 2
Lamp, Arnold W., 2
Lancaster, Kenneth R., 2
Lane, Charles, 2
Lane, Glen O., 4
Lane, Mitchell S., 4
Laney, Billy R., 2
Lannon, Richard C., 5
Lapham, Robert G., 2
Lapland, Kurt E., 2
Laporte, Michael L., 2
Latimer, Clarence A., 2
Laueano, Lopez I., 3
Lauteno, Manuel A., 1
Lautzenheiser, Michael, 5
Lavod, John A., 2
Lawrence, Bruce E., 2
Lawrence, Gregory P., 2
Laws, Delmer L., 3
Laws, Richard L., 3
Lawson, Karl W., 3
Leaver, John M., 5
Ledbetter, Thomas I., 2
Lee, Albert E., 2
Lee, Charles R., 2
Lee, Glen Hung Nin, 2
Lee, Leonard M., 3
Leeper, Wallace W., 4
Leeser, Leonard C., 2
Leet, David, 3
Leetun, Darel D., 2
Lefever, Douglas P., 3
Lehnhoff, Edward W., 2
Lehrke, Stanley L., 2
Lemcke, David E., 4
Lemmons, William E., 2
Lemon, Jeffery C., 2
Leonard, Marvin M., 3
Leonard, Robert B., 5
Leonor, Leonardo C., 4
Lerner, Irwin S., 2
Lester, Roderick, B., 2
Letchworth, Edward N., 5
Levan, Alvin L., 5
Levis, Charles A., 2
Lewandowski, Leonard J., 3
Lewellen, Walter E., 2
Lewis, James W., 3
Lewis, Charlie G., 4
Lewis, Larry G., 5
Lewis, Merrill R., 2
Lillund, William A., 4
Lilly, Carroll B., 4
Lilly, Lawrence E., 2
Lindahl, John C., 4
Lindbloom, Charles D., 5
Lindewald, Charles W., 1
Lindland, Donald F., 1
Lindsey, Marvin N., 2
Lindstrom, Ronnie G., 2
Lineberger, Harold B., 3
Link, Robert C., 2
Lint, Donald M., 2
Lira, Jose T.
Little, Danny L., 2
Livingston, Richard A., 5
Lloyd, Allen R., 2
Locker, James D., 2
Lockhart, George B., 2
Logan, Jacob D., 3
Loheed, Hubert B., 3
Lomax, Richard E., 4
Loney, Ashton N., 2
Long, Carl E., 5
Long, George W., 2
Long, John H., 4
Longanecker, Ronald L., 5
Lono, Luther A., 4
Lopez, Robert, 3
Lopez, Robert C., 5
Lord, Arthur J., 4
Lovegren, David E., 3
Lowry, Tyrrell G., 5
Lucas, Larry F., 3
Lucki, Albin E., 2
Lukenbach, Max D., 2
Luker, Russell B., 5
Lull, Howard B., 1
Lum, David A., 5
Luna, Carter P., 2
Luna, Donald A., 3
Lundy, Albro L., 2
Lunsford, Herbert L., 3
Luttrell, James M., 2
Lynn, Doyle W., 3
Lynn, Robert R., 2
Lyon, Donavan L., 2
Lyon, James M., 2
MacCann, Henry E., 2
MacDonald, George D., 2
Mackedanz, Lyle E., 2
Macko, Charles, 2
MacLaughlin, Donald C., 2
MacNamara, Len, CVL
Maddox, Notely G., 3
Madison, William L., 2
Madsen, Marlow E., 5
Magee, Patrick J., 4
Magee, Ralph W., 1
Magers, Paul G., 2
Magnusson, James A., 3
Mahoney, Thomas P., 2
Mailhes, Lawrence S., 5
Makel, Janie A., CVL
Mallon, Richard J., 2
Malone, Jimmy M., 4
Mimiya, John M., 2
Mancini, Richard M., 3
Mangino, Thomas A., 2
Mangus, Arlie R., 5
Mann, Robert L., 2
Manning, Ronald J., 3
Manor, James, 3
Manske, Charles J., 3
Mape, John C., 2
Marik, Charles W., 5
Mark, Kitt T., CVL
Marker, Michael W., 3
Marshall, Danny G., 2
Marshall, James A., 5
Marshall, Richard C., 2
Martin, David E., 5
Martin, Donald E.
Martin, Douglas K., 3
Martin, Duane W., 1
Martin, James E., 3
Martin, Jerry D., 5
Martin, John B., 5
Martin, John M., 5
Martin, Larry E., 2
Martin, Richard D., 2
Martin, Russell D., 2
Martin, Sammy Arthur, 5
Martinez-Mercado, Ed Ju, 2
Marvin, Robert C., 5
Mascari, Phillip L., 4
Mason, James P., 5
Mason, William H., 4
Massucci, Martin J., 2
Masterson, Michael J., 2
Masuda, Ronald S., 1
Matejka, Alan P., 2
Matejov, Joseph, 1
Matocha, Donald J., 2
Matteson, Glenn, 1
Matthes, Peter R., 2
Mauterer, Oscar, 2
Maxwell, Calvin W., 2
Maxwell, James R., 3
Maxell, Samuel C., 2
May, David M., 2
May, Michael F., 2
Mayer, Roderick L., 2
Mayercik, Ronald M., 4
Mayhew, William J.
Maysey, Larry W., 2
McAndrews, Michael W., 5
McTeer, Thomas J., 5
McBride, Earl P., 5
McCain, Marvin R., 2
McCants, Leland S., 3
McCarty, James L., 2
McCleary, George C., 3
McClellan, Paul T., 2
McConnaughhay, Dan D., 5
McConnell, Jerry, 4
McCormick, Carl O., 3
McCormick, Michael T., 2
McCoy, Meril O., 5
McCrary, Jack, 4
McCubbin, Glenn D., 2
McDaniel, John L., 2
McDaniel, Morris L., 4
McDonald, Herman, CVL
McDonald, Emmett R., 2
McDonald, Joseph W., 3
McDonald, Kurt C., 4
McDonell, R.D., 2
McDonnell, John T., 2
McDonough, John R, 5
McElhanon, Michael O., 4
McElroy, Glenn D., 3
McElroy, John L., 2
McElvain, James R., 4
McEwen, James A., 2
McGar, Brian K., 2
McGarvey, James M., 2
McGonigle, William D., 5
McGouldrick, Francis J., 2
McGrave, Donald P., 2
McGrath, James P., 3
McGrath, William D., 2
McIntire, Scott W., 2
McIntosh, Ian, 4
McIver, Alexander
McKain, Bobby L., 2
McKay, Clyde W., CVL
McKay, Homer E., 5
McKenney, Kenneth D., 2
McKinley, Gerald W., 3
McKinney, Clemie, 4
McKinney, Neil B., 4

McKittrick, James C., 2
McKnight, George P., 2
McLamb, Harry L., 2
McLaughlin, Arthur V., 2
McLaughlin, Olen B., 5
McLean, James H., 1
McLeod, Arthur E., 2
McLeod, David V., 3
McMahan, Robert C., 2
McManus, Truman J., 5
McMican, M.D., 2
McMurray, Fred H., 4
McPhaul, William, 4
McPhee, Randy N., 5
McPherson, Everett A., 2
McPherson, Fred L., 2
McQuade, James R., 3
McRae, David E., 2
McVey, Lavoy D., 3
McWhorter, Henry S., 3
Meadows, Eugene T., 2
Meder, Paul O., 2
Mein, Michael H., 4
Meldahl, Charles H., 4
Mellor, Fredric M., 2
Melton, Todd M., 1
Menges, George B., 4
Mercer, Jacob E., 2
Meroney, Virgil K., 2
Metoyer, Bryford G., 5
Metz, James H., 1
Metzler, Charles D., 4
Meyers, Roger A., 5
Mickelsen, William E., 5
Midgett, Dewey A.
Midnight, Francis B., 2
Milikin, Richard M., 2
Milius, Paul L., 2
Millard, Charles W., 4
Miller, Carl D., 2
Miller, Carleton P., 5
Miller, Curtis D., 2
Miller, George C., CVL
Miller, Glenn E., 3
Miller, Malcolm T., 3
Miller, Richard A., 2
Miller, Michael A., 3
Miller, Richard C., 3
Miller, Robert C., 3
Miller, Robert L., 5
Miller, Wyatt, 4
Milliner, William P., 1
Millner, Michael, 2
Mills, Jame B., 4
Mills, James D., 5
Mims, George I., 2
Minor, Carrol W., 4
Mirrer, Robert H., 3
Mishuk, Richard E., 3
Mitchell, Albert C., 2
Mithcell, Archie E., CVL
Mitchell, Carl B., 3
Mitchell, Donald W., 5
Mitchell, Gilbert L., 5
Mitchell, Harry E.
Mitchell, Thomas B., 4
Mixter, David I., 2
Miyazaki, Ronald K., 2
Moe, Harold J., 5
Mongilardi, Peter, 4
Montez, Anastacio, 2
Montgomery, Ronald W., 5
Moon, Walter, 1
Mooney, Fred, 2
Moore, Herbert W., 2
Moore, James, R., 2
Moore, Jerry L., 2
Moore, Maurice H., 2
Moore, Ralph E., 3
Moore, Raymond G., 4
Moore, Scott F., 5
Moore, Thomas, 1
Moore, William J., 5
Moore, William R., 5
Morales, Frank A., CVL
Moran, Richard A., 5
Moreida, Manuel J., 4
Moreira, Ralph A., 5
Moreland, James L., 1
Moreland, Stephen C., 2
Moreland, William D., 5
Morgan, Burke H., 2
Morgan, Charles E., 2
Morgan, Edwin E., 4
Morgan, James S., 2
Morgan, Thomas R., 3
Morgan, William J., 5
Moriarty, Peter G., 2
Morin, Richard G., 2
Morley, Charles F., 2
Morley, Richard G., 2
Morrill, David W., 5
Morris, George W., 1
Morrison, Glenn R., 3
Morrison, Joseph C., 2
Morrissey, Richard T., 5
Morrissey, Robert D., 4
Morrow, Larry K., 2
Morrow, Richard D., 2
Mosburg, Henry L., 5
Moser, Paul K., 5
Moshier, Jim E., 2
Mossman, Harry S., 2
Mossman, Joe R., 3
Mowrey, Glenn W., 5
Mowrey, Richard L., 5
Mulhauser, Harvey, 2
Mulleavey, Quentin E.
Mullen, William F., 2
Mullins, Harold E., 2
Mundt, Henry G., 2
Munoz, David L., 1
Muren, Thomas R., 5
Murphy, Barry D., 2
Murphy, Larron D., 4
Murphy, Terence H., 5
Murray, Joseph V., 3
Murray, Patrick P., 4
Musetti, Joseph T., 5
Musil, Clinton A., 3
Myers, David G., 2
Nahan, John B., 2
Nash, John M., 2
Neal, Dennis P., 2
Neeld, Bobby G., 4
Neislar, David P., 5
Nellans, William L., 4
Nelson, David L., 3
Nelson, James R., 5
Nelson, Jan H., 2
Ness, Patrick L., 3
Neth, Fred A., 5
Netherland, Roger M., 4
Neville, William E., 4
Neville, William E., 5
Newberry, Wayne E., 2
Newburn, Larry S., 3
Newell, Michael T., 3
Newman, James C., 5
Newman, Larry J., 2
Newton, Charles V., 2
Newton, Donald S., 2
Newton, Warren E., 2
Nichols, Hubert C., 2
Nickerson, William B., 5
Nickol, Robert A., 5
Nicotera, Carl, 1
Nidds, Daniel R., 2
Niedecken, William C., 3
Niehouse, Daniel L., CVL
Nightengale, Randall J., 5
Nipper, David, 5
Nobert, Craig R., 2
Nolan, McKinley, 1
Nolan, Joseph P., 3
Nopp, Robert G., 4
Nordahl, Lee E., 2
Norris, Calvin A., 5
Norton, Michael R., 2
Nyhof, Richard E., 2
Nyman, Lawrence F., 5
Nystrom, Bruce A., 2
Nystul, William C., 3
Oakley, Linus L., 3
OBrien, John L., 2
OBrien, Kevin, 4
Ochab, Robert, 3
Odom, Chester R.
ODonnell, Michael D., 3
ODonnell, Samuel, 4
Offutt, Gary P., 2
Ogden, Howard, 2
OGrady, John F., 2
OHara, Robert C., 4
Okerlund, Thomas R., 4
OLaughlin, Stephen M., CVL
Oldham, John S., 2
Olds, Ernest A., 2
Olmstead, Stanley E., 2
Olsen, Betty A., CVL
Olsen, Floyd W., 2
Olson, Barry A., 2
Olson, Delbert A., 3
Olson, Gerald E., 4
Omelia, Dennis W., 4
ONeil, Douglas L., 3
Orell, Quinlen R., 2
Orr, Warren R., 3
Osborn, Geoffrey H., 5
Osborne, Edwin N., 4
Osborne, Rodney D., 3
Osborne, Samuel W., 5
Ostermeyer, William H., 4
Ott, Edward L. III, 5
Ott, Patrick L., 2
Ott, William A., 2
Overlock, John F., 4
Owen, Clyde C., 5
Owen, Robert D., 4
Owen, Timothy S., 4
Owens, Fred M., 1
Owens, Joy L., 4
Pabst, Eugene M., 5
Packard, Ronald L., 2
Padgett, David E., 4
Padgett, Samuel J., 4
Padilla, David E., 3
Page, Albert L., 3
Page, Gordon L., 4

Page, Jasper N.
Painter, John R., 5
Palacios, Luis F., 5
Palen, Carl A., 4
Palenscar, Alexander J., 5
Palmer, Gilbert S., 4
Palmgren, Edwin D., 4
Panek, Robert J., 2
Pannabecker, David E., 2
Pantall, James R., 5
Parcels, Rex L., 5
Parish, Charles C., 2
Parker, Charles L., 4
Parker, David W., 5
Parker, Frank C., 4
Parker, John J., 5
Parker, Maxim C., 5
Parker, Thomas A., 2
Parker, Udon, 3
Parker, Woodrow W., 2
Parks, Joe, 1
Parks, Raymond F., 3
Parra, Lionel, 4
Parsley, Edward M., 4
Parsons, Don B., 4
Parsons, Donald E., 4
Parsons, Michael D., 4
Partington, Roger D., 5
Paschall, Ronald P., 1
Pasekoff, Robert E., 4
Pastva, Michael J., 5
Pate, Gary, 4
Patterson, Bruce M., 5
Patterson, James K., 2
Pattillo, Ralph N., 2
Patton, Kenneth J., 4
Patton, Ward K., 5
Paul, James L., 4
Pauley, Marshall, 4
Paulson, Meryln L., 2
Pawlish, George F., 5
Paxton, Donald E., 2
Payne, Kylis T., 5
Payne, Norman, 2
Peace, John D., 4
Peacock, John R., 4
Pearce, Dale A., 2
Pearce, Edwin J., 2
Pearson, Wayne E., 3
Pearson, William R., 2
Pederson, Joe P., 1
Pender, Orland J., 2
Pennington, Ronald K., 5
Pepper, Anthony J., 5
Peralta, Benjamin R.
Perisho, Gordon S., 4
Perkins, Cecil C., 5
Perrine, Elton L., 2
Perry, Otha L., 5
Perry, Randolph A., 2
Perry, Richard C., 5
Perry, Thomas H., 2
Peterson, Delbert R., 2
Peterson, Dennis W., 2
Peterson, Mark A., 1
Pettis, Thomas E., 5
Pfaffmann, Charles B., 5
Pharris, William V., 2
Phelps, Jesse D., 4
Phelps, William, 3
Phillips, Daniel R., 1
Phillips, David J., 3
Phillips, Elbert A., 3
Phillips, Marvin F., 5
Phillips, Robert P., 1
Phipps, James L., 2
Pick, Donald W., 3
Pierce, Walter M., 4
Piersanti, Anthony J., 5
Pierson, William C., 4
Pietrzak, Joseph R., 2
Pietsch, Robert E., 2
Puttmann, Alan D., 2
Pike, Dennis S., 2
Pike, Peter X., 4
Pineau, Ronland R., 3
Pirker, Victor J., 2
Piruccello, Joseph S., 2
Pitman, Peter P., 4
Pitt, Albert, 4
Pittman, Robert E., 5
Pizen, John R., 2
Plants, Thomas L., 3
Plassmeyer, Bernard H., 2
Platt, Robert L., 2
Pierman, James E., 3
Plowman, James E., 4
Plumadore, Kenneth L., 2
Pogreba, Dean A., 4
Polard, Perry, CVL
Pollin, George J., 2
Polster, Harman, 3
Pool, Jerry L., 3
Poole, Charlie S., 2
Poor, Russell A., 2
Posey, George R., 5
Potter, William J., 2
Potter, William T., 2
Potts, Larry F., 2
Powell, William E., 2
Powers, John U., 2
Powers, Lowell S., 4
Powers, Verine H., 2
Poynor, Daniel R., 2
Prater, Roy D., 2
Prather, Martin W., 2
Preiss, Robert F., 2
Prentice, Kenneth M., 5
Preston, James A., 2
Prevedel, Charles F., 2
Prevost, Albert M., 5
Prewitt, William R., 2
Price, Bunyan D.,
Price, David S.
Price, William M., 4
Pridemore, Dallas R., 1
Primm, Severo J., 1
Pringle, Joe H., 4
Prudhomme, John D., 3
Pruett, William D., 2
Puentes, Manuel F., 2
Puggi, Joseph D., 4
Pugh, Dennis G., 2
Pugh, Kenneth W., 3
Purcell, Howard P., 4
Putnam, Charles L., 1
Pyles, Harley B., 4
Quinn, Michael E., 4
Rackley, Inzar W., 4
Ragland, Dayton W., 5
Ralston, Frank D., 4
Rambaugh, Elwood E.
Ramirez, Armando, 2
Ramos, Ranier S., 2
Ramsey, Charles J., 4
Ramsden, Gerald L., 5
Ramsower, Irving B., 2
Ransbottom, Frederick J., 2
Rapp, Jeff, CVL
Rash, Melvin D., 4
Rattin, Dennis M., 4
Ratzel, Wesley D., 4
Rausch, Robert E., 4
Ravenna, Harry M., 4
Rawlings, James, CVL
Rawsthorne, Edgar A., 3
Ray, James Michael, 1
Ray, Ronald E., 2
Raymond, Paul D., 2
Read, Charles H.W., 2
Reardon, Richard J., 1
Reed, James W., 2
Reed, Terry M., 2
Reedy, William H., 5
Reese, Gomerd, 2
Reeves, John H., 5
Rehe, Richard R., 1
Rehn, Gary L., 2
Reid, Harold E., 4
Reid, John E., 2
Reilly, Edward D., 1
Reilly, Lavern G., 2
Reinecke, Wayne C., 5
Reiter, Dean W., 5
Reitmann, Thomas E., 2
Renelt, Walter A., 3
Reno, Ralph J., 2
Rex, Robert A., 3
Rex, Robet F., 2
Rexroad, Ronald R., 3
Reynolds, David R., 2
Reynolds, Terry L., CVL
Rhodes, Ferris A., 4
Rice, Thomas, 4
Rich, Richard, 2
Richardson, Dale W., 2
Richardson, Floyd W., 2
Richardson, Stephen G., 5
Rickel, David J., 2
Ricker, William E., 4
Rickman, Dwight G., 4
Riggins, Robert P., 3
Riggs, Thomas F., 5
Riordan, John M., 5
Rios, Noel L., 4
Risner, Richard F.
Rissi, Donald L., 2
Ritchey, Luther E., 3
Ritter, George L., CVL
Rittichier, Jack C., 3
Riverburgh, Richard W., 3
Roark, Anund C., 2
Roark, James D., 5
Roark, William M., 5
Robbins, Richard J., 2
Roberson, John W., 4
Roberts, Gerald R., 3
Roberts, Harold J., 5
Roberts, Michael L., 3
Roberts, Richard D., 2
Robertson, John H., 2
Robertson, John L., 2
Robertson, Leonard, 1
Robertson, Mark J., 2
Robinson, Edward, 5
Robinson, Floyd H., 2
Robinson, Kenneth D., 2
Robinson, Larry W., 2
Robinson, Lewis M., 2

Roby, Charles D., 2
Rockett, Alton C., 3
Rodill, Daniel, CVL
Rodriguez, Albert E., 2
Roe, Jerry L., 4
Roehrich, Ronald L., 5
Rogers, Billy L., 5
Rogers, Edward F., 2
Rogers, Lyle D.
Roggow, Norman L., 3
Romero, Victor, 4
Romig, Edward L., 4
Romine, Albert W., 2
Roraback, Kenneth M., 1
Rosata, Joseph F., 2
Rose, Luther L., 2
Rosenback, Robert P.
Ross, Douglas A., 2
Ross, Jlynn, 2
Ross, Joseph S., 3
Rossano, Richard J., 2
Roth, Billie L., 2
Rowley, Charles S., 2
Rozo, James M., 1
Rucker, Emmett, 3
Rudolph, Robert D., 3
Rumbaugh, Elmwood E., 3
Runnels, Glyn L., 3
Rupinsky, Bernard F., 2
Rusch, Stephen A., 2
Russell, Donald M., 2
Russell, Peter J., 4
Russell, Richard L., 2
Ryan, William C., 3
Ryder, John L., 4
Rykoskey, Edward J., 3
Saavedra, Robert, 2
Sabog, Mateo
Sadler, Mitchell D., 4
Saegaert, Donald R., 1
Sage, Leland C., 3
Salazar, Fidel G., 5
Sale, Harold R., 4
Salinas, Mercedes P., 2
Salley, James, 1
Salzarulo, Raymond P., 2
Sampson, Leslie V., 2
Sanchez, Jose R., 5
Sanderlin, William D., 4
Sanders, William S., 2
Sander, Robert L., 3
Sandoval, Antonio R., 3
Sands, Richard E., 2
Sansone, James J., 5
Sargent, James R., 5
Sause, Bernard J., 5
Savoy, M.J., 4
Sayre, Leslie B., 4
Scaile, Kenneth D., 4
Schaneberg, Leroy C., 2
Scharf, Charles J., 2
Schell, Richard J., 4
Scherdin, Robert F., 2
Scheurich, Thomas E., 4
Schiele, James F., 1
Schimberg, James P., 4
Schimmels, Eddie R., 5
Schnidt, Peter A., 2
Schmidt, Walter R., 1
Schmittour, Eureka L., 5
Schroderer, Eric J., 5
Schoeppner, Leonard J., 5
Scholz, Klaus D., 4
Schoonover, Charles D., 5
Schott, Richard S., 1
Schreckengost, Fred T., 2
Schroefeel, Thomas A., 3
Schuler, Robert H., 4
Schultz, Ronald James, 4
Schultz, Sheldon D., 4
Schumacher, James K.
Schumann, John R., 1
Schworer, Ronald P., 3
Scott, Dain V., 2
Scott, David L., 2
Scott, Martin A., 2
Scott, Mike J., 4
Scott, Vincent C., 3
Scrivener, Stephen R., 2
Scull, Gary B., 2
Scunqip, Vincent A., 2
Schurlock, Lee D., 2
Seablom, Earl F., 4
Seagraves, Melvin D., 5
Searlus, William H., 5
Seeley, Douglas M., 2
Seidl, Robert, CVL
Sennett, Robert R., 5
Serex, Henry M., 2
Setterquest, Francis L., 4
Seuell, John W., 2
Seward, William H., 2
Sexton, David M., 4
Seymour, Leo E., 2
Shafer, Phillip R., 4
Shanks, James L., 3
Shanley, Michael H., 4
Shannon, Patrick L.
Sharp, Samuel A., 2
Shark, Earl E., 1
Shaw, Edward B., 5
Shaw, Gary F., 2
Shay, Donald E., 2
Shea, James P., 3
Shea, Michael J., 3
Shelton, Charles E., 1
Sherman, John B., 2
Sherman, Peter W., 5
Shewmake, John D., 5
Shimek, Samuel D., 2
Shimkin, Alex, CVL
Shine, Anthony C., 4
Shingledecker, Armon D., 2
Shinn, William C., 2
Shoneck, John R., 4
Shorack, Theodore J., 2
Shriver, Jerry M., 4
Shue, Donald M., 2
Shumway, Geofrey R., 2
Siegwarth, Donald E., 4
Sigafoos, Walter H., 2
Silva, Claude A., 2
Silver, Edward A., 2
Simmons, Robert E., 2
Simmons, Willie E., CVL
Simpson, James E., CVL
Simpson, Joseph L.
Simpson, Max C., 3
Simpson, Robert L., 2
Simpson, Walter S., 2
Singleton, Daniel L., 3
Siow, Gale R., 3
Sisson, Winfield W., 4
Sitek, Thomas W., 3
Sittner, Ronald N., 2
Sizemore, James E., 2
Skarman, Orval H., 4
Skeen, Richard R., 5
Skibbe, David W., 3
Skiles, Thomas W., 2
Skinner, Owen G., 2
Skivington, William E., 2
Slater, Freddie L.
Small, Burt C., 1
Smallwood, John J., 3
Smiley, Stanley K., 2
Smith, Carl A., 5
Smith, David R., 4
Smith, Dean, 5
Smith, Edward D., Jr., 2
Smith, Gene A., 2
Smith, George C., 3
Smith, Hallie W., 3
Smith, Harding E., 2
Smith, Harold V., 3
Smith, Harry W., 2
Smith, Howard H., 2
Smith, Joseph S., 2
Smith, Lewis P., 2
Smith, Richard D., 3
Smith, Robert N., 2
Smith, Roger L., 2
Smith, Ronald E., 2
Smith, Victor A., 2
Smith, Warren P., 2
Smith, William A., 4
Smith, William M., 2
Smith, William W., 2
Smoot, Curtis R., 2
Snider, Hughie F., 4
Soucy, Ronald P., 5
Soulier, Duwayne, 5
Soyland, David P., 2
Sparenberg, Bernard J., 5
Sparks, Donald L., 1
Sparks, Jon M., 2
Spencer, Dean C., 4
Spengler, Henry M., 2
Spilman, Dyke A., 4
Spindeler, John G., 5
Spinelli, Domenick, A., 1
Spinler, Darrel J., 2
Spitz, George R., 1
Sprague, Stanley G., 3
Sprick, Doyle R., 4
Springsteadah, Don K.
Springston, Theodore, 4
Sprott, Arthur R., 3
Squire, Boyd E., 2
Stacks, Raymond C., 4
Staehli, Bruce W., 2
Stafford, Ronald D., 3
Stancil, Kenneth L., 4
Standerwick, Robert L., 2
Stanley, Chalres I., 4
Stanley, Robert W., 2
Stanton, Ronald, 4
Stark, Willie E., 2
Staton, Robert M., 2
Steadman, James E., 3
Stearns, Roger H., 2
Steen, Martin W., 2
Stegman, Thomas, 5
Steimer, Thomas J., 5
Stephensen, Mark L., 2
Stephenson, Howard D., 2
Stephenson, Richard C., 5
Stevens, Larry J., 2
Stevens, Phillip P., 3

Stewart, Donald D., 2
Stewart, Jack T., 2
Stewart, Paul C., 4
Stewart, Peter J., 2
Stewart, Robert A., 4
Stewart, Virgil G., 3
Stickney, Phillip J., 2
Stine, Joseph M., 4
Stinson, William S., 1
Stoddard, Clarence W., 5
Stolz, Lawrence G., 1
Stone, Dana, CVL
Stone, James M., 2
Stonebraker, Kenneth A., 4
Story, James C., 4
Stoves, Merritt, 3
Stow, Lilburn R., 2
Stowers, Aubrey E., 2
St. Pierre, Dean P., 2
Strait, Douglas F., 2
Straley, John L., 5
Strange, Floyd W., 2
Stratton, Charles W., 2
Strwawn, John T., 3
Stride, James D., 2
Stringer, John C., 4
Stringham, William S., 5
Strobridge, Rodney L., 4
Strohlein, Madison A., 1
Strong, Henry H., 2
Stroven, William H., 2
Stuart, John F., 2
Stubblerfield, Robert A., 2
Stubbs, William W., 2
Stuckey, John S., 2
Stuilbergen, Gene P., 2
Stuller, John C., 2
Suber, Randolph V., 2
Sulander, Daniel A., 2
Sullivan, John B., 2
Sullivan, Martin J., 5
Sullivan, Robet J., 2
Sutter, FrederickB., 4
Sutton, William C., 2
Suydam, James L., 4
Swanson, John W., 2
Swanson, Jon W., 2
Swanson, Jon E., 2
Swanson, Roger W., 2
Swanson, William E., 3
Swigart, Paul E., 5
Switzer, Jerrold A., 5
Swords, Smith, 3
Sykes, Derri, 1
Szeyller, Edward P., 5
Tadios, Leonard M., 1
Talken, George F., 5
Talley, James L., 2
Tapp, John B., 5
Tapp, Marshall L., 2
Tatum, Lawrence B., 2
Tavares, John R., CVL
Taylor, Danny G., 2
Taylor, Edd D., 2
Taylor, Edmund B., 5
Taylor, Fred, 3
Taylor, James H., 2
Taylor, James L., 2
Taylor, Neil, B, 5
Taylor, Phillip C., 2
Taylor, Ted James, 4
Taylor, Walter J., 4
Templin, Erwin B., 5
Teran, Refugio T., 2
Terla, Lothar G., 2
Terrell, Keavin L., 5
Terrill, Philip B., 1
Terry, Oral R., 4
Terry, Ronald T., 2
Terwillinger, Virgil B., 5
Thackerson, Walter A, 2
Thomas, Daniel W., 4
Thomas, Harry E., 2
Thomas, Darwin J., 2
Thomas, James C., 2
Thomas, James R., 3
Thomas, Leo T., 2
Thomas, Robert J., 2
Thompson, Benjamin A., 4
Thompson, David M., 5
Thompson, Donald E., 2
Thompson, George W., 2
Thompson, Melvin C., 5
Thompson, William J., 3
Thompson, William Joseph, 5
Thoresen, Donald N., 3
Thorne, Larry A., 3
Thornton, Larry C., 4
Thornton, William D., 4
Thurman, Curtis F., 3
Tice, Paul D., 5
Tiderman, John M., 5
Tiffin, Rainford, 2
Tigner, Lee M., 2
Timmons, Bruce A., 5
Tipping, Henry A., 2
Todd, Larry R., 2
Todd, Robert J., 2
Todd, William A., 2
Tolbert, Clarence O., 2
Toms, Dennis L., 5
Toomey, Samuel K., 4
Towle, John C., 2
Townley, Roy F., CVL
Townsend, Francis W., 2
Trampski, Donald J., 3
Traver, John G., 2
Travis, Lynn M., 5
Treece, James A., 4
Trembley, Jay F., 2
Trent, Alan R., 2
Trier, Robert D., 2
Trimble, James M., 5
Trimble, Larry A., 2
Tritt, James F., 5
Trivelpiece, Steve M., 2
Tromp, William L., 5
Trowbridge, Dustin C., 5
Trudeau, Albert R., 5
Trujillo, Joseph F., 2
Trujillo, Robert S., 2
Tubbs, Glenn E., 4
Tucci, Robert L., 2
Tucker, Edwin B., 1
Tucker, James H., 4
Tucker, Timothy M., 3
Tunnell, John W., 5
Turner, Kelton R., 3
Turner, Frederick R., 5
Turner, James H., 4
Turose, Michael S., 3
Tucz, James N., 2
Tye, Michael J., 5
Tyler, George E., 2
Uhlmansiek, Ralph E., 5
Underwood, Thomas W., 3
Underwood, Paul G., 2
Uplinger, Barton J., 5
Upner, Edward C., 2
Urquart, Paul D., 2
Utley, Russel K., 3
Vaden, Woodrow W., 3
Van Bendegom, James L., 1
Van Artsdalen, Clifford D., 2
Van Buren, Gerald G., 4
Van Campen, Thomas C., 2
Van Cleave, Walter S., 3
Vandegeer, Richard, 3
Vanden, Eykel M., 4
Vanrenselaar, Larry J., 1
Varnado, Michael B., 1
Vaughan, Robert R., 5
Vennik, Robert N., 4
Versace, Hurberto R., 1
Viado, Reynaldo R., 5
Vietti, Eleanor A., CVL
Villeponteaux, James H., 3
Vinson, Bobby G., 2
Visconti, Francis, 2
Vlahakos, Peter G., 5
Vogt, Leonard F., 5
Wadleigh, Carl D.
Wadsworth, Dean A., 2
Wagener, David R., 2
Wagner, Raymond A., 2
Wald, Gunther H., 2
Walker, Bruce C., 2
Walker, Kenneth E., 3
Walker, Lloyd F., 2
Walker, Michael S., 3
Walker, Orien J., 1
Walker, Samuel F., 2
Walker, Thomas T., 2
Walker, William J., 5
Wall, Jerry M., 5
.Wallace, Arnold B., 5
Wallace, Charles F., 5
Wallace, Hobart M., 4
Wallace, Michael J., 4
Wallance, Michael W., 2
Waller, Therman M., 4
Walling, Charles M., 2
Walsh, Brian, CVL
Walsh, Richard A., III, 3
Walters, Donovan K., 2
Walters, Tim L., 2
Walters, William, 4
Walton, Lewis C., 2
Walton, Wilbert
Wann, Donald L., 2
Wanzel, Charles J., 2
Ward, Neal C., 2
Ward, Ronald J., 4
Ware, John A., 4
Warren, Arthur L., 2
Warren, Ervin, 2
Warren, Gray D., 2
Washburn, Larry E., 5
Waterman, Craig H., 2
Watkins, Robert J., 3
Watson, Frank P., 5
Watson, Jimmy L., 2
Watson, Ronald L., 2
Wax, David J., 5
Weaks, Melvin L., 4
Weatherman, Clyde E.
Weaver, George R., 5
Weger, John, 2
Weimorts, Robert F., 5

Weisner, Franklin L., 2
Weissenback, Edward J., CVL
Weissmueller, Courtney E., 2
Weitkamp, Edgar W., 2
Weitz, Monek, 4
Welch, Robert J., 2
Wellons, Phillip R., 2
Wells, Robert J., 4
Welsh, Larry D., 2
Welshan, John T., 4
Wenaas, Gordon J., 4
Werdenhoff, Michael R., 4
West, John T., 2
Westbrook, Donald E., 2
Westcott, Gary P., 2
Wester, Albert D., 2
Westton, Oscar B., 2
Westwood, Norman P., 5
Wheeler, Eugene L., 1
Wheeler, James A., 2
White, Charles E., 2
White, Danforth E., 2
White, James B., 4
Whited, James L., 3
Whitesides, Richard L., 1
Whitford, Lawrence W., 1
Whitmire, Warren T., 2
Whitt, James E., 2
Whitteker, Richard L., 2
Whittemore, Frederick H., 5
Whittle, Junior L., 5
Wickham, David W., 5
Widdis, James W., 2
Widdison, Imlay S., 2
Widener, James E., 2
Widner, Danny L., 2
Widon, Kenneth H., 3
Wiechert, Robert C., 3
Wiehr, Richard D., 4
Wilbrecht, Kurt M., 2
Wilburn, John E., 3
Wilburn, Woodrow H., 2
Wiles, Marvin B., 1
Wiley, Richard D., 2
Wilke, Robert F., 2
Wilkins, Calvin W., 5
Wilkins, George H., 2
Wilkinson, Clyde D., 2
Wilkinson, Dennis E., 2
Willett, Robert V., 2
Williams, Billie J., 2
Williams, David B., 3
Williams, David R., 2
Williams, Eddie L., 2
Williams, Edward W., 2
Williams, Howard K., 2
Williams, James E., 2
Williams, James R., 4
Williams, Leroy C., 5
Williams, Robert C., 2
Williams, Robert J., 5
Williams, Roy C., 2
Williams, Thaddeus E., 4
Williamson, Don I., 4
Williamson, James D., 4
Willing, Edward A., 2
Wills, Francis D., 2
Wilson, Claude D., Jr., 2
Wilson, Harry T., 2
Wilson, Marion E., 2
Wilson, Mickey A., 1
Wilson, Peter J., 2
Wilson, Richard, 4
Wilson, Robert A., 2
Wilson, Roger E., 1
Wilson, Wayne V., 4
Wimbrow, Nutter J., 2
Wideler, Charles C., 2
Winkler, John A., 5
Winters, Daryly G., 2
Winters, David M., 2
Wiseman, Bain W., 5
Wistrand, Robert C., 4
Wogan, William M., 4
Wolfe, Donald F., 3
Wolfe, Thomas H., 2
Wolfkeil, Wayne B., 2
Woloszky, Donald J., 2
Wolpe, Jack, 2
Womack, Lonnie H., 4
Wong, Edward P., 2
Wonn, James C., 3
Wood, Don C., 2
Wood, Patrick H., 2
Wood, Rex Stewart, 5
Wood, Stewart S., 5
Wood, Walter S.
Wood, William C., 2
Woods, David W., 5
Woods, Gerald E., 2
Woods, Lawrence, 2
Woods, Robert F., 2
Woodworth, Samuel A., 2
Worchester, John B., 2
Worley, Don F.
Worst, Karl E., 2
Worth, James F., 2
Wortham, Murray L., 3
Worthington, Richard C., 2
Wozniak, Frederick J., 2
Wright, Arthur, 2
Wright, David, L., 2
Wright, Donald L., 2
Wright, Frederick, W., 2
Wright, Gary G., 2
Wright, James J., 2
Wright, Jerdy A., 4
Wright, Thomas T., 4
Wrobleski, Walter F., 2
Wrye, Blair C., 4
Xavier, Augusto M., 4
Yeakley, Robin R., 3
Yeend, Richard C., 2
Yim, John S., CVL
Young, Barclay B., 2
Young, Charles L., 2
Young, Jeffery J., 4
Young, Robert M., 1
Zavocky, James J., 5
Zempel, Ronald L., 5
Zerbe, Michael R., 5
Zich, Larry A., 4
Zimmer, Jerry A., 3
Zissu, Andrew G., 3
Zollicoffer, Franklin, 3
Zook, David J., 2
Zook, Harold J., 2
Zorn, Thomas O., 3
Zubke, Delano D., 2
Zukowski, Robert J., 3
Zutterman, Joseph A., 5

Recommended type of letter that should be written to the President.

President
The White House
1600 Pennsylvania Avenue, NW
Washington, DC 20500
RE: A Matter of the Highest National Priority
Dear Mr. President:

I fully support your effort to make the POW/MIA issue a matter of the highest national priority. Your demonstrated interest is of the primary importance to those American Servicemen who are, in all probability, still being detained. Your maximum interest would be a godsend to the MIA families and enhance the image of your administration. While the efforts of these families have never faultered during the long struggle to help these American Servicemen return to their homes, it will take executive action to help or assist Vietnam in accounting for our MIAs and recovering live POWs.

As you are aware, the history of this issue has always been controversial, but it has developed into a national disgrace which may well make Watergate look like a Sunday School picnic.

Consideration must be given to the following facts:

1. Laos was not invited to attend the Paris peace talks which ended the war even though their Government officials publically stated that they held hundreds of US Prisoners.
2. No on going effort at Presidential Envoy level is being pursued to negotiate with Laos. It must be noted only 6% of the total flyers shot down and listed as missing at the end of the war were accounted for.

Obviously Presidential action is required. Congress has denied payment to Vietnam of the $3.25 billion promised during the Paris peace talks, for war repairs. The Asian mind will never allow the return of our POWs until this commitment is honored at least through US AID.

It must also be considered that a peaceful return of our detained personnel can be accomplished with the assistance of foreign governments.

Explanations and assurances cannot be properly rendered by having the bureaucracy investigate itself. The charges of "Whitewash" and "Coverup" will continue to taint any such investigation.

I recommend that an INDEPENDENT Commission be established to conduct a complete and impartial investigation into all aspects of this issue.

At the completion of the investigation a complete and comprehensive, totally unclassified, report should be given to the American People.

Your reply regarding the feasibility of these recommendations is anxiously awaited, as a day of procrastination on our part is a day of imprisonment for our servicemen.

"You see Mr. President "all is not being done that could be done."

______________________________
(Signature)

______________________________
(Typed or Printed Name)

______________________________
(Street Address)

______________________________
(City) (State) (Zip)

## MAJOR LESSONS THAT SHOULD HAVE BEEN LEARNED IN VIETNAM

1) The short tour (one year) for servicemen in a war is counter-productive. When the experienced officer and NCO leadership changes the new group must start at zero and learn everything about the enemy, the terrain and every other facet of the war. At the beginning of our envolvement it seemed a good idea. After all we should have a combat trained Army in a year or so. But, it really didn't work out that way. Ten years after the war no company NCO's were left with combat experience and no Lieutenants or Captains and few Majors had seen combat. They were all retired under a reduction of forces order. A vast number of Senior Lt. Colonels were retired as "not promotable because they did not get to Command and General Staff school". (They had been fighting the war, some of them for three tours).

Even Senior officers had a short timers attitude from day one of their tour. He only had to stay alive for twelve months. Then it was home to the family for a year or two. In many cases this meant a lot of people were looking for a safe staff job and only a few seeking combat units. Also, maybe thinking would go like this, "I should get out to the field and see how things were going, but then maybe that can wait for two months. "Let my replacement take that field trip". This was the attitude only too often.

2) Troop units must be left in country after a limited war to hold the gains achieved. There were gains in Vietnam and in 69-70 the war could have been ended and a second Korea formed. Southeast Asia would have been stablized. This should have been done without fanfare. The Division size units with air and artillery support air mobile could have been used to support a South Vietnam Army as it came of age.

3) There was a lack of resolve on the part of the Americans. Revolution for the Vietcong was forever. We kept looking for an end of the Vietnam War; the Vietcong were willing to fight for 30 years.

4) The fact it takes 20 years to build an Army of quality was never accepted by our leaders or the American public.

5) Placing civilians, senior advisors into a military situation is a great mistake. The civilians were expected to advise Vietnamese Military commanders at Provance level. That was expecting too much.

6) A resolve to win must be instilled in the people by the Government. Reasons for the war must be explained and accepted by the public or U.S. forces should not be committed. It can be done and Nicaragua is another good example of how not to handle a potential war situation. If Cuba had been properly handled in the early 60's there would be no communist government in Latin America today.

My father once told me "never ask anything of anyone unless you have given him something first." If you like this journal and think the POW issue is worth more than $7.95, send your additional donations to:

The Civil Fact Finding Commission
For P.O.W./M.I.A. in South East Asia, Inc.
Rt. 3 Box 96
Rochester, IN 46975

**It will all be used toward the return of the POWs.**

**F.D.S.**